Breathing Orange Fire

Jose Altuve

Bill Brown

PROLOGUE

Why the title "Breathing Orange Fire"? It takes us back to the era of the late '70s and early '80s, which was the first successful era of a team that began playing in 1962. The title comes from the lyrics of the song "Here Come the Astros." The first two lines were: "Here come the Astros, Burning with Desire.
Here come the Astros, Breathing Orange Fire."

The word "fan" is a derivative of "fanatic." For those who are fanatical about their connection to the team, for those who are lukewarm and for those who are just curious, this book might help bring you closer to the team, its players, its history, and the quest to do what the Chicago Cubs and the Cleveland Indians did in 2016. Both those teams and their long-suffering fan bases found their spirits lifted by their postseason advance to the World Series.

Net proceeds from "Breathing Orange Fire" will be donated to nonprofit Society for American Baseball Research (SABR). That organization has contributed an enormous amount of enjoyment and understanding of the sport to its researchers and its fans. The study of baseball statistics and the stories behind the performers has brought many hours of joy to baseball fans.

Here's hoping that soon Astros fans will have their day in the sun. Thanks for your loyalty and for your patience.

And to all of the hard-working professionals in baseball at every level, may your days be rewarding and your memories be vivid.

DEDICATION

This book is dedicated to longtime friend Ron Soanka. Ron has been a friend since high school days in Missouri. We both shared a passion for sports broadcasting. But it took Ron many years to become a play-by-play broadcaster. He began to broadcast high school sports on the internet as his second career at age 46. For 24 years Ron has brought the action from various sports in Portland, Oregon and Vancouver, Washington to fans of the teams in those areas on both radio and TV and also has broadcast on the internet to relatives of the high school athletes who are scattered across the country. Ron has been at the microphone broadcasting football, basketball, baseball, soccer, volleyball and softball. He has broadcast both boys and girls sports. He has been unable to broadcast in the fall of 2016 due to his battle with cancer. We offer prayers to Ron and his family. For Ron and so many other broadcasters who bring the games to many listeners, we salute them and thank them for their service to their audiences.

CONTENTS

ACKNOWLEDGEMENTS

SPECIAL THANKS TO GENE DUFFEY, WHO WAS INVALUABLE WITH HIS EDITING CONTRIBUTION.

ASTROS FAN LE HOANG NGUYEN SHOT THE COVER PHOTO OF JOSE ALTUVE. IT WAS ON THE WALL IN THE BATHROOM AT A FRIEND'S HOUSE. THANKS TO NGUYEN FOR ALLOWING HIS 2014 PHOTO TO BE THE COVER SHOT.

COMPLIMENTS TO STEVE SPARKS AND GEORGE GENTRY FOR THEIR INPUT, GREG LUCAS FOR HIS SUGGESTIONS AND FOR WRITING THE EPILOGUE, EVAN DRELLICH, JESUS ORTIZ, JAKE KAPLAN AND ANGEL VERDEJO JR. FOR THEIR PROLIFIC WRITING AND TIM GREGG FOR HIS ADVICE.

MATERIAL FROM THE *HOUSTON CHRONICLE, USA TODAY, SPORTS ILLUSTRATED, THE SPORTING NEWS, BLEACHER REPORT AND SPORTS WEEKLY* IS CONTAINED IN THIS BOOK.

Chapter 1

Broomsticks and Bottlecaps

"Enrique winds, he fires, and the BOTTLECAP breaks sharply into the strike zone. Jose swings the BROOMSTICK and the bottlecap flies HIGH and DEEP to left field…."

What? A bottlecap? A broomstick? When you're growing up in Maracay, Venezuela, ten years old, and there is no equipment available for your recreation, you do the best you can. So a baseball becomes a bottlecap and a bat becomes a broomstick.

How does a youngster progress from hitting bottlecaps to contending for the most prestigious award in major league baseball? It's a unique story about a unique player.

Astros minor league manager and scout Omar Lopez had been "sitting on" Jose Carlos Altuve since he turned 16 in the summer of 2006. Lopez mentioned Altuve among several names in a meeting with his superiors. "He has good enough skills, good enough talent to be a ballplayer," Lopez said. "But the problem is he's too short. You need to get glasses to see the kid." In the Houston media guide, scouts Pablo Torrealba and Wolfgang Ramos are credited with signing Altuve September 27, 2006. In that and other baseball publications, Altuve is listed as 5-6. He admits to being 5-5. Thus, his nickname: "Gigante." Translated: "Giant."

The day before, his name was not among those the Astros were interested in signing to professional contracts after a tryout camp. Jose and his father Carlos went home and talked that night. Carlos suggested that they return to the next day's tryout camp. Jose disagreed. He emphasized to his father that the Astros had already made their decision. His father refused to accept it as final, pointing out that Al Pedrique of the Astros front office was not on hand that day but would be attending the next day.

Pedrique, recalled Carlos, had shown interest in Jose previously. Jose then agreed to return the next day.

Pedrique met with the Altuves after the next day's tryout, indicating that the Astros were willing to sign Altuve but could not offer more than $15,000 because they had no more room than that in their budget. The Altuves found that offer to be acceptable. "We projected him as a AA or AAA player," Pedrique said. "We knew his hitting had to stand out enough that he would be taken seriously and get an opportunity."

Said Astros farm director Ricky Bennett, "For five days I watched Jose, and I couldn't take my eyes off him. He played the game with such flash, such passion. He was always in the right place at the right time. I wanted to take him home with me."

The Astros had a tradition of signing prominent major league players from Venezuela. Andres Reiner ran their Venezuelan Academy starting in the 1990s. That academy churned out Johan Santana, Bobby Abreu, Richard Hidalgo, Carlos Guillen and Freddie Garcia.

Jose made his professional debut in the Venezuelan Summer League in 2007. He led the club in batting average (.343) and on base percentage (.429). He played 64 games and hit no home runs in 204 at bats.

"I always knew I would have to work harder than the rest to get here," Altuve said. "But I was always ready for that, and you can accomplish anything through hard work."

The Astros moved Altuve to the United States the next year and he started 38 games at second base for rookie level Greeneville. He hit .284 with two home runs and 21 RBI in 40 games, getting just 141 at bats.

Returning to Greeneville in 2009, Altuve improved his average to .324 in 179 at bats and was named team MVP, earning Player of the Month honors in July and Appalachian League Postseason All-Star recognition. He moved to Tri-City for 76 at bats and hit .250. He stole 28 bases in 66 games at both stops combined.

Altuve heard all the small jokes. "Inside the field, everybody is the same size," he said. "No matter how big or small you are, it's what you can do to play the game. I've always been a guy that believed in myself."

"The first time I saw Jose, I was managing in Venezuela about four or five years ago," said Astros hitting coach Dave Hudgens. "I had never seen him before. He was playing second base for the team in Magallanes, Valencia. I had never heard anything about him. Boy, he could really hit. When you first see him you bring the infield in, bring the outfield in, or bring the corners in, but he could hit the ball by you. For a young guy he could really hit. His bat to ball skills, I knew right away he was exceptional."

Playing at age 20 in 2010, Jose divided the season between Lexington (.308-11-45 in 393 at bats) and Lancaster (.276-4-22 in 116 at bats). He was an All-Star again in the South Atlantic League. His totals for the two clubs were .301-15-67 with 42 steals in 125 games. He had worked his way onto the radar screen of minor league experts.

"Once he hit well in Lexington, we realized he would be a big leaguer," said former Astros scouting director Bobby Heck. "What's impressed me so much is that his body bounces back so well at that size."

"My time in the minor leagues wasn't that easy," Altuve said in a reflective moment after his 1,000th hit in 2016. "I had to work really hard every day to get to this point. I wanted to be better overall. I knew I had to work harder than the rest of the guys because I wasn't a big prospect in the organization."

Front office insiders recall their curiosity in Altuve's early years. "We did the game reports each night, player development reports," said Paul Ricciarini, former Astros senior director of player personnel. "These were entry level games. Every night I would hear the name Altuve," said Ricciarini.

"So I got to spring training and I called Matt Galante, my idol, my mentor, and I said, 'Matty, who's this kid Altuve who's in the game reports all the time?' He said, 'You've gotta see him. You know he's smaller than I am.' (Galante is listed at 5-6 and was the 833rd and last player drafted in 1966). I said, 'Yeah right, nobody's smaller than you.' We were laughing about it. He took me on the back fields and he (Altuve) was at second base. He said, 'He's beautiful, this kid. I told you he was smaller than me and I wasn't lying.' From that day on I started watching him and rooting for him because he probably had to battle for everything he got."

In 43 years of scouting, Ricciarini had not seen a player Altuve's size who reached the major leagues. "It was probably his second full year out where I started really paying attention to him," said Ricciarini. "You saw a kid that just worked so hard and could do things that you refused to believe. That was an unselfish approach, moving runners, having so much fun being on a ball field. He had everything in a player's makeup you'd want to see. I'm sure the world is so against players his size. His makeup was loud. I think I'm more proud about him as a person than his baseball skills."

In spring training in 2011, Brad Mills was managing the Astros. Ed Wade was the general manager. One day some extra players were needed and Altuve was one of the players chosen to join the major league club from minor league camp. Mills remembers he was told, "Don't laugh – he's about 5-5." Then as Mills remembers, "Sure enough, this guy takes off and makes a big impression on us in the game. So I go back to Ed and say, 'He's a pretty good player.' The next time we needed an extra player I said, 'Why don't you send over that Altuve guy?" Mills asked at the end of spring training where Altuve would start the season and he was told at High A Lancaster, California.

Altuve started at Lancaster and hit .408 with five homers and 34 RBI in 213 at bats). Advancing to AA Corpus Christi, Altuve put up more impressive numbers (.361-5-25 in 144 at bats).

He started at second base for the World team in the Sirius XM Futures Game, going 2-for-3 with a double.

The Houston Astros happened to be watching the Futures game on their charter flight as it traveled from one city to another. Soon they would see him in the flesh.

Altuve got word he would be going to the major league club July 19 and made his debut July 20, starting at second base.

He singled in his fifth career at bat.

His first career major league home run was a leadoff, inside-the-park home run August 20 off San Francisco lefthander Madison Bumgarner. No Astro had led off a game in that fashion since Bill Doran April 22, 1987. Altuve tied Russ Johnson's franchise record set in 1997 by hitting in his first seven games, going 11-for-26. Only Ken Caminiti (1987) and Orlando Miller (1994) had 11 hits in their first seven games in the majors for Houston.

Brad Mills said, "I'd be lying if I said I thought he could handle major league pitching when I first saw him. It's the type of individual he is. He's gonna be a success at whatever he wants to do because he listens to the right people. He's developed and that's a tribute to him."

In that first half season in the majors, a .276 batting average proved he could handle the best pitching in the world. That has been his lowest average in a major league season through 2016. Jose's total of 200 hits in 2011 at three different stops provided a strong indicator of his ability to hit. He was named the Astros Minor League Player of the Year for 2011, but he had said his farewell to the minors. He bypassed AAA completely.

"It was a lot of fun," said Altuve at the end of that season. "I didn't come to big league camp last year, and it wasn't in my plans to be a big leaguer. Everything happened quickly.

"I was happy because I got to the big leagues in the same year that I started playing High A so obviously you have to give some credit to yourself. But I wasn't completely satisfied. I knew I could go out there and do better."

Following the season, Jose played for Magallanes in the Venezuelan Winter League and led the league in hits with 82. He finished third in batting average at .339. When the calendar year ended, Altuve had accumulated the staggering totals of 898 plate appearances in the minors, majors and winter ball, including 282 hits!

Brad Mills described Altuve's hitting style in his first major league years. "When he came to the big leagues, he swung at everything," said Mills.

Altuve's work ethic in spring training impressed the Astros strength and conditioning coach, Gene Coleman. "I remember Jose was extremely shy, very quiet and a hard worker," said Coleman.

"We would set up work outside before the game and he would always show up. There would be occasions when he had a really tough game and had run a lot of bases and so forth and he would come in and he would look at me and say, 'I'm a little tired, What do you think?' I would say 'What do YOU think?' He would say, 'I could use a little rest, but if you think I should work, I will stay and work.' I always remember that he was always smiling. He always came in with Marwin Gonzalez and I think one of the reasons Marwin has gotten better is that Jose made him work harder."

Little did anybody know that Altuve would soon become a standard for measurement. It didn't take long after he became a major league fascination that something 5-5 was measured as an "altuve." If a sports fan went jogging, he or she might tell a friend, "I just ran 2,880 altuves this afternoon!" Bryan Trostel developed the website HowManyAltuves.com to aid in calculations.

Altuve is the shortest active player in the majors and the shortest since Freddie Patek retired in 1981 after 14 seasons, nine of them with Kansas City. Patek, who was listed at 5-5 and 140 pounds, was a three-time All-Star, but he never hit more than six homers or drove in more than 60 runs in a season. Altuve had company on the Astros roster in 2016. His teammate, Tony Kemp, is 5-6.

Wee Willie Keeler, who was 5-4 and 140 pounds, had a Hall of Fame career with 2,932 hits from 1892 to 1910. But the world was a much smaller place with much smaller players then and the rules of the game were different.

Jose Altuve quickly reached All-Star status in 2012, his first full major league season. His average climbed to .290, with 167 hits in 147 games. He led the Astros in runs, hits, doubles, triples and steals. He was the second youngest Astro in club history to reach All-Star status. Only Cesar Cedeno at age 21 in 1972 was younger. Bryce Harper was the only younger member on the National League All-Star team. Altuve led NL second basemen in steals with 33. He swung and missed just 10.6% of the time, ranking fifth in the league. "These guys are proving people wrong every day, and I love it," said Chipper Jones of Altuve and Dustin Pedroia of Boston, who is 5-8. "They took a frame that's less desirable and still got a lot out of it. It's hard not to root for somebody like that."

He belted a home run and stole home in the same game June 10 against the Chicago White Sox, the first Astro since Jeff Bagwell in 1993 to do that.

Altuve became the only player in club history to reach 40 doubles and 40 steals in his first 200 games. In 2012 Altuve won his first Astros MVP Award. He again played in winter ball in Venezuela, hitting .336 in 43 at bats after 576 at bats with Houston.

Brad Mills and his son Beau got into the livestock business when Mills was managing in Houston. "We bought this bull," said Mills. "And about a month after we bought it we hadn't named him."

Mills had not yet seen the bull but asked about him.

"He's really athletic – he's small but he has a lot of determination," Mills was told. "That's Jose Altuve!" Mills responded. The bull was named Altuve. The two Altuves once met outside Minute Maid Park. Altuve was taken to his namesake in a golf cart hours before a ball game. What happened to the bull Altuve? "We sold it," said Mills. "It was a championship bull and we had to maximize its value."

In the first season as an American Leaguer for the Astros in 2013, Altuve played 152 games (.283-5 HR-52 RBI). He ranked sixth in the American League with 35 stolen bases, leading all major league second basemen in steals and double plays. When he batted leadoff, his on base average was .376, leading the American League. His 35 hits in April set a club record for a second baseman.

In July, Jose signed a four-year contract with Houston running through 2017 with two club options for 2018 and 2019.

After the season, Altuve stepped up his conditioning program. He worked out pulling a heavy tractor tire from a belt attached to him. "Actually I don't do that anymore," he said. "I quit that. I do stuff similar to that but with less risk. At that time I was doing whatever I could to get better. Now I have my people that really know baseball. The things you can do and not do. I don't think the tire was the big difference. It was more about the cardio program that I did."

A strict diet became a big part of his new program. He eats sweets only on Mondays, his "cheat" day. He follows the diet fanatically.

His gratitude and dedication to the organization soon came full circle. "I'll tell you one story about him," said Paul Ricciarini. "I never managed him or coached him. It was on the back fields in spring training about three years ago. I was just watching the kids in the morning. It was probably about 10, 10:30...he comes over from the big league camp to Field 4 and he's got his t-shirt on, he's got his game pants on, all that.

"He's over there smiling and he's walking with a kind of pace that I said, 'Jose, did they send you down? (joking) He said, 'No, no, man. I've got to check on my boys.' I didn't realize he did this. He'd come over every morning and go from player to player, all the Latin players, and make sure they were doing what they're supposed to be doing.

"I saw him and we talked. I said, 'I will never ever forget this.' He said, 'Hey man, somebody had to do this for me. I needed support and obviously help.' And it was the greatest moment of leadership I ever saw as far as somebody caring that much about the future. That's the most important thing I've ever witnessed about Jose because he really cared that much. It shows up between the lines too. His baseball instincts, his baseball intelligence, his ability to make an adjustment for the sake of the team is what he's all about. He's the quintessential baseball player as far as I'm concerned."

By 2014 Jose Altuve was a headline-maker. He decided to incorporate a leg kick, which improved his timing. He ascended to prominence on the national stage as a batting champion, pounding out 225 hits for a .341 batting average. No Astro had collected that many hits in a season and no Astro had won a batting title. Entering the final game of the season, Altuve led Detroit's Victor Martinez by three points. After an internal debate about whether Altuve should play in the final game at New York's Citi Field or sit out the game and force Martinez to beat the odds to overtake him and win the title, he decided to play. Altuve went 2-for-4 and finished six points ahead of Martinez, .341 to .335.

Altuve also won the Silver Slugger Award as the AL's top offensive second baseman. He joined Ty Cobb as the only players in history with as many as 225 hits, 47 doubles and 56 steals in the same season. Altuve led the league in batting average, hits and steals. Ichiro Suzuki in 2001 was the last to lead the league in all of those categories.

Again Altuve was an All-Star, via the player vote. His 130 hits by the All-Star Break marked a club record. His 500th career hit jumped off his bat June 18 at Washington in his 426th game, faster than any other Astro.

Following the season, Jose traveled to Japan as part of the Major League Baseball All-Star Team. He again won Astros MVP honors and finished 13th in the Most Valuable Player voting in the American League.

By now, the baseball media was cranking out stories on Altuve. Tyler Kepner wrote in the *New York Times*, "The Houston Astros may be the most data-driven organization in baseball, or at least the one most willing to try new ideas. Yet there are no statistical models that would project the smallest player in the majors to be the game's best hitter." Astros assistant general manager David Stearns told Kepner, "He's an anomaly. He's tough to explain, other than the fact he works as hard or harder than anyone, he's got freakish hand-eye skills, he loves baseball and he wants to be great."

"John Mallee and Altuve were inseparable," said Mallee's assistant hitting coach, Ralph Dickenson. The Mallee-Altuve combination started in 2013 when Mallee joined the Astros as the hitting coach. "They were on that stuff. Anything that Jose did, Mallee was there with him."

Mallee explained that height brings leverage, and smaller players often don't generate as many line drives because they don't generate as much bat speed. "Usually the better hitters have the shorter arms and the guys with more power have the longer arms because they have more leverage," explained Mallee.

Brad Mills agreed. "Two things," he said. "His height comes into benefit for him. It's a smaller strike one. His bat to ball skills are amazing. The biggest thing is the experiences he's gone through. He's developed, and that's a tribute to him."

"So I would think that Mallee was probably presenting him a leg kick," said Dickenson. "You take a guy who comes from AA to the big leagues, hitting .260, .270, whatever he did in that first year, which is very good, right? So now Mallee comes along as a first-year hitting coach (in 2013) and wants to add this leg kick in there. So there would be a lot of guys who would be opposed to making a change like that.

"But he (Altuve) wasn't. So he went out and he led the league in hitting that year. And did it out of an entirely different swing than the previous year!"

"He (Mallee) just thought that a leg kick would give me more power," said Altuve. "Not right away, more for the future, but I guess he was right because I did it." Was it complicated to get the timing down? "Absolutely because we talked about mental approach and physically a little bit but not putting it into practice. It was more like theory than practice because we were in the middle of the season.

"But as soon as we finished that season, he was like, 'OK, we've got to go into the offseason now and put it into practice.' And I felt weird, showed up at spring training feeling maybe 50-50, but as soon as the season started I got my work in, I started to play every day and it was worth it."

"Especially me and him, we have a great relationship," said Altuve of Mallee. "He was a little bit young, but just a player and a coach... I think that's why he helped me so much and we had a lot of success that year he was with me. He taught me a lot of stuff and I'm happy he went to the World Series with the Cubs."

Mallee said the first time he met Altuve "his hand-eye coordination impressed me the most." As they discussed his goals, Mallee counseled Altuve. "You can be a .300 hitter who won't be productive or you can be a hitter with a high OPS with a good slugging percentage and a number of walks." Mallee said, "He was a hands first guy. That's all he ever knew. We changed his concept. I suggested that he stay in motion.

"The leg kick made a huge, huge difference. His lower half has to lead his hands. It's a hip turn also. It's hard to learn if it's not a natural move for you. It was natural for him. By the sixth swing he had it. His body just evolved into what is efficient. He just figured it out on his own."

What did Altuve say to Mallee about the results he was getting with the leg kick? "It feels fine. It feels normal." How did the twosome attack his weaknesses? "He was deficient against lefthanded pitching and offspeed pitches," said Mallee. "He had a high chase rate. Since most lefties pitch him away, he had a timing issue. He had an early stride with his toe, which was a pre-stride. The leg kick allowed him to time the pitch better."

Altuve spoke of his aggressive approach in 2014. "That's me," he said. "I just try to make contact with the ball. It's obvious that I like to swing the bat. I'm not thinking of taking a lot of pitches. I'm coming up there ready to look for one pitch. This is the big leagues; pitchers throw a lot of strikes. I feel like they attack me. That's why I go up there and swing."

Why was Altuve, already an established player, willing to try a new technique and risk failure? "He is fearless," said Mallee. "He's not scared of anything. He wanted to be better."

By 2015, Altuve was a major star and a fan favorite. His level of play was at such a peak that maintaining it was the biggest problem because of high expectations. But in 2015 he was named to his third All-Star Game and made his first start. He added his second consecutive Silver Slugger and earned his first career Gold Glove.

Altuve again led the league in hits, with 200 this time. He was the first Astro to have 200 hits in consecutive seasons.

He finished third in batting average at .313. Even though his average was lower than in 2014, he added power in 2015. He reached new career highs with 15 home runs and 66 RBI. He scored 86 runs, a new career high.

Through five seasons (actually 4 ½), Altuve's 830 hits were a club record. He hit .372 against lefthanded pitching, leading the league in that category for the second straight year. He set a club record at Minute Maid Park by hitting in 18 consecutive games there.

Most Valuable Player award voters pegged him for tenth place.

Adding more power in 2015, Altuve lost points on his batting average but created more respect from pitchers because he did more damage on extra base hits. He pulled the ball more often in the air.

"I think when you hit for power, you have to have strength," Altuve said. "But I think most of the time, no matter who hits the ball, if you hit it on the barrel, it's going to carry. And that's what I'm trying to do. I'm not trying to swing hard, not trying to over-swing the bat. I just want to put the barrel on the ball."

Altuve had not reached his peak.

October 12, 2015

After beating the Yankees in the Wild Card playoff game, the Astros took a two games to one lead over Kansas City in the Division Series. They were six outs away from meeting Toronto in the American League Championship Series. In Game 4 of the ALDS in Houston, Will Harris entered in the top of the seventh with a 3-2 lead and pinch runner Terence Gore at first base. Gore stole second, then was thrown out by Jason Castro trying to steal third. Harris struck out Alex Gordon to end the inning. Rookie Lance McCullers Jr. had started the game and pitched 6 1/3 innings, allowing just two hits and two runs. Harris then gave up four straight hits to start the eighth – more hits than he allowed in a game all season! KC overtook the Astros with a five-run eighth and won the game 9-6. The Astros were 70-5 during the regular season when they led after seven innings.

The usually reliable Houston bullpen, finishing fourth in ERA in the American League, had started slumping in mid-September. That downward spiral sucked in the entire relief corps in this game. Earlier in the game, the crowd of 42,387 at Minute Maid Park was rocking when Carlos Correa ripped a two-run homer in the bottom of the seventh and Colby Rasmus followed with a solo shot for a 6-2 Houston advantage. The fans were primed for a big celebration in what would have been the NLDS clincher until the late inning turnabout.

When Game 5 in Kansas City went to the Royals behind Johnny Cueto, Astros fans put the season in context. Again the playoffs were a disappointment considering how close the team came to advancing. But this was a young, improving team. And with KC beating Toronto to get to the Series and knocking off the Mets to win the big prize after falling just short against the Giants the year before, it was no shame to lose to this talented Royals bunch. The idea that this Houston group would have been capable of accomplishing this would have brought some sideways glances if somebody had suggested it six months earlier.

What happened in Game 4 was all too familiar to students of Astros history. It took some longtime fans back to Game 5 of the 1980 NLCS, when Nolan Ryan was on the mound leading the Philadelphia Phillies 5-2 with six outs to go. In that game the Phillies put together a five-run eighth and went on to win the game and later the World Series.

Although the Astros returned to the playoffs in the split season of 1981, they had to wait until 1986 for their next strong bid at a World Series. That year, Bob Knepper stepped up to shackle New York and led the Mets 3-0 in the ninth in Game 6 of the NLCS. But again, a late-inning misstep by the bullpen cost the Astros their lead and eventually they lost 7-6 in the 16th to lose the series and possibly a World Series berth. If the Astros had won, they would have had Mike Scott pitching Game 7. Scott was the MVP of the series.

With essentially the same club in 1987, they went 76-86. How did they lose 20 more games? If you saw it, you could believe it. The numbers will help explain, though. The 1986 Astros scored 654 runs. In 1987, they scored 648. The difference was on the mound. They allowed 569 runs in 1986, compared to 678 the next year. The biggest differences in the pitchers individually came from Nolan Ryan, Bob Knepper and Charlie Kerfeld. Ryan went from 12-8 with a 3.34 ERA in 1986 to probably the unluckiest season in Houston history in 1987, 8-16 despite a 2.76 ERA – the NL's best! He also led the league in strikeouts!

The Astros scored a TOTAL of 27 runs in his 16 losses. Knepper and Kerfeld could not lament about lack of run support, though. Knepper slipped from 17-12 with a 3.14 ERA in '86 to 8-17 with a 5.27 the next year. Kerfeld went from 11-2, 2.59 in relief in '86 to 0-2, 6.67 and a demotion to the minors in '87. Even when good teams avoid crippling injuries, it can become tough to repeat simply because players at the highest level can't always duplicate their performances from one year to the next.

Others watching the loss to Kansas City in 2015 might have flashed back to Game 7 of the NLCS in 2004 with Roger Clemens on the mound, when the Astros led St. Louis 1-0 in the second and Brad Ausmus crushed a ball to left center field with the bases loaded, only to see Jim Edmonds flying through the air to snag what would have been a possible putaway extra base hit. The Cardinals came back to win.

Then there was Albert Pujols' massive home run off Brad Lidge in the ninth inning of Game 5 of the 2005 NLCS in Houston to give St. Louis a 5-4 thriller. Even though the Astros regrouped to win Game 6 in St. Louis to send them on to a World Series, they needed to use ace Roy Oswalt to win that game, which put him on the shelf for the first two games of the World Series against the White Sox. The Astros lost both.

Chapter 2

Valentine's Weekend Reflections

When the Astros sponsored a preseason luncheon for the media in mid-February at Minute Maid Park, many Houston sports fans were searching for flowers or candy for their sweethearts for the weekend. But the turnout was large and the focus was squarely on baseball at the stadium. There were eight television cameras set up on a platform as Astros executives Gene Dias, Reid Ryan and Anita Sehgal previewed the club's plans for 2016. Then Manager A.J. Hinch and General Manager Jeff Luhnow took their turns at the podium. Their reflections concerned an analysis of 2015 and a preview of 2016.

Hinch reiterated several key points he had made to his players in 2015 with remarks categorizing his focus on staying in the moment:

"Every play matters."

"Every game matters."

"A lot of people in this room are gonna tell these players how good they are. I'm sorta paid to tell them how bad they are."

"For me, it's going to be easy to instill in our players that we need to focus on every play. The experts didn't pick us last year and we proved them wrong."

"We're a fun team. Don't ask me a question about panic. I won't panic."

"I think consistency matters with players. If I'm inconsistent I can't expect them to be consistent."

"We're not gonna get better just by showing up and maturing. We have room to get better and we have to work at it."

All of these remarks were geared to approach the mindset of not being complacent in 2016. The average Houston fan might have placed complacency low on the list of priorities. Why? The Astros had shocked many people in the baseball world by improving from a 70-92 record in 2014 to 86-76 in 2015. In 2013, they had a record of 51-111. The jump of 35 wins in two years had attracted a lot of notoriety. The theme was that the Astros would not be sneaking up on any teams in 2016. They had grabbed their share of headlines and their young players were well known.

Hinch told Brian McTaggart of MLB.com in a story February 16, "This game itself will humble you if you're not aware of your surroundings. They're not going to give us anything. I've been in the game long enough to go through a lot of different teams who came to camp feeling good about themselves, and misfortune or injury or underperformance gets in their way. I'll be pretty direct with our guys to make sure we don't look too far back into last season because it doesn't count on this season's record."

Ken Rosenthal of Fox Sports wrote a column detailing Hinch's hiring as Arizona manager in May 2009 by GM Josh Byrnes. Hinch at the time was farm director for the Diamondbacks and had no major league coaching or managing experience. But, even though such hirings at the time were rare, entering 2016 there were 12 of 30 major league managers who had no previous major league managing experience when they were hired. Only five of the 12 had been a major league coach. Hinch, who was drafted in the third round by Oakland and became an everyday catcher, was a backup later in his career and then became the 25th man on the team. The 25th man typically has his head on a swivel, wondering when he'll be told he's going back to the minor leagues. It's insightful for the manager to know what concerns his 25th player so he can address it. Hinch was a .219 career hitter. But he was a communicator par excellence in 2015. Sparky Anderson hit .218 in his one major league season, but he became a Hall of Fame manager.

Earl Weaver, another Hall of Fame skipper, never reached the majors as a player.

Many top major league managers were not good players.

Hinch moved into front office roles after his playing days with Oakland, Kansas City, Detroit and Philadelphia. He accepted the job as manager in Arizona when he was approached about moving from the front office back onto the field as the majors' youngest skipper at age 34. Hinch explained the reasoning involved in bringing him to the manager's office: "The number one priority is the players. Getting a connection with the players. Being able to push each player's buttons, getting the most out of them." Hinch, with his Stanford degree in psychology, explained, "We were onto something then. It wasn't accepted as freely as it is now."

Hinch replaced the popular Bob Melvin as Dbacks skipper and he had rough sledding on his maiden voyage. The bullpen had a 5.74 ERA. Most successful managers have good bullpens. Hinch was fired in 2010, but when he interviewed for the Houston job before Bo Porter was hired and then the Cubs job when Joe Maddon got the call, he was reinvigorated for a manager's job.

He reflected about the changes he needed to make if he got another shot. Byrnes, now with the Dodgers, said, "I give him a ton of credit for working to evolve and keep growing as a leader."

The trust between Hinch and Astros GM Jeff Luhnow, who knew each other as farm directors with the Padres and Cardinals, is a key to success for the organization. Their openness with each other allows the understanding that drives decisions.

As for Luhnow, who took over as the 12th general manager of the Astros in December 2011, he was somber at the beginning of his remarks. He mentioned that he was missing Hall of Fame broadcaster Milo Hamilton at the luncheon. Hamilton had passed away in September 2015. Luhnow was a regular visitor to Hamilton's hospital room in his final months.

When he turned to his baseball remarks, Luhnow began by saying, "Last year was pretty incredible. We knew we had a chance to do something special, but a lot of things happened."

The Astros blazed to a quick start in 2015: 18-7. That put them in the lead position in the American League West, where they stayed for months before fading in September. Nonetheless, they regrouped in the final stages of the season and won one of the two Wild Card spots in the AL playoffs, beating the Yankees in the Wild Card playoff game before falling to eventual World Series Champion Kansas City in five games in the Division Series. As a result, some of the preseason publications had been rewarding them by boosting them into the top spot in their division for 2016. The Westgate Las Vegas Superbook had the Cubs' odds at 4-1 to win the World Series, followed by the Astros at 10-1. Five teams were at 12-1: Boston, Los Angeles, New York, San Francisco and Washington.

The USA Today preseason poll placed Houston atop the AL West, predicting a 90-72 record. Defending division champ Texas was picked in second place at 85-77.

The highly respected Baseball Prospectus publication, crunching more numbers than a college calculus class, also placed the Astros in first place in its preseason rankings, with 86 wins expected. Respect was pouring in for a team lightly regarded and ridiculed in the media just a couple of years before.

Luhnow had presided over the turnaround. It must be noted that a year before, BP predicted eventual world champion Kansas City would win 72 games. The Royals actually notched 95 regular season wins. So much for predictions!

Luhnow brought an analytical approach from the St. Louis Cardinals. He remade the baseball operations side of the organization with that philosophy, but not to the exclusion of relying on scouts and their opinions.

With an MBA from Northwestern University, Luhnow worked his way into baseball just as many organizations were searching for approaches like his. With waiver acquisitions such as Collin McHugh and Will Harris teaming to pitch the Game 1 win over Kansas City and draft choices like Carlos Correa and Lance McCullers, Jr., Luhnow and his former fellow St. Louis employees Sig Mejdal and Mike Elias had brought top talent through the doors of Union Station and onto the playing field, where they excelled.

Taking over an organization with new ownership and a design for long term success, Luhnow was able to institute his blueprint for acquiring as much young talent as possible. He made a series of trades, unloading veterans with value for young minor leaguers. He emphasized building through the draft. His first two draft picks as general manager, Correa and McCullers, became stars in 2015. He stocked the farm system with high draft picks. He had time on his side by virtue of ownership's plan to stay the course and not to panic by patching with free agents. In 2015, seven Astros' minor league affiliates made the playoffs. Only once had that happened since 2005 in the minors for any organization. Luhnow frequently mentioned in interviews that the plan was to have repeating playoff teams. The goal was to avoid a falloff such as the slides after the 1986 and 2005 playoff appearances.

Prior to 2014, Luhnow signed free agent starting pitcher Scott Feldman, who became the Opening Day starting pitcher, and claimed McHugh on waivers.

Prior to 2014, Luhnow signed free agent Chad Qualls. Tony Sipp joined the Astros during that season. Rule 5 draft choice Josh Fields joined the bullpen.

Rule 5 draft choice Marwin Gonzalez became a super sub. The draft yielded Correa and Mark Appel in 2012 and 2013 as the first players drafted overall each year. A.J. Reed was a second rounder in 2014. Alex Bregman arrived in 2015 as the second player drafted.

But the Astros did not keep every player they drafted. Brett Phillips, Josh Hader, and Adrian Houser went to Milwaukee in a trade for Carlos Gomez and Mike Fiers. That trade was geared toward providing immediate help for the major league club in 2015. It was a classic matchup of trading partners with different objectives. The Astros were now acquiring more proven talent and the Brewers were rebuilding.

In the December 2015 trade with the Phillies for Ken Giles and Jonathan Arauz, eyes grew wide around the baseball world at the Phillies' yield in the deal: Brett Oberholtzer, Mark Appel, Vince Velasquez, Harold Arauz and Thomas Eshelman. It was a rare trade with five pitchers going to the Phillies. As the media initially reported it, outfielder Derek Fisher was one of the players headed to the Phillies. But when the deal was finalized, Appel had replaced Fisher. There were rumors that the Phillies had been concerned about Velasquez' arm in the physical before the trade was finalized and they demanded another pitcher before they signed off on the deal. It seemed to many observers that the Astros had dipped too deep into their talent pool. From their standpoint, they got the hard thrower they needed for their bullpen and he could not be a free agent for five more years. Many were shocked that they would surrender Appel, the number one pick in the 2013 draft.

Appel had a 4.48 earned run average at Triple-A Fresno in 12 starts in 2015 after going 5-1 with a 4.26 at Corpus Christi in 13 starts.

He would be 23 in July. His career ERA in the minors for three seasons was 5.12. His Stanford degree and 6-5, 220-pound stature had catapulted him to the top of the list as a projected big league ace someday. What had happened to derail him? *Baseball America*, ranking him as the Astros' number 8 prospect, judged, "He appears to have the makings of a frontline starter, but the sum of those parts rarely adds up."

BA said his fastball appears to be a "plus-plus" offering at 93-95 mph, but "it plays average, if not below because it is too flat and hitters pick it up too easily." In 12 of his 53 pro starts, he gave up more runs than innings pitched. Nonetheless, the rebuilding Phillies would give him every chance to succeed in their rotation. If he didn't, they would have Velasquez and Eshelman as prospects who had good chances to help and the veteran Oberholtzer to fill a spot until they could improve.

Former Astros GM Ed Wade, who was Luhnow's predecessor, is now a special assistant for the Phillies. During his time at the helm from 2007 until 2011, the Astros drafted Dallas Keuchel and signed Jose Altuve. Wade said, "I was happy for Keuchel and Altuve, not only the guys with the Astros but also J.D. Martinez and Mark Melancon. Somebody pointed out to me that there were 37 players last year who played in the big leagues who were in the system when the sale took place (from Drayton McLane to Jim Crane's group), which I thought was a testimony to the work that our guys did and a fact that the system had greater depth than it was probably perceived or portrayed at the time."

With the frequent changes most baseball organizations make, there are few Brian Cashmans (Yankees) who stay in their jobs so long that their accomplishments stand alone and are not connected to a previous front office.

Some were confused the year before when Houston acquired Jake Marisnick, Colin Moran and Frances Martes from Miami in a trade for Jarred Cosart, Kike Hernandez and Austin Wates. Cosart was in the starting rotation and it seemed he was being relied upon to be a lynchpin for the future. But when the script flips and a club goes from youthful to "in the hunt," it's more likely to assume some risk. Marisnick is a defensive superstar and the other two players were good prospects.

Revisiting Trades

Joe Musgrove and Asher Wojciechowski came from Toronto along with Francisco Cordero, Carlos Perez and David Rollins in 2012 for J. A. Happ, Brandon Lyon and David Carpenter. That deal had not yet yielded positive results, but Musgrove did have a big year in the minors in 2015. Perez made the deal look worse for Houston by catching well for the Angels. Happ blossomed with Toronto and went 20-4 in 2016.

Going further back, Lance Berkman was dealt to the Yankees in July of 2010 for Mark Melancon and Jimmy Paredes. Paredes has always struggled defensively and has not found overall success. Melancon pitched well for the Astros and then moved on to Boston following the 2011 season for Jed Lowrie and Kyle Weiland. He has continued to pitch well at the end of games. Berkman had a big year for St. Louis in 2011 and excelled in postseason play for the World Champion Cardinals.

The Astros and Phillies had been frequent trading partners in recent years. When Ed Wade was the Houston GM, he knew the Phillies' farm system well because of his time as their GM. Wade was tasked with moving high-salaried veterans and obtaining prospects for them to facilitate the Houston rebuilding process.

Roy Oswalt went to Philadelphia in 2010 for Anthony Gose, Happ and Jonathan Villar. Gose was then dealt to Toronto for Brett Wallace. Happ and Villar were later moved on.

Oswalt pitched exceptionally well for the Phillies in 2010 and continued that work into the playoffs.

Brad Lidge had preceded Oswalt to Philly in November 2007, accompanied by Eric Bruntlett, in a deal for Michael Bourn, Mike Costanzo and Geoff Geary.

Bourn served the Astros well before he was moved to Atlanta in 2011 for Paul Clemens, Brett Oberholtzer, Jordan Schafer and Juan Abreu. Bourn's production has dropped off in recent years, but overall this trade was a dud for Houston.

Hunter Pence left the Astros in a trade with the Phillies in July of 2011 for Jarred Cosart, Jonathan Singleton and Josh Zeid. Pence was a fan favorite in Houston and he's gone on to claim that same status with big years in Philadelphia and San Francisco. In 5 1/2 seasons after leaving Houston he belted 104 homers and drove in 409 runs, playing on four postseason teams. He was traded at age 28 in the prime of his career and has continued to perform at a high level. For Cosart, Singleton and Zeid there may be more chances to make an impact. If this deal were to be judged now, it would be a tremendous negative for Houston.

Billy Wagner was the first in the series of trades with Philadelphia. He moved to the City of Brotherly Love and vicious booing in November 2003. The return for him was so bad that many don't even remember Ezequiel Astacio, Brandon Duckworth and Taylor Buchholz. After Wagner left Houston, he saved 197 more games with the Mets, Phillies and Braves after nailing down 225 saves for Houston. That is the definition of an awful trade. Even if Philadelphia sports fans do boo airport landings and Santa Claus as the jokes assert, the depths of their passion would have been tested if their club had made that deal in reverse!

Carlos Beltran joined the Astros in 2004 in a three-team deal. Beltran came from Kansas City, with the Royals receiving catcher John Buck from the Astros and Oakland getting reliever Octavio Dotel.

Beltran helped the Astros reach the playoffs and then his talent exploded in the postseason like oil gushing through a West Texas derrick. He had one of the best postseasons in history before his agent Scott Boras priced him out of the Astros' reach in free agency and he headed for the New York Mets. Dotel went on to pitch for nine more years, some of them at a very good level of performance.

Buck went on to an 11-year career as a major league catcher, sometimes a starter and sometimes as backup, hitting .234 with 134 homers. That trade worked well for all teams involved.

As we see from tracking the players involved in these deals, trading for prospects can be VERY risky! But then, there's Larry Andersen for Jeff Bagwell in 1990.......

Astros Daily's Best Trades

(more at www.astrosdaily.com)

Larry Andersen to Boston for Jeff Bagwell 1990

Cash to St. Louis for Jose Cruz October 1974

Cash ($35,000) to Atlanta for Joe Niekro 1975

Ken Forsch to California for Dickie Thon 1981

Don Sutton to Milwaukee for Kevin Bass, Frank DiPino and Mike Madden 1982

Danny Heep to New York for Mike Scott 1982

Eric Anthony to Seattle for Mike Hampton and Mike Felder 1993

Oscar Henriquez, Manny Barrios and Mark Johnson to Florida for Moises Alou 1997

Astros Daily's Worst Trades

Mike Cuellar, Enzo Hernandez and Elijah Johnson to Baltimore for Curt Blefary and John Mason December 1968

John Mayberry and Dave Grangaard to Kansas City in December 1971 for Lance Clemons and Jim York

Rusty Staub to Montreal in January 1969 for Jesus Alou, Jack Billingham and Skip Guinn

(Donn Clendenon refused to report from Montreal and the deal was restructured)

Jimmy Wynn to Los Angeles for Claude Osteen and Dave Culpepper 1973

Joe Morgan, Jack Billingham, Denis Menke, Cesar Geronimo and Ed Armbrister to Cincinnati in November 1971 for Lee May, Tommy Helms and Jimmy Stewart

Bob Watson to Boston for Bobby Sprowl, Peter Ladd and cash 1979

Kenny Lofton and Dave Rohe to Cincinnati for Eddie Taubensee and Willie Blair 1991

Curt Schilling to Philadelphia for Jason Grimsley 1992

Ken Caminiti, Steve Finley, Andujar Cedeno, Roberto Petagine, Brian Williams and Sean Fesh to San Diego for Derek Bell, Ricky Gutierrez, Phil Plantier, Pedro Martinez, Doug Brocail and Craig Shipley 1994

When Luhnow was in St. Louis, 16 of the 25 players on the 2013 World Series roster were drafted while he oversaw player development and scouting. He was following a similar blueprint in Houston.

Luhnow's major acquisitions over the winter of 2015 were Ken Giles from the Phillies in a huge trade and free agent starter Doug Fister, a 6-8 righthander who had an off year in 2015 and was dogged by a forearm injury. Fister was set to replace Scott Kazmir in the starting rotation if he proved to be healthy in spring training. Kazmir, obtained in a July 2015 trade from Oakland, left via free agency, with the Dodgers landing him with a three-year, $48 million deal. Luhnow said at the preseason luncheon, "It hasn't been the flashiest offseason, but we have put players in place." He mentioned fringe acquisitions who were not on the 40-man roster but who might be needed during the six-month major league season. He threw out the names of Danny Reynolds, Brendan McCurry, Danny Worth, Edwar Cabrera, Eury Perez, Wandy Rodriguez, Cesar Valdez and Cy Sneed. Sneed came in a deal with Milwaukee about the time Dallas Keuchel was named winner of the Cy Young Award, giving the Astros two Cys in machine-gun fashion.

The Astros traded several highly regarded prospects to obtain members of the 2016 club. Their farm system was now ranked in the middle of the pack for 2016 by some ratings services. MLB.com ranked their farm system as the tenth best. They spent $19 million to sign their 2015 draft picks, a record for the draft.

Prior to the trades, the Astros had been ranked at the top of the list. But their top players still included blue-chippers such as Reed, Bregman, Frances Martes, Tyler White, Colin Moran, Alfredo Gonzalez and Derek Fisher.

Luhnow gave credit to the players who pulled together the previous year to reach the playoffs despite a September slump. "We know there are going to be struggles this year," he said. "We had fun last year...but if it hadn't been for that unity, that chemistry, it wouldn't have gone as well as it did."

Alluding to the different expectation level around the 2016 team, Luhnow summarized, "Last year was pretty incredible. We knew we had a chance to do something special, but a lot of things happened." Then he reeled off a list of 16 significant developments as compiled by his Baseball Operations staff. They were:

16. Club Astros (the postgame victory celebrations complete with smoke machine and dance music in the clubhouse) built camaraderie

15. Gold Gloves for Dallas Keuchel and Jose Altuve

14. Correa's Rookie of the Year award

13. Keuchel's Cy Young Award

12. Keuchel's Opening Day win over Cleveland and Corey Kluber, the 2014 Cy Young winner, 2-0

11. Colby Rasmus hitting four postseason home runs

10. Altuve's walkoff hit to beat Boston July 23, his fourth hit of the game

9. Lance McCullers' complete game win vs. Baltimore June 3, winning 3-1 with 11 strikeouts

8. McCullers getting a triple play ball at Detroit in his second major league start & first win May 23

7. Marisnick slamming into the Green Monster at Fenway Park with a sensational catch July 5

6. Sweeping a three-game series at San Diego in April

5. Evan Gattis ripping a bases-loaded double on a neck-high fastball in the ninth to win at Oakland April 26

4. The miraculous, five-run 9th after two outs in Anaheim September 13 to rescue a 5-3 win

3. George Springer racing to the right field wall in Arlington and leaping high to rob a potential game-winning grand slam from Leonys Martin in a game the Astros won April 12 in the 14th inning

2. Mike Fiers' no-hitter against the Dodgers, part of a three-game sweep with Clayton Kershaw and Zack Greinke starting two of the games for the Dodgers

1. Keuchel's shutout win in the Wild Card playoff game at Yankee Stadium

-----

February 18, 2016

The Astros addressed the bullpen's failures late in the 2015 season when they made the Giles trade. The day the pitchers and catchers reported to spring training, 2015 closer Luke Gregerson was asked if he still expected to be the team's closer.

"How do you think I did last year? I don't see any reason things should change," Gregerson said. Obviously, bringing the guy we brought in, he's got a strong, power arm, he's shown that he can get guys out at the major league level, and I think he's going to be a great addition to our bullpen no matter where we all fit in. I think we've just gotten better, and that's it."

But was that the end of it? On the MLB Network the next morning, analyst Harold Reynolds said, "I think they've got a problem and they need to address it right now."

He and Matt Vasgersian discussed the acquisition of Giles and both agreed that the perception was that Giles would become the closer, although perhaps not right away. They also agreed that the Astros had given up an expensive package and that could not be justified if Giles was a setup man. They discussed the theory that both Gregerson and Giles could be used to close in different situations or on consecutive nights, but not naming one closer could lead to major difficulties. Both pitchers said there had been no discussions from the team about their roles. Gregerson converted 31 of 36 saves in 2015, Giles 15 of 20. Giles was a setup man for Jonathan Papelbon before Papelbon was traded. Gregerson had been primarily a setup man in San Diego and Oakland prior to 2015.

The Houston Chronicle ran a spring preview article written by Evan Drellich on Valentine's Day. Drellich listed these five things to watch in spring training:

1. Ken Giles fitting into the back end of the established bullpen
2. The first base battle, with Jon Singleton given priority but several candidates contending
3. Managing higher expectations
4. The battle for backup catcher behind Jason Castro, with Max Stassi the favorite
5. Rounding out the rotation, with Fister bidding to beat Feldman behind Keuchel, McHugh, McCullers and Fiers

The Astros opening day payroll was calculated to check in around $94 million.

"I think it's going to be a pretty focused camp," said Luhnow. "We know what our objectives are this year, and that's maybe a little different than in years past."

As Colby Rasmus arrived early in Kissimmee, Florida, he was the highest paid Astro at $15.8 million. Rasmus had been eligible for free agency after 2015. The Astros tendered him a qualifying offer after his best major league season. They showed that they valued his contribution and preferred to have him back in their 2016 lineup. But Rasmus had a decision to make. It was his collectively bargained right to reject the offer and open up conversations with all teams as a free agent. Rasmus became the first player in three years of this system to accept the offer, which guaranteed he would be with the Astros for another year. At that time, he was eligible to explore free agency again. Most players at Rasmus' stage of their careers would have angled for a multi-year contract, but Rasmus had enjoyed his teammates and the team's success.

"I'm just going to try to be positive with these guys and love on everybody and make it just a fun environment to be in," he said.

His lefthanded bat and his stellar outfield play were important to the Astros, who were righthanded heavy in their lineup. They had Altuve, Correa, Springer, Gattis and Gomez from the right side.

Luis Valbuena and Jason Castro were the only other lefty hitters in the lineup, and Castro had not put up good numbers since 2013.

"I'm ready to go out and beat some folks, win some ballgames, chest bump with these guys and eat some gummy bears. You know what I'm saying?" said Rasmus. He added, "I'm just super excited to be an Astro."

Gattis avoided arbitration by signing a one-year, $3.3 million deal that included a club option for 2017 for $5.2 million or a $100,000 buyout. He was the final Astro to agree to contract terms. He had just undergone sports hernia surgery a few days before the agreement and the start of his season would be delayed as a result.

The last time expectations were this high for the Astros, in 2006, they had reached the World Series for the only time in their history the year before.

They finished 82-80 under skipper Phil Garner that year, 1 1/2 games out of first place. Garner was an infielder on the 1987 team which suffered the disappointing season. There were also some excellent teams in 1998 and '99, as well as 2004. But the Astros, who began in 1962 as the Colt .45s, had never brought home the World Series trophy. In Houston, only the Rockets in 1994 and 1995 had won major pro sports championships. (The Houston Oilers won the first two American Football League championships before the merger with the National Football League). It was a city hungry for another postseason parade.

Most average sports fans in the city gravitated toward whichever pro team gave them the best hope for winning it all.

The attraction of this team to sports fans was multi-faceted. It was a young, exuberant team playing a hustling brand of baseball. The players genuinely liked each other and celebrated in the dugout with dance moves.

Many players were near or at the minimum salary in 2015.

Only a few had multi-year contracts. For the fans, this team was filled with players who were at the opposite end of the spectrum from Carlos Lee, who joined the Astros as a $100 million free agent in 2006 and, although he produced as a hitter during his six years, was not known for his effort defensively or his passion for the game. The players were primed, and the fans were primed, for 2016's curtain to open. But first came spring training.

-----

3 Correa and Keuchel

Carlos Correa

February 20---Many position players reported to Kissimmee early to get a head start on their workouts, regardless of their scheduled reporting date the next week. The media swarmed around Carlos Correa. Evan Drellich reported in the *Houston Chronicle*, "Correa belongs in a stratosphere of not just athletic ability, but persona, that above all else, needs to be sought out by his fans and city in the season to come." The reports indicated that Correa took the field with two hours sleep the day before, spending hours for an adidas photo shoot. He had just signed a multi-year contract with adidas, which would buttress him through his early years in the majors until he became arbitration eligible. At that time, his salary would soar because under baseball's system a player could compare himself to other players of similar service time and accomplishments and compare his resume with those of the top-salaried players in their category.

Correa wrote in an article in the Players Tribune about his preparation for the season: "People ask me if I put pressure on myself. Honestly, I don't. To me, pressure creates distractions and there is no time for distractions in baseball. When you work hard every single day and you prepare yourself the right way, there should be no doubt in your mind you are going to perform out there." The photo spread in the Players Tribune illustrated his point. It showed him working out with heavy ropes and running while tethered to a stationary object.

Correa had been asked many times about any lingering effects of his Game 4 error in the Division Series against Kansas City and he had always shrugged it off. "My mind is bulletproof, man," he summarized.

Truthfully, the error was a questionable one. The ground ball by Kendrys Morales was hit hard up the middle.

Lefty Tony Sipp got his glove on the ball after it bounced off the mound, which applied wicked spin to the swiftly moving grounder.

Correa was moving to his left and tried to play it to the left side of his body, but the overspin on the ball caused it to bite hard into the dirt and shoot upwards. Correa gloved it, but the ball kicked off his glove and into the outfield. The Royals, who trailed 6-4 at the time with the bases loaded and no outs, scored the tying runs on the misplay. They later grabbed a 7-6 lead on Alex Gordon's grounder. The Royals paraded 11 men to the plate in the inning, which started with five straight singles. Sipp was the losing pitcher.

Correa had the game of his life offensively, going 4-for-4 with two home runs and four RBI. He also was hit by a pitch, reaching base in all five plate appearances. He blasted a 96 mph pitch from Yordano Ventura for his first homer in the third inning, pulling the ball to left field from its location inside the strike zone. He doubled to right in the fifth and drove in a run. He belted a three-run bomb to right field in the seventh, when the Astros took a 6-2 lead. He also singled to lead off the home ninth off Wade Davis in the 9-6 KC win.

Correa, who was hitting third, was just the third player to bat third in the playoffs as a rookie, following Hall of Famers Joe DiMaggio and Mickey Mantle. The only younger player to have a multi-home run game in the playoffs was Andruw Jones of Atlanta in the 1996 World Series. Only three players in the last 100 years batted third in at least 130 games at 22 or younger for a team that made the postseason. They were Joe DiMaggio, Stan Musial and Cal Ripken Jr. Correa had a good chance to join them if he stayed healthy in 2016 and the team made a return postseason trip. DiMaggio was the only one of those to be a fulltime number three hitter at age 21.

Further, removing the postseason designation, only three players started 130 games or more at age 21 in the number three spot; Eddie Mathews, Al Kaline and Ken Griffey Jr.

When Correa first arrived in the majors, his manager told him he would place him toward the bottom of the order for a few weeks and see if he earned his way into a higher place on the lineup card.

"And that lasted about three days," said A.J. Hinch. By his third game he was fifth. Then second. Then third within about three weeks. Correa remembered, "When I saw my name third in the lineup for the first time, I was like, 'Whoa, Skip, did you mess up something with the lineup?' But he trusted in me, and he hit me third. And I think it turned out pretty well, not only for me, but for the team." Hinch said, "It was so funny. I told him, 'Remember what I told you in Chicago?' He said 'Yeah." I said, 'Forget everything I said. You're hitting in the middle of the order now.' He said, 'You've got it. Put me wherever you want.'" Hinch added, "The moment was never too big for him. And the responsibility of hitting in the middle of the order, in the first couple of months of his career, never fazed him. So I saw no reason not to lean on him in that way."

The media and fans are always looking for comparable players when a multi-talented rookie such as Correa arrives and excels early in his career. The common comparable used by many was Alex Rodriguez. ARod arrived at an even younger age (18) than Correa and reached superstardom quickly with Seattle. He was a teammate of Ken Griffey, Jr. and thereby was not getting the main focus of media and fans. Correa's body type was similar to ARod's and he showed the same combination of the five essential tools of baseball. His throws to first had been clocked as high as 97 mph! His poise, like ARod's, was off the charts. Another comparable was Derek Jeter, who had just retired and is on his way to the Hall of Fame.

Correa's father, Carlos Sr., was not a baseball expert.

But he studied the techniques of Rodriguez and Jeter on television and asked his son to emulate their play. Carlos Sr. worked as a fisherman when he was a boy and he quit baseball when he didn't succeed.

The Astros were 3-10 all-time in postseason possible clinching games. But the hope for the future with Correa, Altuve and others in the lineup kept the spirits of Astros fans from sinking to the basement.

Actually there are few basements in Houston homes because the city is at sea level!

Correa also had a role in a biopic about Puerto Rican hero Roberto Clemente. "The thing I bring to the table is I'm bilingual," he said. Hopefully I can do a lot of great things for the sport of baseball and I can not only help here in the States, but the Latin community as well."

Puerto Rico, an island 110 miles by 40 miles, was the birthplace of Hall of Famer Roberto Clemente, Orlando Cepeda and Roberto Alomar. Pudge Rodriguez and Edgar Martinez were other top stars who grew up there. But there was a decline in baseball luminaries coming from the island in recent decades. Why? The incentive of signing a lucrative deal as a free agent was gone, because Puerto Rico had become a part of the United States and was now part of the U.S. draft territory. Youngsters from other countries such as the Dominican Republic and Venezuela could bargain with all 30 major league clubs when they turned 16, while Puerto Rican kids who were drafted were limited to dealing with only the drafting team. Basketball, soccer and volleyball provided competition for athletes. In the Dominican and Venezuela, soccer was the only real competition for baseball. Cleveland's Francisco Lindor and the Cubs' Javier Baez were drafted one after the other in 2011 in the eighth and ninth spots after being born in Puerto Rico, but both had moved to Florida to improve their exposure to scouts and better competition. "I want to come out of Puerto Rico," Correa said. "I want to show people it can be done from here."

When Correa came to Jupiter, Florida in 2011 to play in a tournament, a Cardinal scout, Mike Elias, witnessed a line drive off his bat shooting like a laser down the right field line.

It struck the foul pole for an impressive opposite field home run.

Elias filed it away. When Correa became the first choice in the 2012 draft, Elias was the Astros' Special Assistant to the GM-Scouting. He was instrumental in making the decision to draft Correa over Byron Buxton and others.

The story of Clemente is well known in baseball circles. New Year's eve in 1972, Clemente was killed in a plane crash. Clemente had reached the 3,000-hit milestone at the end of the regular season that year. An earthquake struck Nicaragua that winter, causing enormous damage and loss of lives. Clemente, with help from his teammates in winter ball, loaded supplies aboard a chartered airplane bound for Managua. One of his teammates, pitcher Tom Walker, helped load the supplies and asked Clemente if he needed help taking the supplies to Nicaragua. Clemente said that he had it under control and wished Walker a good New Year's Eve. The load was not distributed properly. It shifted after the plane took off and caused the plane to go down in the water shortly after takeoff. Walker later became the father of Neil Walker, who had been the Pirates' second baseman for years and now was beginning a new phase of his career with the New York Mets.

Correa said of his quick ascent to stardom, "I always visualized this stuff coming. And I think it came earlier than what I expected. But I was ready for it, and I'm not going to let it get to my head." Correa had explained to Houston media in 2015 that when he was five or six years old he was focused on being a star baseball player. His father, who worked in the construction industry, let Carlos tag along on jobs and directed him to make himself useful by carrying some items. It didn't take Carlos long to realize what he did NOT want to do for a living.

By the time Carlos was eight, he asked his father to enroll him in a bilingual Baptist school.

"I'm watching interviews on TV, and I would see the Latin guys with translators and stuff like that. I'm like 'Dad, I don't want to be one of those guys. I want to speak for myself,'" Carlos told *Sports Illustrated*. His father took on a third job so Carlos could enroll in a private school.

Correa graduated from the Puerto Rican Baseball Academy, where his development was facilitated by baseball instructors when he wasn't in the classroom. Correa told people he was going to be a first-rounder and they laughed.

He turned down invitations to parties because he wanted to stay focused on baseball.

"It comes from my dad," he said of his upbringing. "It comes from how I was raised. He wanted me to be perfect every single time I was on the field. When you have your dad being that tough with you...and then you come here, you go one-for-four with a home run and then the media's all over you and your dad's like, 'You had a terrible game. What happened with the other three at bats?' What the media says, it doesn't affect you as much as what your dad is telling you."

When the Astros drafted Correa with the first overall pick in the 2012 draft, they signed him for $4.8 million, well below the slotted figure for the top pick that year. By design, they wanted to use the savings on subsequent picks. That strategy worked quite well, allowing them to sign Lance McCullers, Jr. for $2.5 million after drafting him with a supplemental pick following the first round. McCullers had good leverage since he, like Correa, was a high school senior who could have passed on a lesser offer and headed for college instead. Correa and McCullers moved along through the farm system and became good friends. Now they were two important cogs in the young machine.

"My goal is not just to be good inside the field but to be great outside the field," Correa explained. He funded a charitable foundation and raised money for a children's hospital with his charity golf tournament over the previous winter.

On his way to becoming the American League Rookie of the Year in 2015, Correa set club records for home runs by a shortstop and also by a rookie with 22. He was the youngest position player in the majors. Correa turned 21 September 2, 2015.

Only 19 players have hit 22 home runs before the age of 21.

He drove in 68 runs in 387 at bats. In 2014, Correa's season ended after 249 at bats at Class A Lancaster because of a broken fibula suffered on a slide into third base.

Surgery was required to allow the bone to heal properly. Correa started 2015 at Class AA Corpus Christi, but he had impressed everybody enough in spring training that it was not surprising how quickly he progressed. After 117 at bats, hitting .385 with seven homers and 32 RBI, Correa was promoted to Class AAA Fresno. With three more homers and 12 RBI at Fresno, Correa then joined the Astros in early June. Hinch announced on the intercom of the Astros charter from Toronto to Chicago that Correa would be joining the team and a cheer went up from the players seated in the back of the plane. Jed Lowrie had begun the season as the shortstop but was sidelined by a thumb injury for a few weeks. Jonathan Villar and Marwin Gonzalez were filling in, but Correa's arrival was expected almost every day for weeks by the media.

"We saw what he did last year in 99 games, but this year he's going to start from Day One," Jose Altuve said of 2016. "It's going to be pretty interesting. He's going to be the best player in the game soon, and I'm very excited and I feel very proud to play next to him."

Five players as young as Correa hit 22 homers in their first 100 major league games. Three had 45 extra base hits, as he had, at that age. No shortstop had done it at his age. But he was focused on improvement, saying, "I feel I can run more" he said. "I can steal more bases. I can play better defense. I can hit for a better average. So I feel like I can do everything better."

If there was a better shortstop in the majors than Correa in 2015, it wasn't apparent. The San Francisco Giants' Brandon Crawford hit 21 homers and drove in 84 runs in 561 at bats. Boston's Xander Bogaerts drove in 81 runs in 654 at bats.

Bogaerts, like Crawford, had an excellent reputation defensively. Cleveland's Francisco Lindor finished second to Correa in the AL Rookie of the Year voting and was an excellent fielder who hit .313, but he lacked Correa's power. As baseball fantasy draft owners prepared for their 2016 drafts, Correa ranked as the top shortstop on the major league list for many.

Cy Keuchel

Dallas Keuchel became the first Astro since Roger Clemens in 2004 to win the Cy Young Award. Keuchel said of Clemens' visit to Kissimmee, "When that guy talks, we listen. Any time he's around, everybody tries to do their best or impress. I don't know if it's always a good thing, but it's definitely a good thing to have him around and pick his brain a little bit."

There were not a lot of obvious similarities between the pitching styles of Keuchel and Clemens. But Keuchel had not only improved his stuff but also thought his way to success. It was obvious that he wanted to continue to grow mentally in how to assess hitters. Clemens had won seven Cy Youngs, and Keuchel was not satisfied that this one trophy was going to allow him to coast through the rest of his career. "The guy's done everything," Keuchel said of Clemens. "He has an MVP, seven Cy Youngs, 354 victories. He reiterated the fact that what he's seen in the last couple of years is that our clubhouse is one of the closest knit that he's seen in a very long time. That's always positive, but at the same time we've got to do some work on the field. It's not just won in the clubhouse. It's won outside."

Keuchel, Altuve and Jason Castro could all enjoy spring training as much as anybody in the clubhouse. After all, they all had lived through back to back 100-loss seasons in 2013 and 2014. Keuchel broke into the majors with a 3-8 record and 5.27 ERA in 2013. He was 3-3 at Minute Maid Park with a 2.95 ERA in 10 starts, a harbinger of future success, but it was a rough learning season for the Tulsa, Oklahoma native.

He also threw a complete game in his second major league start, which became a trend later in his career. The other solid indicator of future promise was his ground ball tendencies.

Keuchel went 6-10 with a 5.15 ERA in 2013, making 22 starts. He was learning his craft, but the statistics did not come close to predicting the kind of success that was to follow. And the Astros' new trend of statistical analysis presented a choice for Keuchel.

"I think when they introduced some of the new-school baseball ways with the over-shifting and the advanced data, guys were a little skeptical because it was a new concept," he said. "Not just a new concept to us but a new concept to baseball. That having been said, guys gave it a try with myself included. It's either you get on board or you get left behind. I was willing to hop onboard. It wasn't like I had room to say anything. I was coming off two pretty sub-par seasons so I did everything I could and just hopped on board."

By 2014, Keuchel was ready to break out of the early statistical pattern and become a ground ball machine, associated with more soft hits than Elton John. With his 12-9 record, 2.93 ERA, 200 innings, AL Gold Glove and 3.63 groundball to flyball ratio to lead the majors, Keuchel and his flowing beard looked the part of a rock star. The University of Arkansas southpaw, drafted in the seventh round in 2009, was destined for a major part in the 2015 season. He also had a consecutive inning scoreless streak of 20 2/3.

Named the Opening Day starter in 2015, Keuchel burst out of the starting gate by blanking Cleveland and reigning Cy Young Award winner Corey Kluber 2-0. "He's such an easy guy to trust and watch compete," Hinch said. "He takes every game as serious as anybody, so it's nice to hand him the ball here in five to six days when we play."

By May 20, Keuchel was 6-0 with a 1.67 ERA. In three of his first four starts, he allowed no runs and that covered 22 innings. He won Pitcher of the Month awards in April, May and August.

At the All-Star break he was 12-4 with a 2.12 ERA, which put him on the mound to start the All-Star Game for KC Manager Ned Yost.

Keuchel has become a fierce competitor who brings many skills to the mound. He is a physical fitness addict who brings an aggressive, skilled approach to glovework. He reminds some Astros fans of lefty Mike Hampton, who starred in the late 1990s and also fielded his position as well as anybody.

Keuchel excels at reading hitters' swings and making adjustments when hitters make solid contact. His release point is the same for his fastball, slider and changeup. He has a talent for throwing a pitch resembling a strike on its way to the plate, but it moves out of the strike zone and often produces weak contact. That's where his fielding comes in handy. Dallas has a 2.84 career groundball to flyball ratio through 2016, the best among active pitchers with at least 800 innings. He ranges along the first base and third base lines to field slowly hit topped grounders, with deft glovework and an accurate throwing arm turning them into outs instead of irritating infield hits. His second straight Gold Glove in 2015 recognized Keuchel's performances after the ball left his hand. He made only one error in 72 chances. In 2016 he made no errors and won his third straight Fielding Bible Award as the best fielder at his position in the major leagues. That award is decided by a panel of 12 experts. He also picked up his third straight Gold Glove.

Keuchel accepted the 2015 Cy Young Award in New York City from Tommy John on a snowy night over the winter. John mispronounced Keuchel's name when he introduced him as Dallas KOO-chul rather than KY-kill. Broadcasters were forced to learn it and the baseball writers were forced to vote for him by the sheer body of his work. Dallas put together a rare season, going 20-8 with a 2.48 earned run average. In his 232 innings, he allowed 185 hits. He walked 51 and fanned 216. Between the whiffs and the ground balls, there weren't many big innings against him. He became only the third Cy Young Award winner in Astros history, behind Mike Scott in 1986 and Roger Clemens in 2004. He also finished fifth in AL MVP voting.

The most remarkable number about Keuchel's groundbreaking year was his 15-0 regular season record at home with a 1.46 ERA. He was the first in major league history to do that. Keuchel stylishly accepted the Warren Spahn Award in Oklahoma as the top southpaw pitcher in the game, meaningful in a larger way because of his Oklahoma upbringing.

Who owns the Yankees? The Steinbrenner family, right? No, Dallas Keuchel.

Tyler Kepner pointed out in the *New York Times* that Keuchel shut out the Yankees for 16 innings in the regular season and six more in the Wild Card game.

Keuchel's family grew up with veteran catcher Charlie O'Brien, who caught for the World Champion Atlanta Braves in 1995, when Dallas was seven. O'Brien's son Chris was a catcher for Tulsa Bishop Kelley, where Keuchel pitched when he wasn't playing centerfield or quarterback on the football team. Keuchel idolized the Braves' Hall of Fame trio of Greg Maddux, Tom Glavine and John Smoltz. O'Brien took him to see those players one day. Both Glavine and Maddux struggled early in their careers. O'Brien said in the *Times* article, "It's almost identical. They had to learn who they were, that's the biggest thing. They knew, 'I can't throw fastballs past people all the time. I've got to pitch. I've got to change speeds, I've got to throw guys' timing off." Said Keuchel, "I feel that I've been slighted, and I'm going to make sure people know who I am. That's my main goal: to make sure people in baseball remember they missed out on Dallas Keuchel, the 221st pick overall in the '09 draft. I mean, that's not all I think about. But it's mainly what I think about."

February 24---Astros owner Jim Crane visited camp on the first day of full squad workouts. Special Assistant to the General Manager Roger Clemens also was on hand. They took in the annual address to the team by the manager before the workout and later spoke with the media. Crane was always asked by the media about payroll plans this time of year. "Listen, we've got an ownership group that is very supportive," he said. "We run kind of a break-even budget, we make a little money, but we're always flexible and will be a little more moving forward."

The payroll would start at $94 million, but, Crane added, "If we've got to make some adjustments (at the trade deadline), we'll do that. We're never gonna put a hard number on the plate, but...as we told you when we bought the team, as the team improves, we continue to spend the money in the right place and spend it in a frugal way."

The biggest multi-year contract by an Astros player was Scott Feldman's three-year, $30 million deal which would expire after the 2016 season. It was a front-loaded contract and it paid Feldman $8 million in the final year. Carlos Gomez was entering the final year of his multi-year agreement, with the Astros assuming the rest of the payments after trading for him with Milwaukee. Jason Castro, like Gomez, Feldman, Rasmus and Valbuena, could become a free agent after the season. The Astros had attempted to sign Castro to a multi-year deal but the two sides had not met agreement.

It was obvious the team's payroll was headed higher, either because of the need to fill gaps through signing free agents or getting current players to sign long-term deals.

The $94 million payroll was reported as the second largest in team history, behind only the $103 million figure for the 2009 team. In 1980, owner John McMullen made Nolan Ryan the first baseball player to make $1 million per season. That seemed like Depression era wages compared to the going rate in 2016! The Los Angeles Angels of Anaheim had a projected payroll of about $165 million. Their owner, Arte Moreno, said he had overspent his budget every year.

But he mentioned not wanting to pay a luxury tax, which would kick in if his payroll grew roughly another $25 million.

Crane discussed his team's situation. "We're in it to win championships," he said. "We'll spend what we have. You know, the business is difficult. When you have big contracts like the Angels have and they don't work, it can really hamstring a team. You'll sign the guys you need to sign. And then you'll stay within the budget."

The Angels lavished a huge, ten-year contract on Albert Pujols when he was 31. It totaled $240 million. Now Pujols was fighting to get on the field after needing foot surgery. He was 36 and still had six years remaining on his huge deal. He had delivered three full, productive seasons in his four years. But Pujols was probably not going to be ready to start the season on time and when he did play he might be relegated to more DH duties than first base assignments. He was not able to run well in 2015.

A few days later, an article in the Bleacher Report ranked the Astros number one in "Moneyball," a system used to evaluate which teams spent their payroll most efficiently. The article predicted that the Houston payroll would rank 23rd in Major League Baseball. It listed Correa, Springer and McHugh as notable pre-arbitration players. Those in that category had no bargaining leverage with their teams. Others were McCullers, Fiers, Giles, Marisnick, Tucker and Harris.

Players in this group tended to play for $500,000-600,000. The article ranked the players by their WAR (wins above replacement) numbers. Altuve, for example, had a 4.5 WAR and a 2016 salary of $3.668 million. The system of evaluating payroll expenses credited each point of WAR as having a worth of $8 million.

That gave Altuve a value of $33.6 million and assigned him a net value of $29.9 million. Keuchel was assigned a net value of $28.75 million, Carlos Gomez $18 million.

These three star players were part of the core of a team developed to contend for the next few years. Of the 11 players who had substantial playing time in 2015, Luis Valbuena was the oldest at 29. In the 2005 World Series year, seven of the 12 position players who had significant roles were at least 29. Jeff Bagwell, who was 37 then, played in only 39 games because of his arthritic right shoulder. In Correa and Altuve the Astros had two young middle infielders who lived to play with each other. They would have a young first baseman the next few years, it seemed, with Singleton and Reed vying for that spot. Springer was a 26-year-old right fielder. More good young players were in the pipeline.

Only five significant players from the 2015 Astros had left the scene. Jed Lowrie was traded to Oakland because Correa had taken his position and there was no position left for him to play ahead of Altuve and Valbuena. Chris Carter was not tendered a contract and wound up signing with Milwaukee. The Astros opted for younger and more inexpensive options at first base. Scott Kazmir had been far above their projected value for him when he signed the three-year, $48 million deal with the Dodgers. Hank Conger was traded to Tampa Bay after being unable to throw out baserunners. Oliver Perez, an aging southpaw reliever, had not been effective.

In 2005, Roger Clemens was 42. In May of 2016, Hinch would turn 42. The 2005 club featured Biggio at age 39, Brad Ausmus at 36, Jose Vizcaino at 37, Jeff Bagwell at 37 and John Franco, who was 44 when he pitched 31 games for Houston. With Keuchel 28, McHugh 29 and McCullers 22 representing the top three starters in 2016, the core of the starting staff was young. With Giles joining the bullpen at 25, their future closer was young and was not able to leave through free agency until 2021.

Chapter 4

Let the Games Begin

February 25---The Port of Houston east of downtown was teeming with shipping activity. Houston was no longer as dependent on the oil business for its success as in the early 1980s, when the oil bust caused the city to crater economically. But there was still a noticeable effect on the city's financial fortunes. People were moving to Houston in big numbers, but a pressing question existed about jobs for them.

Lance McCullers threw his first bullpen. He was days behind the other pitchers by design. The Astros had big plans for him and wanted to keep him on track for a breakout year by limiting his work in spring training based on his large increase in innings in 2015. "I know they're doing what's best for me and the team," said McCullers.

Luke Gregerson was still sidelined by a sore left oblique which flared up before camp opened. He was doing core-stabilization exercises to strengthen the area around the oblique. Pitchers, by virtue of the torque in their deliveries, are susceptible to these core injuries.

Carlos Gomez sat out part of 2015 with a similar injury. Dexter Fowler had the same type of injury when he was an Astro. Oblique difficulties plagued many major leaguers and it was an ongoing problem for years. Why? Mickey Mantle and Ted Williams never had oblique injuries. It was not an issue for Hank Aaron or Cal Ripken, Jr. Perhaps it was a function of players spending so much time in the gym during the offseason and getting their bodies in such good shape by reducing body fat that they overdid it and lost too much fat!

Mickey Lolich pitched overweight for years and he was one of the best of his era. Was this more about looking good in a Speedo than maintaining a high degree of functionality as an athlete?

With lighter bats and players gearing their training for more bat speed, they created more torque in their swings. There were theories, but the industry was losing months and months of down time to these injuries and it seemed no closer to solving the problem than to ending the Zika virus.

Gregerson said he preferred to be the closer. "I get paid to play baseball," he said. "I get paid to throw pitches and help the team win. So that's all I'm here for. So whatever happens, happens. I've already expressed my desire and you know, that's not going to change. But at the end of the day, we're here to help each other, and however that maps out is how it maps out."

Ken Giles

Ken Giles threw batting practice for the first time. The hitters took more pitches than they swung at. They were training their batting eyes by tracking pitches and giving him a chance to establish the strike zone, which worked well for both approaches. "He throws super hard," said Marwin Gonzalez after facing Giles. "It wasn't a good idea to swing against him today."

Giles arrived in Houston for the Astros Winter Caravan with his wife Estela, who was quite a softball pitcher herself until the last few years. She was carrying their first child, with a due date in July. With the nickname "100 Miles Giles," Ken credited his coaches with his development. His pitching coach at Yavapai Junior College in Prescott, Arizona, Jerry Dawson, helped him simplify his mechanics. Incidentally, Yavapai also produced hard-throwing Charley Kerfeld for the Astros' bullpen in the mid-1980s. Dawson remembered Giles throwing his fastball 93-94 mph at the time. The coaching from Dawson included taking away Giles' windup, slide step and splitter. A few months later, Giles lit up the radar gun in triple figures.

When the Phillies drafted him in 2011 in the seventh round, they got a pitcher who did not throw a slider.

The slider came from former Houston closer Brad Lidge, who learned the pitch from Houston Minor League Pitching Coordinator Dewey Robinson at the same Osceola County Stadium spring training complex Giles was using now. Robinson recommended the slider, an amalgamation of different approaches.

Lidge, who worked with Giles when Brad was a special assistant with the Phils in 2014, passed along what he had learned from Robinson. "They don't see the typical slider dot," Lidge said of the hitters' view of the slider.

Hitters tracking the slider talk about seeing a red dot in the middle of the baseball, which is created by the spin of the red seams in flight. The pitcher's focus in his delivery is on making the slider look exactly like the fastball coming out of his hand, gripping it with his fingers on top of the ball rather than toward the side. The late, sharp break to the pitch gives the pitcher an advantage, especially without the red dot to indicate to the hitter what would happen. Giles said Lidge spent hours on the telephone discussing the mentality of closing. "It was more like what you want to do with your fingers kind of thing – when to snap it" said Giles. "Because the biggest thing for me is, I try to make it look like a fastball as long as I can."

The Phillies sent Giles to the Arizona Fall League in 2013 after an injury-plagued season with a 6.31 ERA. Giles said the assignment "opened my eyes, that they thought I had a future." The epiphany for Giles included a commitment to a rigorous strength and conditioning program and refining his delivery. From that turning point, he developed his slider and was in the major leagues by the next June.

Giles was known for his intensity, and it was in the spotlight a few times with the Phillies. He had a publicized blowup with Phillies Manager Ryne Sandberg and pitching coach Bob McClure in a game in June 2015.

Another closer who hit the highlight shows when his hands were around outfielder Bryce Harper's neck, Jonathan Papelbon, was a mentor to Giles with the Phillies. Papelbon was traded to open up the job for Giles. "It's something that's not easy to explain," said Giles. "It's like a trigger to me. Split personality kind of thing." Giles' father Glenn taught special needs children. Glenn taught Ken how to act around others in need, and to be helpful to them. On the field, he took on a different persona. Glenn and his wife Diane have three children, with Ken being the youngest.

Brother Josh, six years older, preceded Ken into pro ball when he signed with the Texas Rangers.

Giles struck out 151 in his first 115 innings through 2015. "I knew I had a gift, and I decided to take advantage of it," Giles said. Jeff Luhnow added, "He's lived a lot of life and doesn't expect anything to be handed to him...He's feels like every day he's out there he's lucky." His longtime friend Andrew Walter pitched at Lancaster in 2015 and was working in the minor league complex about 200 yards away. Another childhood friend, Roman Montano, was further advanced as a player at an early age but died of a heroin overdose.

Jayson Stark wrote in a column for ESPN that only one of 19 relievers who saved at least 30 games in 2013 was still with his same club – Glen Perkins of Minnesota. Only four others were closers for any team. Seven were either injured or out of baseball entirely.

Major league baseball announced a rule change. New rule 6.01(j) required baserunners to make an attempt to slide to the base and remain on the base on potential double plays. In 2015, Chase Utley's hard slide in the playoffs into the Mets' shortstop Ruben Tejada put Tejada out of action for the rest of the postseason and forced him to have surgery to repair a broken leg.

MLB and the Major League Baseball Players Association agreed that for the players' safety this new rule would be helpful.

A runner must now attempt to make a "bona fide slide" in a double play situation, requiring him to make contact with the ground ahead of the base and to slide within reach of the base without changing his path to initiate contact with a fielder. An umpire can call both the runner and the batter out on a violation.

February 26---On this date in 1836, Colonel William Travis and his brave band of Texian revolutionaries were barricaded inside the Alamo, ready to fight to the death against Mexican General Antonio Lopez de Santa Anna and his vastly superior forces. "I am determined to sustain myself as long as possible and die like a soldier who never forgets what is due to his own honor and that of his country," wrote Travis. "Victory or death." Death followed shortly for Travis and his men. But they set the stage for an ultimate victory later when Texas won its independence at the Battle of San Jacinto east of Houston.

Lefty reliever Neil Cotts left the Land of Lincoln, heading from Illinois to Florida with the announcement that the Astros had signed him as a non-roster pitcher and added him to the mix for the bullpen. Tony Sipp was the only strong candidate for the bullpen from the southpaw side. Kevin Chapman also had a major league resume and was on the 40-man roster, but in Cotts the Astros added a 35-year-old veteran with a 10-year career. Two other non-roster lefties, former Astros starter Wandy Rodriguez and Edwar Cabrera, were possibilities for the roster. It was not a given that the Astros would carry two southpaws. That seemed to be dependent on carrying 13 pitchers rather than 12.

"As we know, there's a lot of major league-quality free agents still out on the market, and we felt it's an opportunity to add to our bullpen options," said Hinch. "We have a little bit of a shortage of lefthanded relievers, depending on where Wandy, Chapman and Cabrera fit in. Adding another lefthanded option with his experience will give us some choices at the end of camp.

"He offers us some versatility that we don't have a ton of. I talked to him on the phone last night. He's a veteran, he's been around. I don't worry about him being a few days late to camp."

Cotts pitched very well against the Astros in the 2005 World Series as a member of the White Sox. Chad Qualls, a member of the 2005 World Series Astros, had left via free agency and signed with Colorado over the winter. He had been the last remaining link on the team to 2005.

Now, in Wandy Rodriguez, the Astros might have added another reminder of that successful year. Or maybe Cotts, who held lefties to a .186 average in 2015 with Minnesota and Milwaukee, would claim that spot.

Cotts was not the only veteran player to sign. Veteran outfielder Drew Stubbs agreed to a minor league deal with the Rangers, as did Shane Victorino with the Cubs and Will Venable with the Indians. The Indians needed an outfielder because they lost Abraham Almonte to an 80-game suspension after a performance enhancing drug test revealed Boldenone in his system. It is an anabolic steroid generally used by veterinarians on horses. The 26-year-old Almonte not only would not make it to the starting gate, but he would sit out half the season as the latest example of stupidity revealed by drug testing. Players are still getting caught on tests every year and that leads to suspicion that some are ahead of the testing technology and are going undetected. But an 80-game penalty is a strong reminder of the risks associated with that approach.

Meanwhile, Roger Clemens gave a tutorial on the split fingered fastball to minor leaguers Michael Feliz, Jordan Jankowski and James Hoyt. That pitch propelled Mike Scott to a Cy Young award when former major league pitcher and San Francisco Giants manager Roger Craig taught it to Scott.

Craig was not managing at the time, but when Scott was dazzling Craig's Giants hitters with the pitch, Roger was suffering at the hands of his own good instruction.

George Springer

As George Springer prepared to begin his third major league season, he got many questions from the media about staying healthy. It was an obvious approach. Springer missed 64 games in his rookie season of 2014 with a left quad strain. Then in 2015 he missed two months with a broken bone in his right wrist after being hit by a pitch by the Royals' Edinson Volquez. "Obviously, the goal is to stay on the field, but there's some stuff you can't control," said Springer. "I was able to take some strides and figure some stuff out as a player, and obviously I was happy with some stuff the team was able to do."

Springer talked on a radio show about running into the right field wall making a play at Minute Maid Park in 2015 and suffering some concussion symptoms. He pointed out that better padding was needed for the wall, and he added that the running track wasn't of much help to him on that play. Springer always said that he wouldn't change his playing style, which included many diving and sliding catches and throwing his body into plays with reckless abandon at times. Veteran observers had raised questions about Springer's style, insinuating that he could learn when to play a little more carefully to keep himself in the lineup.

Springer, a centerfielder prior to arriving in Houston, could be saved from some of the injuries threatening corner outfielders by returning to the wide open spaces of center after 2016, when Carlos Gomez might be moving on through free agency. But for now, Springer was preparing for another all-out assault on walls and the ground if it meant taking away hits.

As noted earlier in Jeff Luhnow's mention of the top highlights of 2015, Springer's catch in Arlington robbing a grand slam ranked as one of the top plays of the year.

In many ways it was the ultimate of catches, given the game situation.

Springer prevented a loss by racing to the right field wall, timing his leap perfectly and reaching to full extension to snag a potential winning grand slam by the Rangers' Leonys Martin in the tenth inning. The April 12 game sent Houston on to 6-4 win in 14 innings on a two-run homer by Hank Conger. Pitcher Tony Sipp, who was spared four earned runs by the gem, reacted on the field as if it were the biggest play ever behind him. It might have been. The catch also demonstrated that the Astros would save many runs by their outfield play. When the players came to the clubhouse after the 4-hour and 24-minute game, they earned a win they seemed destined to lose after blowing a 4-0 lead in the seventh. And they had won the series from the Rangers, serving notice that 2015 was a brand new start for them.

"He plays with a style that's very aggressive, but he can do anything on this field," Hinch said of Springer. "There's a vibe and an excitement that comes when Springer's playing." Hinch discussed wanting Springer to travel with the team when he was injured. "I wanted his voice and his energy," Hinch said. "Those are important things to us. To see him in there getting on guys, getting on me, that's part of who we are as a team." Springer explained, "I understand that not everybody every day is going to be 100 per cent – and I'm not either. If I can do anything to get somebody into the game emotionally, get 'em fired up, be positive, I'll do anything to affect somebody's mood to affect how they play. If you're in a good mood, you'll probably have a higher chance to play better." Luhnow referred to him as "the heart and soul of this team." Added Dallas Keuchel: "He's our spark plug. He comes to the park every day with a smile on his face." Springer spent the winter in Houston staying in shape. "There's not one aspect of this game that I can say I've gotten figured out," he said. "I need to improve on everything that I can."

In 2015 Springer improved by realizing that less is more. He said he realized when hitting, "Just swing 80 per cent. With game adrenaline and my style of swing, I'm going to swing hard – but I'm under control. Swing hard, under control. And that's pretty much all I do now."

Springer was trained by his mother early in life in gymnastics. He starred at the University of Connecticut after growing up in New Britain, where Jeff Bagwell starred just before being traded from Boston to Houston. Springer went to New Britain games and found outfielder Torii Hunter of Minnesota to be his favorite player. By 2013 Springer was putting together one of the best minor league seasons in Astros history at AA Corpus Christi and AAA Oklahoma City, belting 37 homers and stealing 45 bases. He was the first Astros minor leaguer to join the 30-30 club. He was Minor League Baseball's Offensive Player of the Year. When Springer joined the Astros April 15, 2014, he quickly began to show the skills that landed him as the 11th overall selection in the 2011 draft. By May, he was AL Rookie of the Month. Although he hit only .231, his 20 homers in 295 at bats demonstrated his power.

Springer's maturity led to this answer about hitting 40 homers and driving in 120 someday: "It's not about that. It's about what I can do to help us that day. If that's a walk, a stolen base, a sac fly, that's what counts, not the stats at the end of the day." He demonstrated that approach in 2015, improving his batting average from .231 to .276 and his on base average from .336 to .367. When he answered questions about his revised approach from the long, powerful swings of 2014, he said, "I'm just trying to get to first base." When Springer did reach base, his stolen bases improved from 5 to 16. His legs were a major factor in the Astros offense, even with his decline in homers from 20 to 16 even with almost 100 more at bats. Springer demonstrated his growth as an offensive player in 2015. He realized that as a top of the order hitter he could impact the game more by reaching base for his teammates. He hit many more ground balls and line drives through the infield and had much better bat control, going from 114 strikeouts in 295 at bats to 109 in 388 at bats.

"The game is starting to slow down for me," he explained. "I'm starting to get more relaxed, and that's a good thing."

The numbers would agree. Springer in just portions of two major league seasons hit 36 homers in his first 180 games, a club record.

His .817 career OPS was fourth highest among Astros in their first two seasons. Only Lance Berkman, Hunter Pence and Jeff Bagwell were better.

Off the field, Springer became a spokesman for the Stuttering Association for the Young. He hosted a bowling fundraiser for the organization and raised more funds through other efforts. He never shied away from an interview because of his stuttering.

Collin McHugh

The tandem of Dallas Keuchel and Collin McHugh was among the best 1-2 punches the Astros had ever had over a two-year period. Their combined records for 2014-15 were 62-33, with a combined 3.00 ERA. Combined prior to 2014, they were 9-26 with a 5.82 ERA! When did two pitchers have a combined turnaround like that? Research by STATS Inc. did not show a better improvement in combined winning percentage than theirs. Both were 28. They had figured out the keys to success at exactly the same time, without any track record of excellence in the majors prior to that. Pitching in the 1-2 spots in the rotation, they made it much more likely the Astros would win a given series.

"I think that's kind of the building block of every pitcher's repertoire," McHugh said of his fastball. "You have to start from the bottom and work your way back up, and for me, that big block at the bottom is fastball command. You've got to refine it, you've got to get better at it early in the season and kind of build on that base." McHugh said of his quick success, "Every once in a while you've got to pinch yourself and remind yourself you're here and this is real and you have a job to do."

Then he refocused, "Last year is last year. Wins are going to come and go. There are going to be years you pitch better and you get less wins and there's going to be years you don't pitch as well and you get more wins because the team behind you is better.

"My goal is to be as consistent as I can be and just go out and pitch my game and let the results speak for themselves."

McHugh was of interest to Luhnow's staff when the Astros claimed him on waivers in December 2013 despite his career big league record of 0-8 with an ERA of 8.94! Why? He was drafted by the Mets in '08 from Berry College in Georgia and had success in the minors, but he was no mystery to major league hitters. The Astros' analytical staff studied tapes of his pitching and formed the opinion that McHugh could be successful with more emphasis on the high, four-seam fastball. His curve came out of the same arm slot and he mixed in effective cut fastballs. Under the tutelage of pitching coach Brent Strom, McHugh blossomed. In 2014 he made 25 starts and compiled the second lowest ERA for a Houston rookie in the club's history, 2.73. He fanned 157 in 154 innings.

Jason Castro, the fixture behind the plate for Houston pitchers, called an intelligent game and McHugh executed the game plan. In 2015, McHugh's ERA climbed to 3.89, but with the run support from the hard-hitting Astros he was 19-7. His run support was fourth best in the league, an average of 5.79 per nine innings. He rolled up 203 innings, with his final regular season start October 3 at Arizona giving the Astros their 86th win. That lowered their magic number for clinching a playoff spot to one, which allowed them to clinch a spot on the final day of the season without winning the game because the Angels lost that day. Then, in the American League Division Series, McHugh won Game One in Kansas City 5-2 with six innings of two-run baseball. He gave up only four hits, including two solo homers by Kendrys Morales. He led Johnny Cueto 2-1 in the fifth inning of Game Five, leaving with two on in the fifth. Those runs and the loss were charged to him when the Royals rallied and that's when the Astros season ended.

But McHugh tied for second in wins in the AL behind Keuchel and they totaled 39.

McHugh was tied with Jake Arrieta of the Chicago Cubs for the most wins in the majors since August 1, 2014.

He was third behind Keuchel for the highest amount of soft contact in the majors the last two seasons.

He and Keuchel were the only two Astros starters who were in the rotation all season.

Off the field, McHugh's golf game suffered because he was a father now. He and his wife Ashley welcomed baby Shaw on Ashley's birthday December 18, 2015. His father Scott said he was focused on a strong start to the season. Collin said, "My wife was always like, 'You can't make an All-Star team until we have a kid so that we can bring our kid to the All-Star Game.' Now that we have a kid, I can officially set my eyes on making an All-Star team."

Colby Rasmus

Colby Rasmus liked his teammates attitudes on the first day of spring workouts. "There's a lot of smiles and everybody's walking around with their chests puffed out right now feeling pretty good about themselves, which is what we need," he said. "We don't need to have our tails between our legs because we lost those games against the Royals. We played 'em good and they knew we were there. Being an Astro is good right now. It's a good place to be."

Rasmus was a first-round choice of St. Louis in 2005. He arrived in the Cardinal clubhouse in 2009, and the experience was not pleasant for him. "I got drafted first round and they all said I was a bonus baby," he said. "I was driving an M5 when I was 21, so they thought that I should buy my own (suits). Albert (Pujols) gave me a little watch after the season, but that was just because he got it for free. It wasn't the same."

Rasmus brought the approach the Astros wanted to their clubhouse, which was the opposite of what he experienced in St. Louis.

They embraced their rookies when they arrived with the major league club, including their time in spring training, and rookies said they felt they were an important part of the team.

Rasmus and Carlos Gomez took six teammates shopping for suits, and the two veterans footed the bill. They also pulled some players aside and counseled them about nuances of playing the game. Rasmus remembered being a rookie. "I didn't talk to anybody," he said. "I just sat in my locker, put my headphones on, and looked at my clothes. It was a tough time. I thought the big leagues were going to be a little something different. I just try to make it fun. It should be fun."

Rasmus demonstrated that he was enjoying himself when the Astros clinched the Wild Card spot by beating the Yankees in New York when he joined his teammates in the postgame celebration shirtless and wearing large goggles to protect his eyes from champagne. There was a promotional day scheduled in 2016 with a Rasmus bobblehead giveaway. Rasmus had his best season in 2015, with a career-high 25 home runs from his vicious uppercut swing, many of them mortar shots. He led the club with four postseason long balls.

The Astros prized their young players, as evidenced by their use of ten rookies in 2015. Their welcome treatment by the veterans was helpful in allowing them to relax and take the field without being intimidated by teammates who were not ice-breakers for them. "This generation of young players is really impressive," said Hinch. "Across baseball, the number of 25-and-unders who are making their debuts, contributing, is hard to fathom, that this many players can make an impact this soon and become, not necessarily the faces of their teams, but very prominent." Keuchel agreed: "This game is getting younger and younger. The teams that are doing the best are the ones who can get the best performance out of young players. That's the way it is."

Rasmus was one of four centerfielders on the Houston roster. Gomez, Springer and Marisnick all were centerfielders, but only one could play center and the corner outfielders gave Hinch added outfield coverage and gave the pitchers confidence that their mistakes could turn into outs.

February 28---The Texas Rangers signed free agent Ian Desmond. Desmond, an elite shortstop with Washington, had a miserable first half in 2015 but rebounded to hit well in the second half. Washington extended him a qualifying offer after the season, and he waited all winter for a better one. The Players Association planned to target the labor agreement clause regarding qualifying offers in their negotiations with ownership, because several players went unsigned most of the winter. Dexter Fowler, Yovani Gallardo and Howie Kendrick were all caught in that vortex and went unsigned until spring training. The primary reason seemed to be the price of doing business. In addition to the signing cost of these elite players, their 2015 teams would receive a first-round draft choice if they extended a qualifying offer, while the signing team would have to surrender a first-round pick. In the case of the Rangers, the situation was not so costly. They had extended a qualifying offer to Gallardo and when Gallardo signed with Baltimore they picked up a first-round choice. So they would forfeit the 19th pick in the draft for signing Desmond but gain the 30th pick for losing Gallardo. Desmond signed for $8 million, an affordable rate for a player who could move from shortstop to left field to cover for the knee injury of Josh Hamilton, who was expected to miss at least the first month of the season. The Rangers players seemed thrilled to have him. Hamilton was always a question mark because of his health, and Cole Hamels mentioned the balance Desmond would bring to the lineup. He is a righthanded hitter and would help balance the lefthanded bats of Prince Fielder, Mitch Moreland, Shin Soo Choo and Rougned Odor.

Desmond turned down a seven-year, $107 million offer from Washington two years earlier.

He was one of six players to hit at least 100 homers and steal at least 100 bases since 2010. He spoke of the need to change the system involving the loss of a draft choice by the signing team.

Both the Astros and the Rangers were in a position to eye each other's moves over the winter. The Rangers overtook the Astros to finish atop the division in the late stages of 2015 and they dominated the season series 13-6. That extended their hold over the Astros to 80-49 in the all-time series. For years the only thing at stake was a trophy given to the winner of the season series, called the Battle for the Silver Boot. In 2015 the prize was the top spot in the division, and the Rangers edged the Astros by two games. There was a real rivalry for the first time now, brought to a heightened state by a dustup on the field in Houston. Rougned Odor slid hard into Altuve away from the bag. Odor also homered and had a big bat flip in front of the Astros' dugout running up the first base line. When he came to the plate later and took his time smoothing out the dirt rather than stepping in the batter's box, catcher Hank Conger let him know that was unacceptable. That brought Prince Fielder, who was on deck, running toward the plate and the benches emptied. Managers Jeff Bannister and A.J. Hinch, who are good friends, were shoving and yelling at each other. In another game at Arlington, Odor jumped over the dugout railing after a teammate's homer and danced on the field from one end of the dugout to the other. That attracted some attention from the Houston bench. The rivalry was now full blown and it seemed it would continue at that level for a while.

Strangely, the other four AL West teams train in Arizona, leaving the Astros in Florida with frequent opponents such as Atlanta, Detroit, Washington and St. Louis. If they had moved to Arizona years ago when they explored that plan, they would be playing the Rangers often in the spring.

February 29---The Baltimore Orioles banned postgame pie-in-the-face celebrations for "safety reasons."

A.J. Hinch named Doug Fister his starter for the exhibition opener March 3. "It made sense to have our newest guy kick us off so we can get into competition with him," said Hinch, who planned to use six or seven starting pitchers during the spring.

Those starters who seemed to be ticketed to AAA Fresno unless they got an opening were Brad Peacock, Asher Wojciechowski, Dan Straily, Jake Buchanan and Michael Feliz. The five of them would give Manager Tony DeFrancesco a potentially strong rotation at Fresno. "I understand there's not much opportunity," said Peacock, who was recovering from back surgery. He hadn't faced live hitters since June, but he felt great. "Wojo" revamped his mechanics. Straily worked with a personal trainer over the winter for the first time. All five had been in the major leagues, although Buchanan and Feliz did not see much time. There was a competition for the rotation involving six pitchers for five spots. If all were healthy and the sixth man became the long man in the bullpen, that would leave 13 pitchers on the staff. The six other short relief spots already were allocated to Ken Giles, Tony Sipp, Luke Gregerson, Pat Neshek, Will Harris and Josh Fields. Every team had to provide for depth because of the demands a six-month season puts on a pitching staff. "You can go from full rotation to an empty rotation pretty quickly in this game," said Hinch. Straily was the only one of the "bubble group" of five who had no more minor league options.

That would potentially force the Astros' hand at the end of camp since they would not have control over Straily at AAA and he could become a free agent. Controlling players is of vital importance this time of year. The Astros went to camp with 39 roster spots secured, leaving one opening.

The Future

Baseball America's Prospect Handbook, a necessity for those who follow top minor league prospects, ranks each team's top prospects. J.J. Cooper wrote of the Astros, "Under General Manager Jeff Luhnow, the Astros have focused on depth. If one prospect is good, five are much better. The Astros also look to include lower-level prospects in many of the trades they swing. That's how they picked up Frances Martes, who went from little-noticed Gulf Coast League arm to the Astros' number two prospect in the span of a little more than a year." He pointed out that pitcher David Paulino was still in Rookie ball when the Astros traded for him, and now he's ranked seventh in their organization among developing minor leaguers.

Martes, a Dominican-born righthander, was listed at 6-1 and 225 pounds. The Astros insisted on him when they traded Jarred Cosart, Austin Wates and Kike Hernandez to Miami in 2014. Third baseman Colin Moran, their ninth ranked prospect, was more well-known and Jake Marisnick was in the deal as well. But Martes, now 20 years old, moved along quickly with a mid-90s fastball and a power curve. He made a rare move up from "complex ball" (Gulf Coast League play is at the Astros' Kissimmee complex) to AA in one year because both his pitches were graded "plus-plus," which translates into "top of the line." Scouts loved his expressionless demeanor on the mound. Martes could probably help in the bullpen if there was a need in 2016.

Paulino, a towering 6-7 215-pound righthander, ranks as their third best minor league pitcher and number seven overall among their prospects.

He and outfielder Danry Vasquez were swapped by Detroit in 2013 for closer Jose Veras when the Astros were rebuilding. Paulino missed all of 2014 with Tommy John surgery but made 13 appearances in 2015 and showed an explosive fastball and a big curve. Paulino also was from the Dominican Republic.

Three other Dominican dandies ranked among their top 20. Michael Feliz, number 11, pitched five times for the Astros in 2015.

His exceptional fastball but lack of development of other pitches rendered him a bullpen candidate. Albert Abreu, number 12, had a big time arm but only 115 innings of pro experience. Jandel Gustave, number 18, went 5-2 at Corpus Christi with a 2.15 ERA with 20 saves. He touched 102 mph after being returned as a Rule 5 draft choice by Kansas City. The Astros placed him on their 40-man roster over the winter to prevent a recurrence of that Rule 5 loss.

Major league baseball has become a melting pot of talent from around the world. These five Dominican standouts represent a strong wave of players who seek fame and fortune in the United States at a time when not as many young boys are playing baseball in this country. Many efforts have been made to attract boys to baseball. Major League baseball has had the RBI (Reviving Baseball in the Inner Cities) program for years, including the Astros Academy in Houston. The philosophy behind it is to build baseball fields in the inner city areas, where kids are playing basketball or avoiding sports altogether, relieving them of the need to seek transportation and purchase equipment. The first RBI Academy, in Compton, California served as the model. The kids who are offered free equipment and coaching often ride their bicycles or city buses. Many of them do not have two parents in their homes and come home after school to an empty house or a house with only children since their mothers are at work.

Baseball is a "father-son" sport, involving spending time playing catch and practicing. If there is no father at home, there will be coaches ready to act as father figures at the academies.

Another initiative aimed at getting kids back to the baseball fields again as they were decades ago is under the charge of Hall of Famer Cal Ripken, Jr. He and Commissioner Rob Manfred devised a plan to put more action in the sport.

Ripken founded his Cal Ripken Baseball Leagues years ago and is well equipped to run a program for modern day kids, who want activity rather than too much "screen time."

The design involves changing the rules for kids. Sometimes the inning will begin with two men on base for the batter.

Sometimes the inning will last until five boys have batted. It won't require three outs, but the motive is to have more action in the game with baserunning and fielding plays. The hope is that kids will leave their IPads and IPods at home and ditch the interactive games for physical activity. In poor countries such as the Dominican Republic, kids don't have options involving purchasing technology. Those who pursue baseball and do well at it can make nice lives for themselves and their families.

Years ago there were limits to how many foreign born players any organization could accumulate for the U.S. minor league clubs, based on immigration laws. Each organization was allowed a certain number of foreign work visas per year. Those visas applied to players from foreign countries who play in full-time summer leagues in the United States. Every team has summer league teams in countries such as the Dominican Republic, and players are not required to have visas if they were born in those countries. The common tactic was to sign a young player and play him in one of those leagues until he became proficient enough to award him a work visa and bring him to the U.S. Dominican players from poor families are more likely to play baseball at the Class A level for extremely low salaries than American players from middle class or wealthy families who have other options, such as college.

But the U.S. government changed the system 5-7 years ago, as Astros Director of Minor League Operations Allen Rowin recalled. He explained that the system now allowed for foreign born players to play in the U.S. with no limitations.

Their visas were changed from H1B to P1 visas, which are used for professional entertainers.

The Astros had options for the future at third base while Valbuena manned the hot corner for the major league club, perhaps with help from Matt Duffy and Marwin Gonzalez. Valbuena could become a free agent at the end of the season. Colin Moran was drafted in the first round (sixth overall) in 2013 and hit .306 at Corpus Christi with 67 RBI and a .381 on base average. The University of North Carolina product was known for his line drive hitting style and his good contact approach with a small load to his swing. The Astros could certainly use more hitters of that kind. The knock on Moran was his lack of power and lack of speed and slow first step at third base. But his progress was hampered in 2015 when a throw from the outfield hit him in the jaw when he slid into a base. He missed a month with a broken jaw. Another third baseman with hit tools, J.D. Davis, was a third round pick in 2014 from Cal State-Fullerton. The 6-3, 200-pounder was described by Baseball America as a "fringe-average defender," but his 26 homers, 101 RBI and .370 on base average at Lancaster had him on the radar screens. His strong arm had given him 94-95 mph offerings from the mound as a college closer. He seemed right behind Duffy and Moran on the third base chart of succession. Former Astro Morgan Ensberg coached him at Lancaster on softening his hands.

If a shortstop would be needed any time soon other than the capable super sub Marwin Gonzalez, the number 3 minor league prospect, Alex Bregman, was wearing number 82 in his first big league camp as a non-roster invitee. From his LSU background and his status as the second player drafted in 2016, Bregman was expected to move quickly.

He was assumed to be the AA Corpus Christi everyday shortstop in 2016 after reeling in a $5.9 million signing bonus. He was termed "one of the safer college picks in recent years," and was earning praise from his teammates.

J.D. Davis said of his competitiveness, "really, it's very unique. He wants to be first in everything.

He's one of the hardest-working guys I've seen. Defensively, he's unbelievable." Bregman wasn't gifted with Correa's tools, but his intelligence allowed him to put his body in good fielding positions and he was known for making plays.

Joe Musgrove, prospect number six in the BA rankings, was 23. He arrived in the ten-player Blue Jay trade sending J.A. Happ to Toronto. He had injuries in 2012 and 2013. He climbed the ladder in 2015 from Class A Quad Cities to High A Lancaster to AA Corpus. He totaled eight walks and 99 strikeouts! He was shut down after 101 innings in August, but was given a chance to reach the majors some time in 2016.

March 1---On Super Tuesday, the action took place after dark when the election polls closed. Donald Trump and Hillary Clinton both fared well and continued to be pacesetters in their parties.

Astronaut Scott Kelly left the International Space Station and headed to earth after almost a year in space. He was headed for NASA at the Johnson Space Center the next day. Kelly was actually two inches taller after a year in space, and he would be compared with his twin astronaut brother Mark for the next few months to gauge the effects of spending a lengthy time in space. There was always a close relationship between the Houston club and NASA, going back to renaming the Colt .45s as the Astros in 1965, the same year the Astrodome opened. A group of astronauts threw out first pitches at the first game in the Dome, and some lifetime friendships were formed between Houston players and astronauts.

Through the years at spring training, some front office personnel and even a few players had met in the middle of the night in Kissimmee and traveled to the Kennedy Space Center on the Atlantic Ocean to watch a launch of a space shuttle.

The Astros had the day off.

March 2---Texas celebrated its 180th anniversary.

In football news, columnists were calling for the Houston Texans to waive running back Arian Foster. He would turn 30 soon, and he had been able to play in only 25 of the previous 48 games. He joined the Texans in 2009.

In baseball, new Yankee closer Aroldis Chapman was slapped with a 30-game suspension by Commissioner Rob Manfred under the new domestic violence policy. Manfred and Players Association Executive Director Tony Clark agreed on the policy a few months earlier. Under the guidelines, Chapman would lose 30 days of pay, totaling $1,856,557. Chapman was the first player penalized in this fashion under the new policy. The Rockies' shortstop Jose Reyes was sitting out in Hawaii on an indefinite paid leave suspension until his trial April 4.

Chapman reportedly pushed and choked his girlfriend Oct. 30, 2015. But there were conflicting accounts of the incident and authorities did not file charges against him. It was reported that Chapman was pushed into a garage by his girlfriend's brother, where he was locked in. Then he fired eight shots into a wall and window of the garage. The suspension would prevent Chapman from pitching against the Astros in the season-opening series April 4 at Yankee Stadium. When the Yankees traded with the Cincinnati Reds in December to get him, he joined Andrew Miller and Dellin Betances in one of the most fearsome bullpens in the majors.

Phase I

March 3---Happy Opening Day! For the Astros, anyway. They began the spring campaign in Clearwater against the Phillies and the game was televised on the Major League Baseball Network. Doug Fister started the first game and looked sharp with two shutout innings, striking out four. He faced nine batters on a 75-degree day and touched 90 mph, which is an effective number for him.

The Astros held off the Phillies 3-2.

Young Jandel Gustave gave up an unearned run in the ninth but got the save, keeping the radar readings for his fastballs in the mid to upper 90s. Matt Duffy, playing third base, blasted the first Houston long ball of the spring. Jon Singleton started his campaign for the first base job by going 0-for-3. George Springer had a pair of doubles. The Astros began with 62 players in camp, 32 of them pitchers.

In Kissimmee, Evan Gattis took "flips" in the batting cage for the first time after sports hernia surgery three weeks ago. A coach on one knee just to the side of the player flips the ball and the player hits it into a net. Gattis reported that he was coming along well and on schedule. He was not allowed to run the bases yet and doctors told him that would be one of the most difficult tasks. His availability for Opening Day was undecided.

Luke Gregerson threw off a mound for first time since his minor left oblique strain. He reported no problems.

A "micro" camp opened for ten selected minor leaguers ahead of the reporting date for the bulk of the minor leaguers.

Kolten Wong of the Cardinals and Salvador Perez of the Royals signed multiyear contract extensions.

A handful of people came to the Sam Houston statue in Herrmann Park to celebrate Texas Independence Day. The inscription at the base of the gigantic Sam Houston statue along I-45 just outside Huntsville is a quote from the former Governor of Texas, "Govern wisely and as little as possible."

March 4---If Tuesday was Super Tuesday, this was Super Friday for baseball fans. A full slate of spring training games signaled that the long winter was over and daily baseball news was returning for passionate fans of the sport.

This was the beginning of the Astros' final spring in Kissimmee. They opened Osceola County Stadium in 1985 against the New York Yankees. Yogi Berra was the New York skipper at that time and Bob Lillis had the reigns of the Astros. Berra later became the Astros' bench coach at the request of his longtime friend and New Jersey neighbor, Dr. John McMullen.

McMullen was a passionate sports fan who also owned the New Jersey Devils of the NHL. When he owned the Astros, he directed General Manager Bill Wood to call him in the wee hours of the morning and wake him up with results of any late night games on the West Coast. He listened to a brief summary of the game, then rolled over and went back to sleep. He got more information from Wood the next morning.

This was the 32nd year in Kissimmee. During that time, two U.S. Presidents had thrown out first pitches, George H.W. Bush and Bill Clinton. Of the 24 300-game winners in the history of the game, 11 were at the stadium in some capacity during the 32 years. They included Warren Spahn, Steve Carlton, Phil Niekro, Don Sutton, Gaylord Perry, Early Wynn and Randy Johnson. Johnson never had a spring training with the Astros, joining them in a midseason trade in 1998 and leaving via free agency before the next spring. Kissimmee, near Orlando, served the Astros well, with its 5,300-seat capacity ballpark.

Owner Jim Crane, whose number 24 was retired by his alma mater University of Central Missouri on this day, teamed up with the Washington Nationals to plan their future at the Ballpark of the Palm Beaches in West Palm Beach. On this day, the new logo of that complex was revealed to the media. The new complex was built on a landfill.

It was designed to give the fans unusual access to the minor league fields as well as the major league stadium, which would be shared by the two clubs. They would each have their own minor league clubhouses and complexes. The Ballpark of the Palm Beaches would be a short drive from Jupiter, Florida. That complex housed the Cardinals and the Marlins. The Mets would not be far away in St. Lucie.

The proximity to these other teams would reduce some of the long bus rides the Astros currently had to make to other Florida stadiums. The West Palm complex was being designed to allow fans to walk from the parking areas through the minor league practice fields on their way to the stadium. Features from local golf courses, including some higher landscaped areas, would add to the ambience.

The stadium, with seating for about 6,500, plus another 1,000 seats available, was designed to maximize shaded areas with the sun setting behind the backs of fans sitting behind home plate.

Kissimmee's complex was still in good condition, but attracting another tenant would be difficult. Washington would be moving with the Astros to South Florida from a nearby facility at Viera.

A good crowd watched the Astros beat the Cardinals 6-3 with Wandy Rodriguez starting and fanning four in two innings to get the win. Marwin Gonzalez, Luis Valbuena and Preston Tucker all went deep on a beautiful spring day with the Astros winning their home opener for a 2-0 start. Jeff Bagwell was in camp to work with the first basemen on fielding.

March 5---Former Astros manager Terry Collins brought the New York Mets to Kissimmee and they beat the Astros 3-1. Collins, who managed the Astros 1994-96, is the oldest major league manager at 66. He took his team to the World Series in 2015.

The spring debut of Ken Giles went badly, with Giles losing a 1-0 lead and absorbing the loss. He was clocked from 94 to 98 mph, but made a mistake for a triple to Michael Conforto on a slider. Both Matt Duffy and Jon Singleton fanned as pinch hitters in the ninth. A.J. Hinch and hitting coach Dave Hudgens talked before the game about several hitters working on changes. Altuve was working on his stride, trying to avoid stepping too much toward home plate. Jason Castro is focused on his hands, trying to lift them higher before beginning his swing so he can hit high fastballs better.

Carlos Gomez was trying to "tone down" his swing. "We'd like him to play under control maybe a touch more, but he's never shy on effort, he comes from a good place and effort's never an issue," said Hinch.

The Astros scored their run on a Colin Moran RBI single. Moran said he was more comfortable this second spring with the Houston organization. He mentioned that when he suffered the broken jaw last year he studied video of his hitting for the first time, because he was not allowed to participate in any physical work. He worked on a few mechanical changes for the second half of the season. His work paid off with a .333 batting average from July on, including a .416 on base average and .536 slugging percentage.

March 6---Nancy Reagan died at age 94. The tributes were flowing in for her life, her marriage and her service. She was called a "true partner" to President Ronald Reagan.

NFL quarterback Peyton Manning retired after winning the Super Bowl with Denver. He joined the Mt. Rushmore of NFL quarterbacks along with Johnny Unitas, Joe Montana and Tom Brady.

PGA golfer Adam Scott won a tournament for the second straight week by one stroke over Bubba Watson at the World Golf Championships-Cadillac Championship at Trump National Doral. Donald Trump helicoptered in to meet some of the golfers. But the future of the tournament at Doral was in doubt because the sponsor had a clause in the contract allowing Cadillac to take the tournament elsewhere.

Three months later it was announced that the tournament would be moved to Mexico City.

Chase Utley's two-game suspension was overturned. The decision was based on an inconsistent interpretation of the rule through the years. It seemed to be a proper resolution of the dispute, getting Utley off the hook but establishing a new directive with the players fully aware of their new responsibilities sliding into second base.

Puerto Rican singer Marc Anthony came to camp with his father to watch and meet Carlos Correa. Correa used a recording of Anthony's song "Preciosa" in 2015 for his walkup music. Anthony told Correa he would write a new walkup song just for Carlos for 2016.

Another beautiful Florida morning dawned, with an early departure for A.J. Hinch. He left with the traveling squad on a trip to Bradenton. He would manage the road team on a split squad day, with Brad Peacock starting for Hinch's team in Bradenton against the Pirates while bench coach Trey Hillman managed the home team in Kissimmee against the Toronto Blue Jays. Scott Feldman pitched for that Houston squad.

Hillman brought a wealth of baseball experience and a high energy level to the job. The native of Amarillo, Texas joined the Astros in 2015 after a year in the Yankee organization. He spent the previous 11 seasons as a manager and bench coach in the majors and in Japan.

The UT-Arlington grad, now living in Liberty Hill, Texas, seemed to know people in every major league ballpark. He was a tireless worker, throwing batting practice daily during the regular season. He worked closely with Hinch to communicate with the players during games and also in the preparatory stages to give each position player an idea of where he fit into the picture.

As the Blue Jays worked out on the main stadium field, the Astros again did their pregame routines on the back diamonds of the minor league complex. In the stadium, a cool breeze was picking up and blowing the flags in right center field toward the right field corner.

The Canadian and Texas flags were being blown by a strong wind just to the left of the 390-foot designation on the right field fence.

Former Blue Jay Colby Rasmus homered to right field off Marcus Stroman in the second inning. The wind helped the fly ball sneak over the right field fence. Starter Scott Feldman worked two perfect innings in his debut.

Asher Wojciechowski, another former Blue Jay, took over next, contributing two more perfect innings.

Singleton struck his first blow of the spring in the fifth, lining a homer just over the fence in right close to the foul pole for his first spring hit after starting 0-for-7 with four strikeouts. In the eighth he ripped a two-run double to the wall in right center field, which was jarred out of the center fielder's glove when he slammed into the fence. The Astros won 7-1.

In Bradenton, Jake Marisnick threw out Josh Harrison at the plate. His average velocity on "competitive" throws from the outfield in 2015, according to Statcast, was 98.6 – tops in the majors. Statistically, these statcast numbers rated the Houston outfielders the best in the majors by far in terms of arms. Their outfield coverage was thought to be as good as any also, although Gomez noted the proficiency of the Pirates' trio of Andrew McCutchen, Gregory Polanco and Starlin Marte. Marisnick also homered in the game.

Matt Duffy, playing third base, belted his second and third long balls of the spring. Brad Peacock didn't make it through the second in his first competitive outing since June 11. But the Astros came from behind and won a wild one 11-8. Tyler White also unloaded a bomb. Before the game, AAA Fresno manager Tony DeFrancesco said he told Hinch a few days earlier that White would give him professional at bats if he got a chance to play in the majors.

First base competition ramps up

With two homers from Duffy, clouts from White and Singleton and three hits from Reed, it was quite a day in the Race for First Base. Before the Bradenton game, Hinch told the writers that the real battle for that position would begin in earnest in the middle of March when the Astros had home games scheduled with Washington, Detroit and Toronto.

By then, the first round of cuts would have been made by all of the clubs and the level of competition in some of the at bats would be ramping up. Nonetheless, a day like this didn't hurt any of the contestants.

A.J. Reed

Houston's number one prospect, first baseman A.J. Reed, was closing in on a major league job. When he was at the University of Kentucky, some organizations had a hard time choosing whether he should pitch or play elsewhere. He was Kentucky's Friday night starter, going 19-13 with a 2.83 ERA in three years. The 6-4 lefty threw his fastball from 88-92 mph, but what got him to second round draft status by the Astros was his bat, which produced a .336 average with a NCAA-best 23 homers and a .735 slugging percentage in 2014, when he was named Baseball America's College Player of the Year. He, ex-Vanderbilt pitcher David Price and former Astro and ex-Alabama first baseman Dave Magadan were all unanimous Southeastern Conference Players of the Year.

In 2015, Reed was runner up for BA's Minor League Player of the Year. He led the minors in homers with 34, RBI with 127, slugging percentage with .612 and OPS with 1.044. Reed was slowed by his weight of 285, which came from being undisciplined in his diet. He was on his own after being supervised at Kentucky by advisors in the athletic department and he admitted he did not stay on that program.

He had been advised by the organization to shed some pounds so he could move around better at first base. Over the winter he stuck to a lower calorie diet so that he could avoid hitting the wall that blindsided him in the Arizona Fall League, when he looked exhausted. He was the California League MVP and the ESPN.com Prospect of the Year.

Reed came to camp as a non-roster invitee, but he was being watched carefully. Since he hit .332 in 225 at bats at Corpus Christi and slugged .571, his Opening Day destination seemed to be AAA Fresno.

Nothing was certain, but with the gaggle of first base contenders with more experience that seemed logical.

There were other factors as well. The first was service time. The previous two years, George Springer and Carlos Correa were promoted from the minors in mid-April (Springer) and June (Correa) respectively, which gave the Astros six more years of their services AFTER the remainder of their first major league seasons. That could mean millions of dollars in payroll savings. It is a common practice in baseball.

The other factor was Jeff Luhnow's strong preference for minor leaguers to make a stop at each level before arriving in the majors. Jeff Bagwell observed right away that Reed's footwork was solid at first base. The defensive component of the position was stressed to all of the contenders for the position. Bagwell also pointed out the need for the Astros to have a strong power hitter behind Correa in the lineup so that opponents could not pitch around Correa.

With the competition at first among Singleton, Duffy, White, Marwin Gonzalez and even Preston Tucker, Reed was here to impress the top brass for later in the season unless something unexpected came along.

Tyler White

Tyler White came to Florida riding a wave of confidence after being named the MVP of the Dominican Winter League. The 5-11, 224-pound corner infielder was one of the biggest success stories in Astros camp. He was asked to improve his defense at first base to gird himself for the battle at that position. He wound up not only working to improve a deficiency, but with fans in San Pedro de Macoris chanting "MVP" when he batted for his Estrellas de Oriente team. He sported a .936 OPS in winter ball.

"He's like a legend in the Dominican," said Corpus Christi manager Rodney Linares, who witnessed White in winter ball. "They love him in San Pedro. He doesn't say much, but they love him down there."

White was a rarity, a 33rd round draft choice after his senior year at Western Carolina. He hit .325 there. That got him a $1,000 signing bonus. He broke into pro ball in 2013 with a .322 average in 64 games. In 2014, White blasted 15 homers and drove in 64 runs while hitting .290 at Quad Cities and Lancaster. He continued to impress while climbing the ladder to Corpus Christi and Fresno in 2015, ripping to a .325 average with 14 homers and 99 RBI.

Beyond the solid numbers, White drew attention for his solid approach to hitting. He compiled a .422 on base average in his career, drawing more walks than strikeouts. That was a rarity in any organization, but especially in the walk-challenged Astros group. "He's a guy that has opened eyes throughout his career, but certainly throughout this camp," said Hinch. "He's not going to sneak up on anybody in our organization."

"He's hit his whole life, not just this spring," Luhnow added. "This is not something new. He hit in college, he hit in every single level of the minor leagues. I'm not the least bit surprised he's hitting here. He certainly has put himself in a good spot to make this team."

White explained of his defensive emphasis, "I think working only at first base has helped out." White credited Linares with helping him during early fielding work in the Dominican. Linares was the bench coach for Estrellas. "He was really committed to getting better defensively. That was one of the things that Jeff (Luhnow) and the whole organization expressed to him before he left. We knew he could hit."

White, a native of Mooresboro, North Carolina was now in a position to maximize a big opportunity, but it might take the right combination of circumstances including an injury to another player or a slow recovery by Evan Gattis from his surgery.

Jon Singleton

Jonathan Singleton was getting the chance of his life this spring. He was one of the top prospects of the Philadelphia Phillies after they drafted him in the eighth round in 2009. Two years later, Singleton went to Houston in a trade along with Jarred Cosart, Josh Zeid and Domingo Santana for Hunter Pence. Now he was the only piece of that deal left in Houston, although Cosart and Santana were moved along in separate deals, yielding even more players.

Singleton, now 24, was named the frontrunner in the first base scramble before spring training. The Astros identified him as a big part of their future by signing him to a five-year, $10 million contract two years earlier. Now, after hitting .254 at Fresno with 22 homers and 83 RBI, he was trying to cement the position he wanted to hold down for years to come. In his previous major league trials in 2014 and 2015, he hit 14 homers in 357 at bats and struggled to hit .171. Singleton said about his big league struggles, "It got to me. It definitely bothered me because I knew what I was capable of and I wanted to be that person so bad.

And I was just so aggressive and kept pushing and kept pushing and kept pushing. Now I'm trying to just sit back and play the game."

Singleton was playing the game a little bigger this spring, by about 15 pounds of muscle he added through intensified workouts.

March 7---Peyton Manning announced his retirement from the NFL and his final word was "Omaha." Appropriate, since fans heard him make that call from the line of scrimmage thousands of times on televised games.

The New York Times ran a story about a baseball discovery in an attic. A great grandparents' attic was being cleaned out after they passed away.

Anonymous family members discovered a bag resembling a trash bag and almost threw it away.

But, upon further examination, the bag contained seven Ty Cobb baseball cards dated 1909-11 and they were authenticated, making them worth approximately one million dollars! But a 1984 Darryl Strawberry card worth $15 in 1990 had declined to $3.

A trip to Tampa to play the Yankees at Steinbrenner Field was the highlight of the day. These two teams would square off in the season opener at Yankee Stadium April 4. During the game, the Astros overshifted every time Brian McCann batted and twice he burned them with ground ball hits inside third when the third baseman was playing near second. The third time he batted, he pulled a grounder and grounded out.

Andrew Aplin doubled in a run off Dellin Betances in the seventh. Joe Girardi put together a lineup with several frontline Yankees and used his top bullpen arms in the game. The Astros made the run hold up and won 1-0 for a 5-1 start to spring training. Mike Fiers made a good debut appearance. Michael Feliz worked three scoreless innings and Juan Minaya picked up his second save. Tyler White had two more hits. "I'm pleased the most with how clean baseball we're playing," said Hinch.

One of the scouts at the game was former Astro pitcher Brandon Duckworth, now scouting for the Yankees. He was complimentary of Ken Giles in a conversation. Duckworth lives in the Philadelphia area and saw a lot of Giles with the Phillies.

Ironically, Duckworth was traded by the Phillies to the Astros along with Taylor Buchholz for Billy Wagner, the all time Houston save leader.

March 8---Tennis star Maria Sharapova failed a drug test. She held a news conference and took full responsibility.

The Cardinals lost starting shortstop Jhonny Peralta for two to three months with a torn ligament in his left thumb.

That was the same injury that dogged Yadier Molina last year. Peralta was injured fielding a ground ball. The Cardinals' stock was freefalling like an oil drilling stock.

The *Houston Chronicle* reported that the Astros had given A.J. Hinch a contract extension over the winter.

The club had made no announcement about it and there were no specifics in the report, which suggested that the extension carried through the 2018 season. No length of the original contract had ever been revealed. Hinch confirmed the new deal but did not reveal specifics. "Jim (Crane) and Jeff (Luhnow) have been great to me, and I'm really proud to be the manager of this group," said Hinch. "I love it here and how I've been treated."

"We could see last year he really had a lot of continuity in the locker room, and he continues to get these guys to jell," said Crane. "He communicates well with the front office, and he and Jeff work well together. We thought we had a good combination there.

"And we wanted to reward him for last year and give him some security and move the contract down the line a little bit."

The third televised game of the spring matched the Washington Nationals and the Astros. They would be together in spring training 2017 in Palm Beach County as co-tenants of the Ballpark of the Palm Beaches.

A year ago, one of the Las Vegas sports books gave the Nationals the best odds on winning the World Series. They failed to make the playoffs.

But they plummeted from 96 wins in 2014 to 83 and their season came unraveled, symbolized by closer Jonathan Papelbon trying to choke NL MVP Bryce Harper in the dugout during a game. Matt Williams was relieved of his duties as manager, replaced by Dusty Baker when Bud Black declined an offer of a contract for only one year.

The Nats beat the Astros 4-2 with Max Scherzer winning a 15-pitch battle to get Reed to bounce into a force play at the plate with the bases loaded, then whiffed Singleton to end a 37-pitch first inning. Reed's at bat got a lot of attention because of his approach. He took close pitches and fouled off several, reaching a 3-2 count and making contact against the former Cy Young winner, who had thrown two no-hitters the previous year.

Doug Fister walked three in two innings and gave up one run in his second start. "He wasn't as sharp today as he's going to be...but I love the angle he's coming at," said Hinch. "He's generating some swings and misses, some ground balls." Fister said of his rush to get to the mound every inning, "I really have to get out there and get going. But a lot of it's for defense. Been a few guys that have noticed it so far and they said they have loved the pace."

The loser was Ken Giles, who lost both of his first two outings. He gave up a run in his one inning appearance. Giles said he was working on mechanics and he "felt fine, just need to make adjustments, that's all it is." Hinch said of Giles, "I don't think pressure is (the issue)."

Luke Gregerson, who hadn't pitched in a game yet, seemed to be gaining traction by not pitching.

Wandy Rodriguez threw well, allowing one run in three innings. Jon Singleton struck out in both of his at bats.

March 9---The Zika virus had spread to more than 30 countries and territories, with researchers discovering that it targets fetuses' brains.

The battered bull market had its seventh birthday, two years longer than the average bull run. Investors were $16 trillion richer than they were when it started. One market strategist said the U.S. could be dragged into a recession should other countries around the globe slip and fall.

The movie "Spotlight" got an impressive 140% jolt at the box office after winning Best Picture at the Academy Awards.

Dos Equis announced plans to retire its spokesman, veteran actor Jonathan Goldsmith, 77, as The Most Interesting Man in the World after an advertising campaign lasting about nine years.

The biggest sports story of the day was the Houston Texans signing of free agents Brock Osweiler, Lamar Miller and Jeff Allen. The NFL world was topsy turvy over Osweiler being lured away from the Super Bowl champion Broncos to play quarterback for the Texans.

Owner Bob McNair told the media that quarterback would be his organization's priority, and General Manager Rick Smith followed through with a four-year, $72 million deal.

That addressed a weak area for the Texans and created a major problem for the Broncos, who now had to replace TWO quarterbacks after the retirement of Peyton Manning. GM John Elway chose not to match the offer by the Texans. The Broncos chose to make linebacker Von Miller, their Super Bowl MVP, the franchise player. The Texans moved swiftly and quietly to spirit away Osweiler.

The Orioles signed Pedro Alvarez to a one-year deal for $5.75 million to be their DH. That was the only position for him due to major fielding issues. His addition gave them five everyday players who had blasted at least 33 home runs in a season. Chris Davis, Adam Jones, Manny Machado and Mark Trumbo were the other four.

Former Astro Scott Kazmir was attacked in a 13-13 game between the Dodgers and the Angels, allowing five earned runs in 1 2/3 innings.

In Kissimmee, Carlos Correa was profiled in *Sports Weekly* in its baseball preview issue with a feature spread on the Houston shortstop. "The most important thing I learned was how to work hard but smart, don't overdo anything or get carried away," said Correa of the 2015 season. "I used to work really hard, then be tired by game time."

In the press box dining area, former Seattle Mariners General Manager Woody Woodward, once a major league shortstop, was asked about the comparison of Correa to Alex Rodriguez. Rodriguez was an 18-year-old shortstop when he came to the majors and Woodward said he drew the same comparison as he watched Correa in 2015. He said scouts told him that Rodriguez might gain too much weight to stay at shortstop and the Mariners might have to move him to third base or left field. "I told them that they were describing a player with enough power to play a corner infield or corner outfield position, and that is quite a compliment," he said. Woodward was impressed with Correa and saw no problems with his range, which he described as well above average.

The Atlanta Braves made the short drive from the Disney complex for the game, matching their ace Julio Teheran against Cy Young winner Dallas Keuchel, who was making his spring debut.

The Braves, like the Phillies, Reds and Brewers, were on a youth movement. They were building a new stadium in Cobb County and hoping a young group would give their fans encouragement to come to Cobb County to see the 2017 Braves.

Keuchel worked two scoreless innings and got four ground ball outs. He was one of seven Houston pitchers involved in a 9-5 win, supported by Jason Castro and Marwin Gonzalez homers. Gonzalez also made some excellent plays at third base. Altuve had a pair of doubles and drove in two runs. Keuchel said he's a "nobody now in 2016." Of his 34-pitch effort, he said, "I'd like to have a few of those fastballs back. It felt like I was all over the plate. All in all, I'll take it, but I've got to fine tune more and more each time."

Castro caught for the second straight day after others caught the first six games. He was being eased into catching with plans for extensive use during the regular season. Castro ripped a high fastball to the opposite field off Julio Teheran and the wind helped it clear the left field fence by a big margin for his first spring homer.

His retooled batting stroke, which involved starting his hands a little higher, allowed him to get the barrel of his bat to the high pitch. In the third inning he left the game after Ozzie Albies' bat hit him on the left elbow on the follow through of his swing, prompting a visit from the manager and trainer. Max Stassi entered the game, and on the first pitch he saw the batter foul the ball right into his protective cup and sent him sprawling in pain in the dirt, but he stayed in for several innings. The catching situation seemed shallow, with huge dependence on Castro and a plan to have the inexperienced Stassi as his backup. Evan Gattis' surgery changed the design to have him catch in spring training and be available as a third catcher during the season. All of the other catchers in the organization were young.

Jason Castro

Jason Castro, entering his "walk" year, had other important developments in his life. His wife Maris was pregnant with their first child. He was about to go through major life changes, including fatherhood and free agency. He lost his arbitration case over a small difference in salary. Now his value was on the line and he could reap a lucrative contract if he could return to the level of All-Star play he showed in 2013.

Castro had his best year by far that season, with a .276 average. That was 39 points higher than his career mark. He blasted 18 homers and drove in 56 runs on his way to Team MVP honors. He set club records for homers, doubles (35), runs (63), extra base hits (54), slugging and OPS in a season by a Houston catcher. Only Craig Biggio had been a Houston All-Star catcher before Castro did it.

The tenth overall pick in the 2008 draft, Castro became indispensable to Houston's pitching staff with his thorough game preparation of scouting reports and his pitch framing. After missing 2011 with knee surgery, he worked his way back and became a leader in the clubhouse. Castro was one of three finalists for the Gold Glove Award in the AL in 2015.

His lefthanded bat could provide some bonus offense in 2016 if his offseason work could restore his hitting to 2013 style, when he often ripped balls to left center field for extra bases.

March 10---The wind was howling in from left field at Space Coast Stadium. It affected many batted balls during the evening. The players on the left side of the field had a nightmarish challenge for the first few innings before the sun went down. They had to battle both the strong wind and a bright sun in their eyes. The play of the game was by Matt Duffy on a popup. Playing third, he pursued the popup onto the infield grass and then made a lunging catch near the mound. He never gave up when the wind kept taking the ball away from him and toward the first base line. He made some plays at third but went 0-for-4. Singleton was 0-for-3, putting him at 2-for-19 for the spring.

The Astros beat Washington 4-3 to run their record to 7-2. It was their best through nine games since an 8-1 start in 2000. They won only 72 regular season games that year, so not too much could be made of it. Collin McHugh opened with three scoreless innings.

Hard throwing Jandel Gustave survived a liner off his left wrist by Bryce Harper in a scoreless frame. But Hinch, noting Gustave stayed in the game, praised his work. "He's got wipeout capabilities if he can keep it in and near the strike zone with both his fastball and his slider," said Hinch. Jake Buchanan picked up the save. Marwin Gonzalez ripped another homer in a 2-for-3 game.

The only negative was an injury to Colin Moran. Moran, who was 2-for-3 with an RBI, had outstanding at bats. In the sixth, after his RBI single, he scored on Jon Kemmer's single but also left with an injury after the run.

He was headed for home plate and catcher Jose Lobaton was on his knees catching a throw from the outfield in foul territory up the third base line.

He was blocking Moran's path to the plate, forcing Moran to veer quickly to the infield side of the base line. His quick shift allowed him to get past Lobaton and slide into home safely, but the move quickly to his left caused a leg injury and forced him from the game. No injury report was announced immediately after the game. In the eighth, pinch hitter A.J. Reed whistled a line drive past the Washington pitcher and into center field for a single.

March 11---Venezuelan born Dave Concepcion, now the president of the winter ball team in Maracay, visited camp. He joked that Altuve took batting practice with his team but chose to play for Magallanes when he played winter ball. He said that would be the equivalent of an Astro taking batting practice with the Pirates.

Altuve no longer played winter ball because of the risk it presented, but he remarked before spring training that next winter he was planning to take that risk anyway. Correa, Valbuena and Altuve met with Concepcion, the shortstop for the Cincinnati Reds of the 1970s. Concepcion was a nine-time All-Star who played 19 seasons with the Reds. "I made sure I shake his hand because...those guys paved the way for us to be here now," said Correa.

The Astros cut four players from the roster in their first round of cuts. All were considered good prospects. Shortstop Alex Bregman, third baseman J.D. Davis and outfielders Derek Fisher and Jon Kemmer were reassigned to minor league camp.

Bregman said he was "just trying to soak everything in, see what I can use in my game, what has helped the veterans be successful. I also learned that I definitely can play at this level and play at this level soon." All four were potential major leaguers, but it was time to trim the number of major leaguers in camp and relocate these players with their minor league clubs so they could get more attention and the focus could narrow for the decision makers.

"We want to thin out the room," said Hinch on his pregame radio show. The day started with 62 players in camp. "We've got a touch too many pitchers in camp. I've had a hard time getting a look at all of them." Only two of 32 pitchers had not pitched. Gregerson was throwing well and the plan was for him to pitch soon. McCullers was the other who hadn't pitched. "This time last year he was in minor league camp and he hadn't even pitched in a game yet," recalled Hinch. McCullers was due to pitch soon.

With former Astro catcher Brad Ausmus at Kissimmee to lead Detroit, the Astros resembled the 1927 Yankees in a 10-4 bashing to run their record to 8-2. Rasmus ripped a three-run homer in the first and added an RBI single to raise his spring average to .556.

The media asked him after the game about buying suits for some rookies and he disclosed that he purchased a red velvet suit for himself for the opening trip to Yankee Stadium. Correa had three hits and lifted his average to .500. Feldman went three innings and felt good. Giles allowed a homer but Hinch liked his slider. Moran came off the bench to rip two doubles, proving that his leg was fine after leaving the game a few hours before in Viera.

In his postgame remarks, Hinch referred to an extra base hit by Detroit that was not fielded cleanly by Eury Perez in the outfield. No error was charged to him, but the hitter took third base on the play. Hinch called it "our first drop in the outfield." With an errorless game leaving only two errors in ten games, the nitpicking was notable.

In Houston, Anadarko Petroleum's deep cuts of 17 percent of its workforce reverberated through The Woodlands, where the twin towers built by Anadarko stood as a symbol of achievement in the oil field.

Phase II

A.J. Hinch divides spring training into three phases. The first cuts happened to fall on the day of the tenth game, roughly one-third of the way through the spring schedule. Arbitrarily, this was the start of the second phase. There would be many more cuts in this phase. The third and final phase would be the final games and he would expect the team to play with regular season focus.

March 12---The morning newspaper reports about Lance McCullers were a red flag to doubters. McCullers reported shoulder soreness earlier in the week according to the reports. He went for an MRI, which showed his shoulder to be "clean." McCullers threw a live batting practice earlier in the week, which created the soreness. His load of innings increased from 104 in 2014 to 164 in 2015.

An increase of 60 innings for a young pitcher from one year to the next was significant. McCullers planned to take a few extra days off.

In the game at Jupiter, the Astros lost a 3-2 lead in the ninth and the Cardinals overtook them 4-3. Brady Rodgers absorbed the loss when catcher Alberto Gonzalez made a throwing error to end the game. Danny Worth homered and doubled off Cardinal ace Adam Wainwright. Mike Fiers threw three perfect innings, with Neshek and Asher Wojciechowski keeping the no-hitter alive through five. Jon Singleton's spring was in the crosshairs and his chances seemed dire after going 0-for-3 with two strikeouts, lowering his average to .087. The winning pitcher was named Poncedeleon. Juan Ponce De Leon was the first Spanish explorer of Florida in 1493 on Christopher Columbus' second voyage to the Americas. He had heard of a mythical fountain of youth. He searched for gold and also a fountain capable of making people young again. He found neither. The question after this day centered on Singleton. Would he ever find the success he searched for, or would he share the same fate as Ponce De Leon? De Leon returned to Florida in 1521 on another voyage and he was shot in the thigh by an Indian's arrow and seriously wounded, dying at age 61 in Cuba of his wounds.

March 13---Kevin Chapman and Jake Buchanan reveled in the glow of winning the team's basketball shooting contest. Chapman's winning shot beat the buzzer sounded by Dallas Keuchel. Correa, wearing a James Harden Houston Rockets jersey, set off an explosion by his teammates with a Steph Curry-like bomb. George Springer wore a Houston Texans helmet but would not reveal where he got it.

Backup catcher Max Stassi headed back to Houston for an examination by a hand specialist on his left hamate bone, which bothered him more gripping the bat than catching. This bone had been removed in many baseball players through the years. It contained a hook which was not a necessary part of the bone for hand strength. Stassi had all of 21 major league games on his resume. None of the other young catchers in camp had any.

The Astros might need to move quickly to bring in a catcher from another organization.

Boston had five catchers with major league experience and not all could be protected in the Red Sox organization.

In a wild one, Houston beat Atlanta 7-6. Altuve hit a go-ahead three-run homer in the fourth. "I think I'm having success in what I'm working on," said Altuve. He saw 20 pitches in four at bats. "I don't want to go out there and make weak contact and put the ball in play early in the count. I feel like I'm doing good this spring."

Doug Fister gave up a homer on a pitch he was trying to add to his repertoire, a high fastball to Adonis Garcia. He said he would continue to throw the pitch and thought if he could master it, it could add to his effectiveness. Wandy Rodriguez allowed one run in three relief innings. Jandel Gustave notched his third save.

After the game, the NCAA Basketball Tournament brackets were revealed. The Final Four was set for NRG Stadium in Houston April 2-4. North Carolina, Virginia, Kansas and Oregon drew the top seeds. Early round play would begin Tuesday.

March 14---The squad was cut in order to accommodate those who had an actual chance to make the 25-man roster. As the starting pitchers stayed in games longer to get ready, fewer innings were available for other pitchers. Joe Musgrove, Danny Reynolds, Juan Minaya and David Paulino were optioned to minor league camp. Two others, Brady Rodgers and Brendan McCurry, were reassigned to minor league camp. Since Rodgers and McCurry were not on the 40-man roster, no option was necessary to send them out.

Musgrove went right to work in minor league camp. "He's very competitive," said Hinch. "He has a chance to help us sooner rather than later if he continues to progress the way that he has. As one of the prospects not traded this winter, it's important for him to take a step forward and start to think like a big leaguer and think about how we game-plan, how we approach every start, how to take care of his body, how to be ready to face lefthanded hitters at the major league level. I felt like he adapted and blended in very well as a keen observer of how we do things." Luhnow added, "I think he has a chance to pitch for us this year as a starter or as a long man if we need him. He's a big, physical guy. He's got stuff that can get hitters out at a big league level."

Joe Musgrove

Big Joe Musgrove got into the March 6 game at Bradenton, his first in a major league spring training camp. He gave up one run in two innings. The 6-5 righthander from Southern California had some of the best command of the strike zone in pro baseball in 2015, walking eight and striking out 99. He explained that everything he did was based on placing his two-seam and four-seam fastballs in effective spots. His slider was also a go-to pitch, but he wanted to improve his changeup. Musgrove was the Astros' Minor League Pitcher of the Year. He made the 40-man roster for the first time a few months ago to protect him from being drafted by another team.

The Astros could only protect 40 players by baseball rules. Some players who have four years of pro baseball experience and others who have five, depending upon their age when they signed, have to be placed on the team's 40-man roster or they can be cherry-picked by another organization in the annual winter Rule 5 draft. The Astros had a good number of excellent prospects, and they wanted to carefully identify which ones they would prevent from leaving the organization through that draft. Typically organizations in a rebuilding stance are open to plucking young talent from other clubs in this fashion.

Rule 5 draftees must remain on the team's major league roster all season. That was a steep requirement for some, because they felt they needed to play the young player enough to avoid deterioration of his skill set. In a few cases they could keep the player and send him to the minors, but only if they first offered him back to his original organization and that club declined to accept him back.

Musgrove was drafted by Toronto in 2011 with the 46th overall pick. He was shipped to Houston in the 10-player trade in 2011. When he joined the Astros organization, pitchers did more throwing than he had experienced and injuries resulted because of his lack of experience with that approach. He admitted that he wasn't taking care of his body properly either. He suffered from right hip dysplasia and had a small labrum tear as well, but he opted not to have surgery in 2015. He didn't pitch after August 12, but went on a rest and strengthening program. One reason he chose not to have surgery was the long recovery time. Another was that he had a previous surgery on a dislocated collarbone after the 2014 season. So far he was dealing with a minimum of discomfort in the hip.

Musgrove spent a lot of time with Collin McHugh in spring training. When he was optioned to minor league camp, he talked of learning even more from McHugh when he returned. He was in the mix to be a replacement for an injured starter when the need arose.

In Florida, the sun was shining at Space Coast Stadium in Viera and the Astros were 9-3 as they took the field. Altuve hit the first pitch from Joe Ross for a ground ball single up the middle. Correa blasted his first spring home run. "I always tell (Altuve) I've got more pop than him," joked Correa. "Yesterday he was messing with me, saying that he had hit the homer first before I did. So today was like, 'OK, we'll see.' And I was able to hit one." Keuchel retired the first eight batters on his way to three scoreless innings, throwing 30 of 43 pitches for strikes and fielding a couple of comebackers. He said he made it a point to throw inside on all of the Washington hitters. Ken Giles worked his first scoreless inning. The game was halted after the ninth, tied 1-1.

March 15---The NCAA Basketball Tournament began in Dayton, Ohio.

Adam LaRoche walked away from his White Sox contract, leaving $13 million on the table.

The Angels were dealing with two injured starting pitchers. Jered Weaver had chronic neck pain and C.J. Wilson had more shoulder problems.

Bad news came from Houston. Max Stassi underwent surgery on the hamate bone in his left wrist and would miss six weeks.

A red flag went up for the front office to obtain a veteran catcher to fill in. Other catchers would be getting their release papers soon and some would be free agents. A trade seemed to be the first priority, though.

With Tyler White hitting .370 with 15 total bases and A.J. Reed hitting .318, Jon Singleton was languishing at .111 with 11 strikeouts in 27 at bats.

"He's going to have to earn it," Luhnow said of Singleton's pursuit of the first base job. "It's not going to be handed to him or anybody. He was a top 50 industry prospect. Sometimes those guys succeed immediately in the major leagues. Sometimes it takes them longer." Singleton described the tattoos on his chest: Faith and Hope.

"Faith is a big thing," he said. "You've got to believe in something even though it's not there. And you definitely have to be hopeful every day that you're breathing."

The Nationals rallied with three in the ninth off Jake Buchanan to win 6-4. Marwin Gonzalez blasted his club leading fourth homer. George Springer was hit by a pitch for the third time.

March 16---President Obama nominated federal judge Merrick Garland for the vacancy on the Supreme Court. Republican leaders vowed not to bring the nomination to a vote until there was a new President in office.

The new hitting coach of the Miami Marlins, 50-year-old Barry Bonds, beat Giancarlo Stanton 4-3 in home runs on a back field away from cameras when they worked on hitting breaking balls.

The Astros announced that Lance McCullers would open the season on the disabled list. The plan was for him to be throwing bullpens by Opening Day but he would not be ready to compete in games or be able to pitch six innings by then. The immediate need was for McCullers to rest the shoulder and allow the soreness to recede.

Chris Devenski, nicknamed "The Dragon," was optioned to minor league camp after throwing two scoreless innings the day before. Devenski and Brady Rogers were in the plans to start two games in Mexico City against San Diego and they needed to be "stretched out" and ready to pitch several innings in those games.

The action on one of the back fields was probably more important than what the Houston TV audience saw on Root Sports from Osceola County Stadium. Detroit beat Houston 7-3. Brad Peacock was the starter and loser and Jon Singleton drove in all three runs with a homer and a single.

But on a field out of camera range, Scott Feldman pitched four innings and liked his new changeup grip, Luke Gregerson threw one inning with no ill effects on his oblique and Evan Gattis batted third in every inning for both teams in an effort to maximize the afternoon and get as many opportunities as possible to face live pitching and get game ready. Peacock surrendered a pair of home runs.

Hinch was displeased because two more Astros, Castro and Gomez, were hit by pitches from Jordan Zimmermann. The Astros had been hit by pitches more than any other team in the spring. "I can do without our guys being smoked," said Hinch. "We'll pay attention to that – let's put it that way."

In an interview on the MLB Network, Jeff Luhnow stated that whoever won the first base job would probably be a contact hitting type of player. That was not Singleton's forte.

March 17---Seventy years ago on this date, Jackie Robinson made his spring training debut at City Island Ballpark in Daytona Beach after three other ballparks locked him out. After church services with sermons from pulpits about Robinson, black churchgoers walked hand in hand to the ballpark.

The story of the day was Adam LaRoche's retirement from baseball. It took over talk shows and news shows. Almost everybody on the air seemed to giving an opinion, many of them completely uneducated about baseball clubhouses. LaRoche's reason for leaving spring training in Arizona was to be with his family.

He walked away from a $13 million salary. His reason went deeper than that, though.

LaRoche, who signed a two-year, $25 million deal with the White Sox prior to 2015, was allowed to bring his 14-year-old son Drake to the ballpark almost every day in 2015. Drake also was in the clubhouse on the road for many games. The White Sox vice president, Ken Williams, made the decision to limit clubhouse access to children in 2016. He said he talked with LaRoche twice and asked him to limit these clubhouse visits by Drake to less than half of the games. LaRoche walked away rather than comply. LaRoche, in a written statement, said Williams at one point asked him not to bring his son to the ballpark at all.

ESPN's Karl Ravech said the White Sox players threatened to boycott the next game, but Manager Robin Ventura talked them out of it during a two-hour meeting. "This young man we're talking about – Drake – everyone loves this young man," said Williams. "In no way do I want this to be about him. I asked Adam, said, 'Listen, our focus, our interest, our desire this year is to make sure we give ourselves every opportunity to focus on a daily basis on getting better. All I'm asking you to do regarding bringing your kid to the ballpark is dial it back."

The typical major league clubhouse rules allowed players' kids to be in the clubhouse before and after games. Most players allowed their kids periodic visits. There were concerns about a young man being exposed during games to cursing, displays of temper and unsuitable language and conversations from which children should be shielded.

LaRoche had not been playing because of back spasms. Now 36, he was returning from a .207 average in 2015 with 12 homers. He did not meet with reporters right away, so his reasons went unexplained.

Williams posed the central question of the day. "You tell me, where in this country can you bring your child to work every day?" There were reports that LaRoche had already filled out his retirement paperwork.

Williams, the team's former general manager, said, "He seemed pretty convicted in his decision. He didn't come back to talk to me about it before he made his decision.

"I thought there was enough flexibility built in." Questions were popping up about the White Sox as an organization. Would they be thought of highly by free agents considering them? Could this issue have been kept off the news shows if it had been dealt with over the winter? Could the White Sox have kept their promises to LaRoche in 2016 and then instituted a new policy in 2017?

Their owner, Jerry Reinsdorf, got involved in meetings about the issue. The Players Association studied filing a grievance against the White Sox.

The White Sox had acquired Todd Frazier to play third base and wanted to make a push to return to the playoffs after going 76-86 in 2015. Their last trip to the playoffs was in 2008.

St. Patrick's Day---St. Patrick was a fifth century patron saint of Ireland who was captured as a boy and held in slavery by pirates, tending to flocks of animals for six years before escaping. He returned to Ireland as a Christian missionary.

With green uniform tops and white shamrocks on the left sleeves, green caps and white pants, the Astros took the field in Kissimmee and another Houston team played at Disney against the Braves. Both Houston teams won to improve their spring record to 11-5-1.

In Kissimmee, Michael Feliz looked good in his three shutout innings against Toronto. His slider was better than last year and he threw some split changeups. The Astros jumped on Brad Penny for three in the first on their way a 7-5 win. Correa and Tucker went deep.

Tyler Heineman caught all nine innings and got his first three hits of the spring. Duffy made some nifty plays at third base. Springer had two hits and scored three runs.

At the Disney Wide World of Sports complex, A.J. Reed's first home run of the spring was a big one with two on in the eighth, providing a 5-3 victory. Danny Worth also homered. Roberto Pena caught all nine innings.

After the games, Jordan Jankowski and Alfredo Gonzalez were sent to minor league camp. Now 49 players remained in camp. Only two, Heineman and Pena, were left in the battle to back up Castro.

March 18---In Dunedin, Toronto stung Houston 7-2. Fister surrendered five earned runs in 3 2/3 innings including a long, three-run bomb to Jose Bautista. There were reports that Toronto showcased catcher A.J. Jimenez for Houston by starting him. He went 1-for-2 in the game.

March 19---A rare day off for the Astros. Hinch spent the day with his wife Erin and daughters Haley and Kaitlin. "It's important for all of us to include our families the most we can," he said. His daughters were planning to join him in Mexico City in another week. Dallas Keuchel threw 67 pitches over four innings in a minor league game.

Ken Giles needed nine pitches for one inning.

March 20---In one of the most surprising NCAA Tournaments, Texas A&M advanced to the Sweet 16 against Oklahoma by rallying from 12 down with 44 seconds to play to beat Northern Iowa in double overtime. But the dream ended for Stephen F. Austin with a one-point loss to Notre Dame.

Wandy Rodriguez was excellent as the starter and Ken Giles hit 101 mph with his first pitch in relief in a 5-4 loss to the Phillies at Bright House Field in Clearwater.

This was the second consecutive day on the mound for Giles, a plan all the relievers had on their schedules.

Giles said he was working on balance and timing drills to get his hands in the right position. Giles was carrying a couple of grapefruits in his ERA of 10.80, but he seemed unconcerned.

Rodriguez gave up two hits and a run in four sharp innings with five strikeouts. Colby Rasmus ripped a three-run homer, giving him 11 RBI.

Four players were sent back to minor league camp: righthander Asher Wojciechowski, who got the blown save and loss, outfielder Andrew Aplin and infielders Nolan Fontana and Tony Kemp.

March 21---President Obama was in Cuba for the first visit to that country by a U.S. President since Calvin Coolidge went to the island in 1928. The Tampa Bay Rays were in Havana also, preparing for an exhibition game against Cuba's national team. Evan Longoria and Chris Archer spoke of how honored they were to be a part of the event.

White Sox Chairman of the Board Jerry Reinsdorf issued a statement about the Adam LaRoche retirement decision. The statement was an attempt to move on from the episode and silence all front office employees from making any further comments.

Chris Sale also commented that the players wanted to focus on getting ready for the season.

The Astros lost to Washington 5-3 and starter Scott Feldman allowed three earned runs in 3 2/3 innings, running his ERA to 5.19. Dan Straily was the losing pitcher, allowing one run in one inning to run his ERA to 5.19. Colin Moran hit his first homer, leaving his average at .320. Jon Singleton's average stood at .146 after going 0-for-1. Jeff Luhnow, on the Astroline radio show on KBME in Houston, spoke of the need to make better contact than last year's club when asked about the first base position. He made a lukewarm mention of Singleton while discussing the different options at first base.

Phase III

March 22---The Tampa Bay Rays played a Cuban national team in Havana, where Jackie Robinson began his groundbreaking 1947 season with spring training. His widow Rachel and daughter Sharon arrived with President Obama and the first family aboard Air Force One. While politics raged daily in the U.S., Cuban citizens at a café in Havana talked about the lack of freedom of expression to talk about politics in their country.

Baseball Commissioner Rob Manfred said he was confident that by the end of the year a new system would be in place governing the transfer of Cuban players to the United States, ending the need for them to escape their country and establish residence in a foreign country so they would not be subject to the draft.

Negotiations between MLB and the players association were ongoing as part of the new collective bargaining agreement. The governments of both countries also were involved. Cuba had allowed its citizens to play in other countries only if a large percentage of their wages went to the Cuban government. Cuban born outfielder Dayron Verona was the leadoff batter for Tampa Bay in the game.

A.J. Hinch might have previewed his Opening Day lineup except for the starting pitcher. Viewers on Root Sports Southwest watched the game with this lineup: Altuve 2B, Springer RF, Correa SS, Rasmus LF, Gomez CF Valbuena 3B, Gonzalez 1B, Tucker DH, Castro C. Mike Fiers started the game against Atlanta.

Marwin Gonzalez was a possible starter at first base by virtue of sharing time with younger players and being one of the hitting leaders in the spring. Tucker was the possible DH against Masahiro Tanaka in Yankee Stadium because Gattis might open on the disabled list. Tucker still had not played any first base in the spring and obviously was not a candidate to share time at that position.

The Astros fell behind the Braves 6-1 when Fiers struggled to hit his spots. A long home run off the batter's eye in center field by Correa led a furious comeback to a Houston 8-7 victory. White came off the bench to go 2-for-2 with two RBI and raised his average to .371. Altuve banged out three more hits and ended the day at .353.

Hinch hinted he would carry 12 pitchers. He cited some off days early in the season and referred to having some starters available in long relief until the off days disappeared from the schedule. Lefthander Edwar Cabrera was returned to minor league camp. "You're going to see some player movement this week," said Hinch. "Maybe not every day, but close to every day. I'd like to have a smaller camp."

March 23---The Astros were featured on the cover of *Sports Illustrated*. Correa, Keuchel and Altuve were pictured in uniform with the caption "Liftoff" on the cover. This endorsement as the best team in the sport in 2016 was taken with many grains of salt. The Cleveland Indians were featured on the cover in 2015 and they were nothing special. The SI cover jinx was well known in the sporting world. The cover featuring Springer and predicting the Astros to win the 2017 World Series came many months ago and was the source of surprise at the time because many gave the team no chance to be elite that quickly. Reporters started digging and unearthed some details of SI's marketing plan. Actually four teams were featured on four different regional covers – The Mets, Cubs, Astros and Giants.

This type of marketing strategy was common and catered to fans of each of those teams in their home areas, which translated to more magazine sales.

"I worry about the psyche of our team being ready to compete and I've got two weeks to make sure that we get started in the right direction," said Hinch. "The season will be decided over the course of the next six months, not the first six games." The schedule in April presented a stern test, with 24 games including just eight against teams not thought to have a chance for the playoffs.

Evan Drellich, who was about to leave the Astros beat for the *Houston Chronicle* to join a Boston newspaper, stated in a column that Tyler White should be the first baseman. "He always does things that are right," Hinch told Drellich. "He's made probably one or two mistakes on the bases, and that's about it this spring." But Hinch said Gonzalez would be at first in some games.

In the night game, the Astros shaded the Phillies 2-1 on a combined two-hitter. Giles got his first save. Feliz cited his offspeed stuff as being instrumental in his four innings of a one-hit start. Castro went 3-for-3. Right-hander Brad Peacock was optioned to the minors.

March 24---In March Madness, Texas A&M lost to Oklahoma across the highway from Disneyland in the Sweet 16.

In the game at Port St. Lucie, it was a matchup of aces with Dallas Keuchel facing the Mets' Matt Harvey. Keuchel threw five shutout innings, escaping trouble from the outset.

He struck out Yoenis Cespedes and got Lucas Duda on a double play ball with runners at first and third and no outs. The Astros jumped on Matt Harvey for six runs in an 8-5 win. A.J. Reed was credited with a weird "inside the park" home run when Cespedes failed to pick up the ball at the base of the center field wall, holding his hands out and indicating to umpire C.B. Bucknor that it should be called a double because the ball was wedged in the padding at the base of the wall. Bucknor did not comply, and Reed circled the bases while Cespedes and the umpire looked at each other. The lumbering Reed, who had three hits, said, "I told the guys they witnessed history. That's probably never going to happen again." Wandy Rodriguez pitched well in relief. Decision day was imminent for the Astros on keeping Rodriguez and lefthander Neil Cotts. Both had opt out dates in their contracts in the next few days. Young righthander Jandel Gustave did not retire a batter and gave up five earned runs.

March 25---Gustave and Kevin Chapman were optioned to the minors. Cotts was given his unconditional release. That left 40 players in camp. Evan Gattis was not going to be ready to open the season. The plan was to have him finish minor league spring training and join an affiliate to continue to rehab from sports hernia surgery.

In the game at Disney's Wide World of Sports complex, Dan Straily made a strong bid for a spot on the Opening Day roster with four innings of no-hit work as the starter. The decision seemed to be between him and Rodriguez. Straily was out of options and Rodriguez had an opt-out clause in his contract, so this decision was imminent. Could the Astros market the loser in this battle and obtain a backup catcher in a trade? The game wound up a 1-1 tie after seven innings because of a black, fast-moving rain cloud that ended play just after Singleton struck out and walked slowly back to the dugout.

Collin McHugh was named the starter for the second game of the season.

March 26---In Nevada, a drone delivered a package to a residence in a small town. It was the first drone delivery in that type of setting. The company named Flirtey recently moved its headquarters from Australia to Nevada. The FAA predicts a bright future for the growth of drones and their commercial use in the U.S.

The first two NCAA entries to the Final Four in Houston were Oklahoma and Villanova, who would play each other at NRG Stadium.

In Mexico City, Jeff Luhnow recalled his childhood as a native of that city who made summer trips to San Antonio in the late 1970s and attended his first games in the Astrodome.

His American-born parents worked in Mexico City. The Astros and Padres opened their two-game Mexico City Series with Altuve, Correa and two Mexican minor leaguers making the trip. This was the first spring training series in Mexico since 2004. The Astros had some fan support from Mexico. MLB opened its first business office there and wanted to have a more prominent marketing role in Mexico, with expansion a possibility someday. Hinch was in Mexico City to manage the club on a split squad weekend, with Trey Hillman in Florida managing that Houston team.

The Astros walloped the Padres 11-1 in Mexico City. That afternoon, players from both teams gave clinics. Commissioner Rob Manfred and Players Association chief Tony Clark attended and spoke highly of Mexico's prominence in growing the game internationally. Mexico's top slugger, Vinny Castilla, went out of his way to introduce himself to Altuve and thank him for making the trip. Castilla hit 320 homers in the majors and also played for the Astros.

In the game, Correa and White hit back to back homers and Tijuana native Leo Heras contributed a sacrifice fly. Chris Devenski pitched scoreless ball for 4 1/3 innings despite the 7,200-foot altitude.

In Kissimmee, the Astros were rained out of their scheduled final game at Osceola County Stadium, ending a 32-year run for them at the facility. It might have been the final major league game at the facility, although if the Astros' new stadium was not finished in 2017 it could be used on a temporary basis. The World Baseball Classic also could host a team or some games there in 2017.

Luke Gregerson

Luke Gregerson made the jump from setup man to full-time closer in 2015, and he performed almost flawlessly. Although he never had more than nine saves in a major league season, the Astros added him to their bullpen with a three-year contract in December 2014.

He stepped up to the promotion by nailing down 31 saves in 36 opportunities, striking out 59 in 61 innings.

Gregerson maintained his excellence despite off the field turmoil, dealing with his father Duke's surgery on a cancerous brain tumor. "It was almost surreal, almost like not wanting to believe it," said Gregerson. After he pitched a scoreless inning in a minor league intrasquad game in Kissimmee, the 6-3 reliever from Park Ridge, Illinois embraced his family. "I know a lot of us look at our fathers and ourselves sometimes, and we feel like we're invincible and nothing can stop us," he said. "There's certain things in life that really put things into perspective, and you're really able to sit back and reflect and look at everything as a whole picture, and you realize our life is real fragile, and it can be taken away from you just as quickly as it was given to you."

Hinch said, "I've seen his makeup and how professional he is up close and personal for a number of years. He has incredible concentration to anchor a really good bullpen on a playoff-caliber team with all that was going on in his world."

Gregerson made his first game appearance March 16 in the minor league contest. His six-month old son Logan was there. Gregerson left the team twice in 2015, for his father's illness and the birth of his son. He credits his father for his strong work ethic and also a stubborn streak. Duke Gregerson played in the annual Thanksgiving family football game until he was 56, reluctantly retiring from the game after a broken sternum.

Gregerson pitched and played right field at St. Xavier University on the far south side of Chicago before St. Louis drafted him in the 28th round in 2006. In seven major league seasons, he made 499 appearances to lead all relievers. San Diego traded for him in 2009, and he went on to make 363 appearances in five seasons with the Padres, third most in club history. Including 2015, Gregerson was one of only three relievers to make 60 appearances or more for each of the last seven seasons.

Carlos Gomez

Carlos Gomez, a native of the Dominican Republic, was a big part of the Latin contingent. He joined Correa, Altuve, Valbuena and Marwin Gonzalez in the lively Houston clubhouse in a trade the previous July. He and Mike Fiers provided Houston's return in a major package of prospects including Josh Hader, Brett Phillips, Adrian Houser and Domingo Santana. There were reports that the New York Mets rejected Gomez in a proposed trade because the Mets' doctors were wary of results from his physical.

Gomez, beginning his tenth season in the majors, was headed for free agency after the 2016 season. After he arrived in Houston, he took over in center field. His offensive production, a .242 batting average, was far short of his career standards of .260. He belted just four homers in 149 at bats, driving in just 13 runs. He played through intercostal discomfort, adding home runs in the Wild Card game against the Yankees and in the Kansas City series in the divisional playoff round. But Gomez clearly was not at his best.

The two-time All-Star was one of 12 active players with at least 100 long balls and 200 steals. He joined the 20-40 club in 2013 and the 20-30 club in 2014 with his elite combination of power and speed. He made National League All-Star teams both of those years, and in 2013 added a Gold Glove as well. Since his debut in 2007, he saved more runs defensively than any other center fielder in the game (88) according to Fangraphs. Gomez also was an excellent bunter.

"All of the things that you see, it's pretty authentic," said Hinch. "It's him. He's that classic guy that can drive you nuts when you play against him and then you enjoy it when he's in your foxhole." Recalled reliever Pat Neshek: "When I played for the Cardinals, everybody hated him. I hated him, too. I hated playing against him." Why? His style was over the top. He flipped bats and hot dogged catching fly balls. He brought that style to the majors and he never lost it.

"I just interviewed him knowing that he's a guy that's high on life," said John Smoltz, an analyst for the MLB Network. "And I love those kinds of guys." Goose Gossage wouldn't like his antics, but players from the 1970s did not allow that type of behavior on the field. Gossage and Bryce Harper exchanged opposite points of view in articles regarding players celebrating on the field.

"Baseball gives me the opportunity to be who I am right now," said Gomez. "So every single day, I pray. I say, 'Thank you, God. Thank you to give me the opportunity to be a baseball player.' Every time I step on the field, I feel like it's a dream come true. I feel like it's a new game, my first game every time." How could a fan find fault with that approach?

Chapter 5

April Flooding

April Game by Game Accounts

April 4---The players were headed to Yankee Stadium on the team bus from Manhattan when Twitter informed them that the Yankees had postponed Opening Day.

It meant another day with down time and a longer wait for the season to start. The next day's forecast called for dry weather but much colder – around 38 degrees at game time. But nobody disagreed with the decision not to play with steady rain falling and a forecast for steady rain throughout the day. A.J. Hinch told reporters he would use the same lineup the next day. His lineup was: Altuve 2B, Springer RF, Correa SS, Rasmus LF, Gomez CF, Valbuena 3B, Tucker DH, Gonzalez 1B, Castro C. Keuchel would take a 28-inning scoreless streak against the Yankees into his delayed Opening Day start.

Hinch announced that Luke Gregerson would be his "primary closer." It was understood that Ken Giles would get some save opportunities as well.

The prediction business was going strong. Many of the TV network analysts were picking the Astros to be a playoff team and advance deeper into the playoffs than in 2015. The Cubs were a popular pick to win the World Series for the first time since 1908.

It was a good day for reading and watching some of the other openers. The book called "the most important baseball book in years" by Hall of Famer John Smoltz, "The Arm" by Jeff Passan, presented some sobering thoughts to executives everywhere. Passan pointed out that every year baseball teams spent $1.5 billion on pitchers. Yet more than 50 per cent of pitchers would wind up on the disabled list every year, averaging two months. And one quarter of major league pitchers today have had Tommy John surgery. Scary!

The book details the elbow injuries to teenage pitchers and the pattern of abuse of their arms in the name of competing and earning either college scholarships or multimillion dollar pro contracts.

Villanova claimed the NCAA Basketball Championship, beating North Carolina in a fantastic game at NRG Stadium. Kris Jenkins drilled a three-point shot at the buzzer for a 77-74 thriller some thought was the best finish in a title game.

Opening Day

April 5---The season did open, but a polar vortex swept through New York and morning temperatures were frigid. In the morning, the Yankee Stadium grounds crew had to clear a sheet of ice off the field after removing the tarp. By game time, a 36 degree temperature presented difficult playing conditions and the wind added to the dilemma. Pitchers had a hard time gripping the baseball and hitters struggled to get loose. It was the coldest opener ever for the Astros. It was the coldest game in the Bronx since April 8, 2003. Dallas Keuchel tweeted after the game: "Tough, hard fought team win in Game 1. Side bar: Baseball should never be played in 30 degree weather."

Yankee right-hander Masahiro Tanaka mowed down the first nine. Keuchel gave up two runs in the second on a double by Starlin Castro. Carlos Correa mishandled a Chase Headley grounder which could have been an inning ending double play, but Correa was able to get one out on the play. Correa atoned with a fourth inning RBI and a sixth inning homer to tie it. He became the youngest Astro to go deep in a season opener, months younger than Terry Puhl in 1978 against Cincinnati's Tom Seaver at Riverfront Stadium. Correa also stole two bases and scored two runs. He was involved in the biggest play of the game, sprinting to first base on a slow roller near the first base line and reaching on an errant throw by losing pitcher Dellin Betances. The play came with one out in the eighth and led to three unearned runs off Betances.

Yankee manager Joe Girardi intended to file a protest regarding the umpires' interpretation of the rules. Umpires typically had ruled no interference on the batter-runner unless the throw hit the runner on the inside of the first base line. Correa was on the inside of the base line instead of in the runners' 45-foot lane to the foul side of the line, but Betances' throw was a bad lob over the head of first baseman Mark Teixeira. Crew chief and home plate umpire Dana Demuth told Girardi that the throw was too high and would not have retired Correa. Demuth later said, "In my judgment he didn't impede or hinder the first baseman from fielding the ball. The pitcher launched it...the runner does not have to be in a 45-foot baseline. Joe thinks he does."

Although Girardi's contention was that Correa actually caused the bad throw by not running in foul territory, the protest would not be upheld because this was the commonly used call by major league umpires and it was a judgment call. In fact Girardi never filed the protest.

If the protest had been upheld, the game would have been resumed at a future date and completed starting with the overturned ruling that would have declared Correa out for interference. From that point the game would have been played to conclusion. Only two protests were upheld in MLB since the George Brett pine tar incident at Yankee Stadium in 1983. Both of them dealt with how the umpires handled weather problems with game stoppages.

The Astros set a club record by winning their fourth straight season opener. Ken Giles told the media before the game that the decision to use Luke Gregerson as the closer was a surprise to him. He worked the eighth inning and surrendered a homer to DiDi Gregorius. Gregerson nailed down the save with a perfect ninth.

There was more baserunning controversy elsewhere. Toronto lost by a run at Tampa Bay. Jose Bautista was ruled out at second for the game's final out when he slid past second base. Umpires instituted the new Chase Utley rule with their call.

The Connecticut women's basketball team won its fourth straight NCAA title.

April 6---The Yankees clubbed the Astros 16-6, shelling Collin McHugh in a six-run first to hand him the loss in his shortest major league start. Michael Feliz threw 107 pitches in a 4 1/3 inning relief stint. But because he labored so much, he was sent down the next day in order to get a fresh arm to New York. Chris Devenski replaced Danny Reynolds on the 40-man roster and headed from Las Vegas to New York instead of starting the season for Fresno.

Devenski, who was left unprotected over the winter and could have been plucked in the Rule 5 draft by any other team, now was a member of this select 40-man group. He was about to lift off on a journey to a magnificent season that would take him to a fourth place finish in American League Rookie of the Year voting by the Baseball Writers Association of America. He would become a bulwark of the Houston bullpen, finishing the season with a 2.16 ERA for 108 1/3 innings, 83 2/3 of them in relief. He was always smiling, almost always available to pitch and an exemplary member of the team.

Carlos Correa went 4-for-5 and blasted two homers, one off the facing of the center field private club. The next day, Alex Rodriguez referred to Correa as a "possible first ballot Hall of Famer."

April 7---The forecast for steady rain was not accurate. The game started 12 minutes late and proceeded without interruption. The Yankees came from behind to win 8-5 to capture two of three in the series. Mike Fiers was spotted with 3-0 and 5-2 leads but could not hold them. He left with the game tied 5-5 after five innings. Nathan Eovaldi allowed a two-run homer to Tyler White (his first in the majors) and a two-run single to White. Preston Tucker made it back to back long balls with a second deck shot to right field in the second inning.

The Yankee bullpen shut out the Astros in the last four innings. Will Harris was the loser. He left a man on base but Ken Giles gave up the winning three-run homer to Mark Teixeira in the seventh. Giles took full responsibility after the game for failing to do his job. The Astros' top three hitters were 0-for-12.

In the minors, Fresno lost its opener despite an RBI from A.J. Reed. Joe Musgrove led Corpus Christi to a 2-0 win.

April 8---There were snow flurries during the day in cold Milwaukee. Miller Park's roof was utilized quite well for the night game. The Brewers built a 6-0 lead but held off the hard-charging Astros, who scored four in the ninth.

They had two men on with one out when Jose Altuve grounded to second baseman Scooter Gennett, who fired to Jonathan Villar for the force play at second on Colby Rasmus. Rasmus slid past the bag on the right field side and his slide took him too far toward left center field to be able to reach the base. Second base umpire Dan Bellino called a double play because of an illegal slide and that call ended the game in controversy.

A.J. Hinch ran out to challenge the call, but replay officials in New York confirmed the call. "It was interpreted right, but the rule needs clarification because I think it's wrong," an incensed Hinch said after the game. "Especially when you're asking athletes to compete at the highest level as fast as they can in last-minute decisions. It is a joke we lost the game based on that when there wasn't intent or contact. It was a baseball slide."

Dallas Keuchel tweeted, "Are we even playing baseball anymore? #unbelievable"

Crew chief Tom Hallion told the media, "My second base umpire determined that it was not a bona fide slide because Rasmus did not attempt to stay on the base. He could not stay on the base. With that, that is the rule of interference."

"Since I got into this game we've been taught how to play and to me that was very mild of a slide, so it's kind of hard," said Rasmus. "It's so bang-bang. It's quick and it happens fast....They didn't even attempt to make a throw, and they can end the game on that."

The central issue regarding the new rule was giving the umpire leeway to rule a double play when the infielder (Villar) made no attempt to throw to first and would not have been able to get a double play on Altuve. As with all baseball rules, the interpretation of it was the important factor. The umpires and managers had been sent interpretations by MLB, and some of those instructions indicated that the ruling of a double play was not automatic.

It seemed that if the infielder was protected from injury with the new rule, giving umpires the judgment to call a double play in the case of little or no contact near second base and no attempt to make a throw was too severe a penalty.

Tyler White continued his rampage with a three-run ninth inning homer to right field. He started the season 9-for-13 with two homers and seven RBI.

Chris Devenski made his major league debut in relief of losing pitcher Scott Feldman, working three scoreless innings. Former Astros Chris Carter, Jonathan Villar and Domingo Santana all made an impact against their former club, combining to go 4-for-10 with a homer and four RBI.

At the Masters, Jordan Spieth shot a shaky 74 but maintained the lead. The defending champ set a record by leading the Masters for six consecutive rounds.

April 9---A two-run Houston first staked Doug Fister to the lead in his Astros debut. Fister turned it into a win, departing after five innings ahead 6-3. The bullpen made the lead hold up. Luke Gregerson nailed down his second save after Ken Giles mowed down Ryan Braun, Jonathan Lucroy and Chris Carter in the eighth. Colby Rasmus and Tyler White connected in the fifth for back to back home runs.

White wound up with the best five-game start of an Astro beginning his career, going 10 for 15 with three homers and nine RBI.

April 10---Milwaukee held the Astros to three hits in a 3-2 series winning game for the Brewers. Milwaukee starter Jimmy Nelson survived a long ball by Jose Altuve on the game's first pitch and another by Preston Tucker in the fifth, fanning nine. The Astros lost three baserunners on the bases. Keuchel was the loser, walking four of the first six batters and a total of six in his 5 2/3 innings. The first road trip wound up with a 2-4 record. "It was really sloppy today," said Keuchel. "It started with me, and I've got to get my act straight because everybody else is looking toward me. It was just really sloppy."

Hinch added, "We didn't play very well mentally and made a couple of physical mistakes as well. But we'll clean it up."

Evan Gattis texted Hinch one word: "Ready" after going 3-for-4 with a three-run homer for Corpus Christi in his third rehab game. Hinch said Gattis could be joining the Astros in a few days.

April 11---Home Opener vs. Kansas City! The defending world champion Royals came to Houston with a 4-1 record, fresh from a three-game sweep of the Twins in Kansas City. They got their shiny new World Series rings and their trophy in their opening home stand. They defeated the Mets on Sunday night baseball to get the season started. Facing the Astros was a rematch of the AL Division Series from 2015. The last time these two teams played at Minute Maid Park, the Royals pulled off that dramatic comeback with six outs left to win Game 4. It was one of their eight comeback wins in the postseason after 40 in the regular season.

Collin McHugh turned back the clock to 2015 and 2014, stifling the Royals with cut fastballs and curve balls in seven shutout innings before a crowd of 43,332. Most were wearing orange as requested in the pregame buildup. Roger Clemens, a seven-time Cy Young winner, threw out one first pitch to Dallas Keuchel.

Standing beside him, Jeff Bagwell, a former Rookie of the Year, threw out another to Carlos Correa. Earlier in the pregame ceremonies, Keuchel and Correa were presented portraits by sports artist Opie Otterstad and Chevy trucks by Astros owner Jim Crane.

The stoked crowd made it a noisy atmosphere, made even louder because the roof was closed with the threat of rain.

Carlos Correa doubled in a run in the first off Chris Young, followed by a Colby Rasmus two-run homer. The Astros banged out 14 hits and beat the Royals soundly 8-2.

April 12---The vaunted Kansas City bullpen worked four shutout innings after starter Kris Medlen left and held off the Astros 3-2.

All of the scoring came in the first inning. Mike Fiers allowed a three-run homer to Lorenzo Cain and trailed 3-0 after three batters. He righted the ship and stayed in for six innings. The Astros' starting pitchers had an ERA of 5.63 through eight games. The Astros whiffed 13 times, including George Springer's called third strike against Wade Davis to end the game with two on.

Evan Gattis rejoined the team and was in the starting lineup as the DH. Matt Duffy was optioned to Fresno.

April 13---Salvador Perez clobbered a 1-2 slider from Ken Giles into the seats in left field for a winning eighth inning, two-run homer in a 4-2 KC win. Jose Altuve homered and ripped two doubles, driving in both Houston runs. Yordano Ventura gave up the homer and Altuve's second double came off Luke Hochevar in the seventh, but Giles failed to keep the score tied. Scott Feldman allowed just two unearned runs in his 6 1/3 innings.

"He's been effective except for one pitch or two pitches in an outing, and it's hard to take him out of his role when it's really one mistake," Hinch said of Giles.

Giles said after the game, "I mean, it's not fun. I'm not having fun right now. I've just got to keep a straight head and just keep going after guys like I always do. I've been successful so far. I just need to get around that one pitch." The three homers allowed by Giles were one more than he allowed in 70 innings in 2015.

Before the game, Gattis went through some catching drills.

The Houston Rockets clinched a playoff berth with a 116-81 torching of the Sacramento Kings. They won a first-round date with the record-setting Golden State Warriors, who finished with their 73rd win.

April 14---Ian Kennedy threw five no-hit innings and KC led 1-0 on a Mike Moustakas home run with two outs in the top of the sixth. With two outs and one on, Doug Fister induced a fly ball to shallow right field and the inning appeared to be over. But George Springer lost Lorenzo Cain's ball in the lights and the play, ruled a hit by the official scorer, opened the floodgates to a five-run inning. KC went on to a 6-2 win, its third straight in the series.

"It's bright," Springer said of the new LED lights. "It's not easy to see the ball. It cost us a game today." When asked what could be done about the lights, Springer said, "play during the day so they don't turn them on. It is what it is and we're just going to have to learn to play with it."

"They're there," said Hinch. "They're bolted in." He continued, "We're a unique stadium, and the lights are lower than most of them. The lights can only be adjusted so much. We'll make the proper adjustments, we'll get used to it. We'll make better plays."

The Astros were 3-7 in their first 10 games. Hinch used 10 different lineups. The offense was generally pretty good, but the team ERA ranked in the bottom tier of the majors.

April 15---Dallas Keuchel snapped the three-game losing streak on a beautiful night with the roof open, stopping hard-hitting Detroit 1-0 in the series opener. A first-inning RBI single by Colby Rasmus off Mike Pelfrey accounted for the only run. Luke Gregerson got the final three outs after Keuchel allowed five singles in eight innings.

Keuchel won his 17th in a row at home. With a 1.36 ERA at home over the 20 starts involved in that stretch, the fans who flocked to Keuchel's Korner and donned their beards for his starts were thrilled. Keuchel wore the number 42, as did all players in the majors to commemorate the career of Jackie Robinson, who wore that number while he broke baseball's color barrier in 1947.

Alex Bregman hit his fourth long ball of the young season for AA Corpus Christi.

Lance McCullers was unable to make his next scheduled start for Corpus Christi on his rehab assignment. It was disclosed that his 48-pitch outing four days earlier caused continuing discomfort and McCullers would be unable to make his next scheduled start Saturday night. "We're trying to iron some things out as far as just recovering," said McCullers. Hinch added, "He wasn't sore while he pitched. It's more of a recovery issue." GM Jeff Luhnow amplified, "His last start, he felt good during the start. The next morning, he didn't feel quite the same as he had prior to the start, and any time anything is off we're going to be cautious because he's still building up his arm strength and durability."

April 16---The Houston Rockets were blasted in the first game of the playoffs by the Golden State Warriors.

Justin Verlander allowed the Astros three runs in the first on homers by George Springer and Tyler White. He slammed the door after that with bullpen help for the final three innings in a 5-3 Tiger win. Collin McHugh failed to protect the lead and allowed 10 hits and four runs in 5 1/3 innings, absorbing his second loss.

April 17---The Astros won their first series of the season wearing their new Sunday alternate jerseys. The navy blue jerseys with rainbow trim down the sides and orange caps with navy bills worked well in a 5-4 tight one over Detroit. Jose Altuve blasted his sixth career leadoff homer to right field off Anibal Sanchez after Mike Fiers retired the Tigers in order. Altuve later drove in two more with a single, giving him the only Houston hit in 10 at bats with a runner in scoring position. Altuve became the first Houston second baseman to belt four homers in his first 13 games of the season.

Fiers survived three Tiger long balls and left with a 5-4 lead after 5 2/3 innings. At that point, Hinch made an unusual move.

He called in lefty Tony Sipp to face switch hitter Jarrod Saltalamacchia. Saltalamacchia was 2-for-2 with a homer, his second in as many games. Both came while he batted left-handed. Sipp's insertion turned him around. Batting right-handed, Saltalamacchia struck out against Sipp. The move was somewhat unconventional, especially with Sipp being the only southpaw in the Houston bullpen. But it was based on sound thinking with statistical support. Pat Neshek, Ken Giles and Luke Gregerson each worked scoreless ball over the last three frames to hold onto the lead. The Astros won two of three while their pitchers only allowed three walks in the series.

Correa, who was given the day off, met with Houston Christian High School student Neil Kerrigan, the 18-year-old brain cancer patient he befriended in 2015. Correa took off his cap and gave it to Kerrigan, who was wearing a Correa jersey. "It's real inspiring," said Correa. "It makes you appreciate things a lot more. I feel like God has put me here for a purpose and I feel like I can impact people in a positive way, and I feel like that's what I'm going to do my entire career."

The Epic Flood

April 18---On this off day for travel, a long line of violent thunderstorms arrived and kept coming in a "training" effect, following each other as if on train tracks. The brunt of the storm was in northwest Houston, which received 16-20 inches of rain. Lakes were at record levels. Schools were closed and people were advised not to drive because 13 of the 22 creeks and bayous in the area were out of their banks.

The death toll was at five when the news rolled in the next morning. Mayor Sylvester Turner called the flooding in the city "unprecedented." Nearly 900 water rescues were performed in the city alone and 1,222 in the metro area. The National Weather Service called it a "historic event."

After deliberating, the club's travel plans remained as originally scheduled, calling for a 3 p.m. departure on buses from Minute Maid Park to Bush Intercontinental Airport. The two buses carried the travelers on their journey without incident and they departed for Dallas, arriving without problems at their hotel in Ft. Worth. More rain was expected in Houston.

Altuve was named co-Player of the Week in the American League. He hit .407 with three homers, seven RBI, two steals and a 1.336 OPS in seven games. Tyler White and Altuve were winners in the first two weeks, making this the first time in history the Astros placed two players in that spot the first two weeks of the season. "It's about alignment to him," Hinch said of Altuve's surprising power. "His bat-to-ball skills are elite. That's not news. But his alignment, when he keeps his body in order and doesn't dive and can hit to all fields – now I think he's learning as he gets older and stronger and more mature, he can juice the ball everywhere."

April 19---A.J. Hinch was surprised to learn of his selection to the Pac-12 All-Century team. He was one of three catchers and 30 players selected by a panel put together by the Pac-12 Network. Hinch was a two-time Conference Player of the Year and three-time All-American. He was inducted into the Stanford Athletics Hall of Fame in 2014. He was honored to join such elite names on the Pac-12 team as Barry Bonds, Randy Johnson, Tom Seaver, Mike Mussina, Dustin Pedroia, Chase Utley, Tim Lincecum and Terry Francona.

The Astros woke up to cloudy skies in Ft. Worth before taking on the Rangers for the first of 19 games this season. Newspaper articles in Dallas and Houston previewed the series with background from 2015, when the Rangers dominated the Astros 13-6 in the season series and finished in first place by two games, beating Houston in eight of the last 10 meetings to overtake the Astros. The teams were two games apart as the series began, with the Rangers holding down the top spot in the AL West and the Astros in the cellar at 5-8.

Former Astros' farmhand Delino DeShields, who got away from Houston in the Rule 5 draft prior to the 2015 season, had some observations. "They had a young team last year, and I think they may have gotten a little too into the rivalry instead of just playing," said DeShields. The rivalry came to a flashpoint in July when Hank Conger told Rougned Odor to get into the batter's box and Odor took issue. Prince Fielder ran from the on deck circle toward the two and soon both benches emptied, with angry comments and fingers pointed toward opponents.

The Rangers were handing out Jeff Banister bobbleheads. Banister's bobblehead was in the same powder blue throwback uniform the Manager of the Year wore the night of that fracas in Houston in 2015 and the figurine was pointing just as Banister did at A.J. Hinch during the blowup. Hinch had a similar reaction that night. The two were good friends, though.

Odor instigated some animosity with his bat-flipping after a home run and his slide into Altuve in two of the games. Hinch and Banister both observed that they loved the rivalry. This was the first time since 2000 that both of these teams met after making the playoffs the year before. In 2000, both of them backslid far out of the playoff picture. Few expected that to happen in 2016.

The Rangers captured the series opener 7-5 for their eighth straight win over the Astros at Globe Life Park. Scott Feldman fell behind on a two-run homer by Prince Fielder after a Correa error. The Astros got back-to-back clouts from Altuve and Springer when they trailed 6-2, but they were 2-for-10 with runners in scoring position.

April 20---The ship was taking on water and some of the fans were looking for lifeboats. The Astros had Cole Hamels in trouble from the outset and could not score. He hit the first two batters and got a caught stealing and two punchouts to end that threat.

In the second, the Astros loaded the bases on three singles with nobody out and didn't score. Marwin Gonzalez hit a fly ball to shallow right field. Nomar Mazara threw home and Carlos Gomez got caught too far off first base. In the ensuing rundown, Colby Rasmus was tagged out between second and third for a double play. Tyler White's homer in the sixth provided the only run in a 2-1 loss. Odor's two-run homer off loser Doug Fister after a walk provided the only Texas runs. "Two things that have plagued us in the first two weeks are walks and homers, and that came back to back for the two-run homer by Odor," said Hinch. "Very symbolic for how things have gone the first two weeks."

"We've lost too many games, but we've lost because of small things, and it's very much something we're going to address," Hinch said of the base running fiasco. "We're going to get better at it. We've got to find a way to conquer the little things that are biting us in the behind every day." Banister said, "We got in a situation where there was a jail break, but more than anything else our guys showed the presence of mind to stay calm and under control."

The Astros stood at 5-10, with nine straight losses at Globe Life Park.

April 21---Add one more loss to the numbers from the previous day. The Rangers swept the series and pounded Dallas Keuchel, piling up 13 hits and six runs in six innings on their way to a 7-4 chest-beater. Colby Rasmus belted two homers for the second time in the season, but Rangers starter A.J. Griffin put in a quality start and overcame back to back doubles to open the game by Altuve and Springer. The short flight home returned a 5-11 team to Minute Maid Park.

April 22---On a beautiful night with the roof open, Collin McHugh's ERA ballooned to 7.56 in Boston's 6-2 series opening win. On the two-year anniversary of his Houston debut, McHugh got only 12 outs with his 92 pitches. Knuckleballer Steven Wright kept his favorite pitch dancing and it proved most elusive to Houston hitters. When George Springer tried to make something happen, he was gunned down trying to steal third trailing 5-0. The first inning ERA for Astros' pitchers mushroomed to a major league worst 11.12. The loss put the Astros at 5-12, tied for the worst record in the league.

April 23---The sun blazed down on Minute Paid Park on another day with the roof open, with 40,223 fans filling the ballpark and many coming early to claim the 10,000 Carlos Correa giveaway, white jerseys. As the game moved to the fifth tied 1-1, Boston's Clay Buchholz from Nederland, Texas dueled with Mike Fiers. Again Houston surrendered a first inning run, but Fiers went to his split changeup after the first three batters reached and kept the Bosox from scoring again until the sixth.

In the Houston fifth, Colby Rasmus worked the count to 2-0 with the bases loaded and two outs. Then Buchholz got him to swing and miss at two curve balls. Buchholz fired a fastball on the 2-2 offering. Rasmus was waiting to drill it. With his well-timed uppercut swing, the ball took off toward right center field. It rocketed through the sunlight and then landed in the shade of the seats, sending the crowd into an explosion of joy. The 8-3 win included 5 RBI for Rasmus and snapped a four-game losing streak.

April 24---ESPN Sunday Night baseball featured the Astros and the Red Sox. It was longer than Ben Hur! Five hours and three minutes after starting, the Red Sox walked off the field winners 7-5 in 12 innings. The game was all too familiar to the Astros, who fell behind 3-0 in the first when Scott Feldman faced eight batters. Only one run was earned because of an error charged to Jose Altuve, whose foot was not touching the base on a force play. The reigning Gold Glove winner made two errors the day after receiving his Gold Glove for 2015. Falling behind 5-1, the Astros kept battling and tied the game with two outs in the ninth on a two-run homer by Colby Rasmus off Red Sox closer Craig Kimbrel. Rasmus was named the AL Player of the Week the next day. He followed Tyler White and Jose Altuve to give the Astros a bit of recent history. It was the first time in the majors since 1974, when the Player of the Week award began, that three members of one team won the award the first three weeks of a season. Ken Giles took the loss when Boston bumped his ERA to 8.31 with a two-run 12th.

Chris Devenski pitched 3 1/3 innings in relief of Feldman. It seemed that Feldman might be on a short leash after only four starts with a 4.58 ERA. Collin McHugh's ERA was higher: 7.56. So was Mike Fiers': 5.73. But Feldman was older and in the final year of a front-loaded three-year contract. After the game the Astros optioned Jake Marisnick to Fresno so that they could get a fresh arm in the bullpen. They recalled Michael Feliz from Fresno.

Lance McCullers was on his way to Florida for more work in extended spring training with the hope he could be brought along toward returning to the rotation, but a more imminent move was called for unless the club turned it around.

The offense was not off the hook either. A 15-strikeout game against Boston included three key punchouts with men in scoring position. These were the strikeout leaders through 19 games: Springer 22, White 20, Castro 20, Gomez 19, Rasmus 17, Correa 16.

Although the Astros led the AL in extra base hits before this game, their 2-for-13 performance with runners in scoring position continued the club's failures in the clutch.

The biggest number to ponder was the 6-13 record. The Astros headed for Seattle with that won-lost albatross around their necks.

April 25---Mariners starter Tijuan Walker improved his career mark against the Astros to 5-1 with an 11-strikeout performance in seven innings, winning 3-2. Doug Fister walked a career-high seven in six innings, allowing three runs. The sleep-deprived Astros, who arrived at their hotel at 4 a.m. Seattle time, outhit Seattle 10-4 but lost two more runners on the bases while falling to 6-14.

April 26---In Houston, the landmark Cleburne Cafeteria on Bissonnet burned down in its 75th anniversary year. Longtime owner George Mickelis vowed to rebuild.

The Astros managed only two hits in seven innings against Nathan Karns, who beat Dallas Keuchel 11-1. Robinson Cano blasted a grand slam off Michael Feliz and drove in six in the game.

"We're still playing sloppy and it's not going to change until something or some people, you know, play well," said Keuchel. "This is the highest level you can go and I think people take it for granted sometimes. It's not the way it should be. We have people busting their tails and doing everything they possibly can, and it seems like we're not a cohesive unit. Until we are, it won't look pretty. That's just the way it is."

Tyler White snapped an 0-for-18 slump with a single. "I think the five home runs (in the team's first 15 games) might have gotten to my head a little bit," admitted White. "I'm like, 'Hey, I can hit a home run every time.' Just trying to do too much."

Before the game, Chris Devenski was told that he would be making the start Saturday in Oakland instead of Scott Feldman.

Hinch made it clear that Feldman would be returning to the rotation but for the short term would be in the bullpen.

Hinch said he talked to Carlos Gomez about being thrown out trying to steal in the ninth inning of Monday night's 3-2 loss. "What he needs to remember is if you don't get the max lead, if you don't get your max jump, you always have the next pitch where you could possibly go," said Hinch. In addition to some poor base running decisions, Gomez was hitting .211 with no homers and two RBI in his first 71 at bats. His .500 OPS was the second worst in the majors for players with 70 plate appearances.

April 27---The Houston Rockets were eliminated from the NBA playoffs by the Golden State Warriors 114-81 in the fifth and final game of the series. The Warriors thrashed the Rockets three times by at least 26 points in the series. Steph Curry sat out the final game for Golden State with a knee injury. It seemed to many that James Harden and Dwight Howard had played their last game as Rockets' teammates. Howard could opt out of his contract. Number one on the Rockets' agenda was finding a head coach to succeed J.B. Bickerstaff.

Jose Altuve hit his third leadoff homer of the season and seventh of his career, jolting Seattle starter Hisashi Iwakuma and getting the Astros started on a 7-4 win. Altuve added a pair of doubles and finished the night with a 1.081 OPS for the season. Collin McHugh went five for the win and the bullpen chipped in with four relievers protecting the lead.

April 28---The NFL draft commanded the attention of sports fans. The first player drafted was Cal quarterback Jared Goff. His father Jerry was a catcher in major league baseball, finishing his career with the Astros. In his final major league game May 12, 1996 at Montreal, Jerry Goff belted his seventh major league homer but also committed six passed balls to tie a major league record. He was released after the game.

The Houston Texans added a speedy wide receiver, Will Fuller from Notre Dame, with their first pick.

An off day in Oakland. Lance McCullers asked the fans for patience on his Twitter account with three imogees crying, saying, "Be patient with me. We are making the right strides." McCullers pitched three innings the day before in Florida and "felt really good, was very encouraged by his outing," according to his manager. He threw 45 pitches. If he recovered well, he could head for a rehab outing soon. Joe Musgrove finished his April work for Corpus Christi with a 0.52 ERA. He had 21 strikeouts and two walks in 17 1/3 innings.

Jason Castro thought back to a month ago. He recalled, "I thought with the way spring went, everything was clicking and we were playing really well," said Castro. "We got into a funk early on, and we need to reassess with the off day, and hopefully everybody can clear their minds and come back ready to play our baseball. I don't think we've done that yet."

April 29---A story about Collin McHugh hit the publications and internet. McHugh reportedly signed a deal with a company named Fantex which paid him $3.96 million up front in exchange for 10 per cent of his future earnings on and off the field.

Fantex planned to sell stock to investors guaranteeing them a return if McHugh made more than $39.6 million for the rest of his career. McHugh was not eligible for arbitration until 2017 and his current salary was slightly more than $500,000. Four other baseball players signed similar deals.

Dee Gordon of the Miami Marlins, who won the NL batting title in 2015, was handed an 80-game suspension for using performance enhancing drugs. A spring training drug test revealed a positive result. Gordon claimed he did not "knowingly" ingest any illegal substances, repeating a stupid statement many athletes had made when they were caught on drug tests. These athletes did not deny the validity of the test. They seemed to be claiming innocence in a way by leaving open the possibility that the substances somehow entered their bodies without their knowledge.

In Oakland, the A's promoted hard-throwing lefty Sean Manaea from the minors for his major league debut against the Astros and he served notice to the hitters that he was ready. The A's got him and another pitcher from Kansas City the previous July in a trade for Ben Zobrist. Oakland was 11-12, 1 1/2 games behind Texas. Coco Crisp ripped a two-run homer off Mike Fiers in the second for a 2-1 lead.

The Astros took a 4-2 lead with three in the eighth and Fiers made his exit after seven strong innings. Then the bullpen imploded. Ken Giles allowed a homer to Marcus Semien, the first man he faced. Jed Lowrie tied the game with a sacrifice fly. It was Giles' first blown save and his ERA ballooned to 9.00. Tony Sipp got two outs and the game was tied 4-4 after eight. Carlos Gomez smashed a double off the left center field wall. On his way to second he saw Crisp going for the ball and decided to head for third. Center fielder Billy Burns, backing up the play, threw out Gomez at third for the first out in the top of the ninth of a tie game. Another base running blunder! Pat Neshek gave up the winning three-run homer to Yonder Alonso with one out in the last of the ninth.

The loss assured the Astros would not win back-to-back games once in April. They had allowed 121 runs, worst in the American League by 15 runs.

April 30---A.J Hinch provided the epilogue for April the night before. "What's been consistent is every mistake we make is magnified," said Hinch. "They've come back to haunt us."

In Oakland, The Dragon was breathing fire. Chris Devenski was about to make his first major league start after compiling a 0.66 ERA in six relief appearances. With Scott Feldman in the bullpen, Devenski was taking Feldman's place in the rotation for at least this one trial. Devenski's AA Corpus Christi manager, Rodney Linares, told the story of Devo's nickname. Linares visited Devenski on the mound in 2015. "You know what I want you to do?" Linares told Devenski. "I want you to unleash the dragon." After Devenski struck out the hitter, he charged into the dugout and said, "I've unleashed the dragon."

Devenski asked Linares to list him as "Dragon" on the lineup card.

He also bought a toy green dragon. As he took the field at Oakland-Alameda County Coliseum, the dragon rested in his locker. He took on Jesse Hahn, who was recalled from AAA to make his first major league start of the season.

Devenski did well, giving up a two-run single to Billy Burns in the second for the game's only runs. He threw 91 pitches, 50 more than in his previous relief appearance April 24. Feldman was perfect in three innings of relief, saving the rest of the bullpen. But Hahn was better, teaming with two relievers to shut out the Astros for the first time. Ryan Madson induced a game-ending double play ball from Evan Gattis with the bases loaded. The 2-0 loss sank the Astros deeper into the April floodwaters, closing the month at 7-17.

Gomez sat out the game with sore ribs from diving in the outfield the night before. X-rays were negative but he was expected to miss a few games.

"I hope we can wash it away quickly," Hinch said of April. "Hopefully, we can do that by turning the calendar."

April Summary

The Astros' 7-17 start dropped them 6 1/2 games behind first place Texas. Their 3-11 road record cost them dearly. Their opponents outscored them, 123-90. Their staff ERA was a burdensome 4.97.

Colby Rasmus (7 HR, 19 RBI) and Jose Altuve (.400 OBA, .611SLG) were the pacesetters offensively. Luke Gregerson had a nice start with 4 saves and a 2.00 ERA.

Noteworthy Achievements: Tyler White, Jose Altuve and Colby Rasmus won Player of the Week honors in the AL the first three weeks. Altuve became the first player in major league history to collect 11 doubles and nine steals in the month of April.

Biggest problem: Pitching. The starters were 7-13 with a 5.10 ERA. The bullpen was 0-4 with a 4.75 ERA.

April Analysis

The 7-17 start in April of 2016 was opposite the club's 17-7 start through the first 24 games of 2015. There were other reversals and they clearly explained the differences between the two years.

In April of 2015, the starting pitchers had a 3.50 ERA. In 2016, it was 5.10. The bullpen ERA was 2.18 in April of '15, 4.75 in '16. It was obvious that pitching was not in the same area code as the year before. There were other contributing factors, though. Base running was ghastly and fielding was at times unsteady. For the offense, the strikeouts were a major limiting factor and the bottom of the lineup was not helping much.

With the Rangers pacing the way at 14-10, the Astros were seven games out of first place. They were 1-7 against the teams in the AL West. It was clear that May needed to show a reversal or a summer of fighting from behind would be next.

The immediate task was to get rolling soon. The upcoming 10-game home stand brought Minnesota (also 7-17), Seattle and Cleveland to Minute Maid Park. A losing home stand would be extremely harmful. Only 15 per cent of the season had been played, but May brought an immediate challenge. The worst April in club history, 1969, brought a 4-20 record. Season over, right? No, actually, that club worked its way back into contention before fading. Still, patience was in short supply

6 Mayday, Mayday!

"Mayday" is an emergency procedure word used internationally as a distress signal in radio communications. It's used primarily to signal a life-threatening emergency by aviators and mariners. The word was not being used in the Astros' clubhouse and it might not have been welcome anywhere else, but the fans felt some urgency to the situation. It had been 20 years since a team fell to 10 games under .500 at the end of April after reaching the playoffs the previous year. The 1996 Red Sox were 7-19 in April after a playoff appearance. Since the start of 2012 when a second wild card team in each league was added to the playoffs, only six of 40 playoff teams had a sub-.500 record in April. None was as far below .500 as ten games. The Astros had two playoff teams in their history with losing April records. The 1981 Astros were 7-12 in April, while the 2005 club was 9-13 on its way to a 15-30 start before playing furiously for the rest of the season.

Johnny Bench welcomed May 1 each season as his Hall of Fame career with the Cincinnati Reds progressed. Bench did not usually do much damage in April, and May was the time he generally exploded offensively.

His annual April struggles were shared by several Astros in 2016. Jason Castro, Carlos Gomez and Luis Valbuena were notable in their need for a more productive May.

Valbuena hit .183 with zero homers and 4 RBI. Castro finished the month at .140-0-2. For Gomez, the numbers were .213-0-2. Gomez was not in the lineup when May began, waiting to be examined in Houston before the sore rib cage area would be cleared for further action.

Around the majors, the top April batting average belonged to the Cardinals' Aledmys Diaz at .423. Like Trevor Story, with 10 homers for Colorado, Diaz was playing because of an injury to another player.

Seattle's Robinson Cano had a comeback April, leading the AL with 24 RBI and ripping eight home runs.

The Chicago Cubs, leading the majors with a 17-5 April mark, rode a strong pitching staff. Their starters were 14-4 with a 2.27 ERA. Other top teams in baseball shared that characteristic. Washington was 16-7, with a 2.28 ERA for Stephen Strasburg and company. The Mets had a 2.85 ERA for starters and they were 15-8 with the fabulous Noah Syndergaard throwing 98 mph bullets.

The mission was clear for the laggards in MLB: If you want to play with the big boys, improve your starting pitching.

May brought a much improved Houston team to the diamond.

May Game by Game Accounts

May 1---The starting pitching improved dramatically, at least for one day. Jose Altuve led off the game with a blast on a 1-1 breaking ball from Oakland lefty Rich Hill, who had a 2.42 ERA for four starts and had allowed one long ball in 26 innings. Altuve jumped on a high pitch. He said after the game he had decided to swing at it no matter what the pitch was. It was his fourth leadoff homer of the season and the eighth of his career. Craig Biggio was the last Astro to hit four leadoff homers in a season, with four in 2006. He set the National League record with 53 in his career.

Doug Fister held onto the early run support and stopped Oakland on one run in 6 2/3 innings. The bullpen trio of Tony Sipp, Will Harris and Luke Gregerson protected a 2-1 lead. The Astros won with only two hits! Oakland had eight. But Houston drew seven walks to Oakland's one. And the defense was superb. George Springer robbed Coco Crisp with a diving catch in the seventh inning, when Oakland scored its only run. Carlos Correa made seven plays to tie his career high. Tyler White aided the cause with good glove work on two plays at first base and Jason Castro picked a pitch out of the dirt when Oakland threatened. The team left Oakland for a ten-game homestand.

Texas and Seattle both lost.

In the last four games of the road trip, Astros starting pitchers combined for a 2.66 ERA.

This was only the 14th time in club history the Astros won a game while getting just two hits.

May 2---Dallas Keuchel led Minnesota 1-0 after two frames on a Preston Tucker home run. Keuchel was paired with rookie righthander Jose Berrios from Puerto Rico. Berrios was a first-round draft choice in 2012 and a longtime friend of Carlos Correa from their amateur days. Berrios got tougher, while Keuchel had control issues and walked five, four in the Twins' three-run fourth. Keuchel lost at home for the first time since 2014, snapping an 18-game home winning streak including postseason. His ERA soared to 5.11, and during his three-game losing streak he allowed 16 earned runs in 16 1/3 innings.

"I guess the book on me is that 40-something per cent weren't strikes last year," said Keuchel. "And I got a lot of chases out of the zone, but a lot of that entails me filling up the zone early and kind of expanding on my own instead of expanding early and having to come to the plate late. I knew their game plan all along was to make me throw strikes and attack the zone. First three innings were a different story and it seemed like it just snowballed from there. Don't feel like I got any help, but I have to do better than that."

May 3---On a crystal clear and beautiful evening with low humidity and the roof open, Minnesota's Danny Santana led off the game by bashing Collin McHugh's 0-2 pitch for a homer off the right field foul pole. But the Astros came back from a 2-0 deficit against Alex Meyer on Jason Castro and George Springer home runs and won 6-4. The bullpen was spectacular with 3 1/3 innings of hitless baseball.

May 4---The run of gorgeous Houston nights continued. This time fans were treated to the best offensive extravaganza of the season, a 16-4 pounding of the Twins. Jose Altuve belted his fifth leadoff home run of the season and had two more hits.

Carlos Correa followed suit with a homer and two other hits. Jason Castro homered and drove in four. But Mike Fiers could not last five with a 9-4 lead to qualify for the win. The bullpen pitched in with 4 1/3 innings of no-hit baseball. For the first time all season, the Astros had back to back wins. It was the deepest they had gone into any season without a two-game winning streak.

May 5---As it turned out on this Cinco de Mayo Day, there was nothing to celebrate. It looked good, with Chris Devenski holding the first place Seattle Mariners to one run in six innings and departing with a 2-1 lead. Altuve hit ANOTHER leadoff homer, this one on the train tracks in left field, off Wade Miley. Baltimore's Brady Anderson was the last player to hit six leadoff blasts before June 1 in 1996, when he hit 50 home runs. Altuve went 4-for-4, raising his average from .306 to .330. He took over the major league lead in extra base hits with 23.

Before the game, Altuve met a boy with terminal cancer, 10-year-old Dylan Tindall-Heathcock, who asked Altuve to break his bat in his first at bat so the boy could have the bat, then hit a home run. Altuve sent for a bat from the clubhouse to give the boy, who still requested that he hit a home run. "Eh, I was like, 'I hit a home run yesterday, so don't expect me to hit one today, but I don't want to make you feel bad if I don't,'" said Altuve. He said Tindall-Heathcock told him, "Yes, you're going to make it. We'll see."

"As soon as I hit the home run and I got out to play second base, I remembered what he said," said Altuve. "I really like the kid. He was really happy to be here. I hope God blesses him for what he's been through right now."

Ken Giles walked the first man he faced and that mistake blew up in the seventh when Tony Sipp gave up a go-ahead, two-run double to Robinson Cano.

Altuve bombed a 400-foot double to center field in the bottom of the inning to tie the game, but Jason Castro was thrown out at the plate trying to score the go-ahead run. Luke Gregerson absorbed the loss on a three-run ninth inning double by Cano, who drove in four to give him 14 RBI in four games against the Astros. Seattle won, 6-3.

May 6---Dylan Tindall-Heathcock was back and Altuve and Correa met with him and gave him autographed items, including the home run baseball from the night before. Altuve held a large media session regarding the encounter the night before. "More than the homer, what makes my day was to see the kid happy," said Altuve, whose wife was pregnant, expecting a girl.

Tony Sipp was away on paternity leave, replaced on the roster by Michael Feliz. Astro killer Tijuan Walker, who was 5-1 against Houston, started for Seattle. He dominated the Astros two starts ago, fanning 11 in seven innings of a 3-2 win over Doug Fister. Fister opposed him again on this clear, beautiful night with the roof again open.

Fister breezed through the first six innings, keeping the Mariners scoreless. Correa struck for another opposite field, two-strike homer in the first. Marwin Gonzalez delivered a two-run blast in the second. It was his first career homer with a man on base! He had hit 25 solo homers to start his career, a major league record. Walker left after two innings with neck spasms and the Astros went on to a 6-3 conquest. Correa turned in a spectacular diving catch of a line drive off the bat of Chris Iannetta with the bases loaded and one out in the seventh. Will Harris pitched his 13th straight scoreless relief appearance and Luke Gregerson earned his 16th straight save.

The big shocker came after the game when Hinch announced that Evan Gattis was optioned to AA Corpus Christi so he could catch in some games. Sipp returned to the roster after the birth of his daughter Zoe Chanel. The Astros needed their only bullpen southpaw against Seattle lefthanded hitters Robinson Cano, Seth Smith, Kyle Seager and Adam Lind.

KKKKKKKKKKKKKKKKKKKKKKKerry Wood

May 6 was the anniversary of one of the best games ever pitched. In fact, it was THE best game ever pitched according to the Bill James Game Score. James devised a ranking system for games pitched, based on plus rankings for strikeouts and minus rankings for runs, hits and walks allowed. Kerry Wood of the Chicago Cubs struck out 20 Houston Astros May 6, 1998 at Wrigley Field. The Bill James Game Score for Wood was 105. It beat a score of 101 for Sandy Koufax in his perfect game in 1965 and Nolan Ryan's 101 in his 16-strikeout, two-walk no-hitter for Texas in 1991.

The Astro team Wood beat that cloudy, warm afternoon won 102 games, a club record. Every player in the lineup, including pinch hitter Bill Spiers, struck out. Three players struck out three times: Jeff Bagwell, Moises Alou and Jack Howell. Ricky Gutierrez got the only hit, a tainted infield hit off third baseman Kevin Orie's glove. Craig Biggio was the only other player to reach base. He was hit by a pitch. Wood did not walk a batter. He threw 122 pitches, 84 of them strikes.

It was Wood's sixth major league start at age 20. He went on to a 13-6 season with a 3.40 ERA and Rookie of the Year honors. His career record was 86-75 with a 3.67 ERA. He developed arm problems and underwent Tommy John surgery. After that, he did not have the same dynamic stuff. Cubs' manager Jim Riggleman was criticized for allowing Wood to throw too many pitches. But Wood never blamed Riggleman, saying that with his delivery his arm would have blown out no matter how he was handled by managers.

Scherzer Joins the Club

Six days after the anniversary of Wood's gem, Max Scherzer of Washington joined the 20K club. Scherzer struck out 20 Detroit Tigers May 12 in Washington, beating his former club 3-2. He pitched two no-hitters for Washington in 2015, fanning 17 in the second one. He joined Wood, Roger Clemens and Randy Johnson in the 20K Club. He also won the 2016 Cy Young Award in the National League. He left the Tigers for a $210 million, seven-year contract. His mound opponent and losing pitcher, Jordan Zimmermann, left Washington for a five-year, $110 million deal with Detroit.

May 7---Robinson Cano took over from Albert Pujols as Astros Enemy #1. He blasted two homers, including a tenth inning winner off Tony Sipp in the 3-2 Seattle win. Dallas Keuchel was much better than in other recent games, surrendering two solo homers. Luis Valbuena ripped his first homer in 78 at bats since last October leading off the home ninth to tie the game at 2-2 off Steve Cishek.

May 8---On Mother's Day the players wore special uniforms with pink letters and trim, accessorizing with pink shoes and socks for some. In special pregame ceremonies some players' mothers threw out first pitches to their sons. Collin McHugh stepped up his game, holding the Mariners to five hits and one run in a 5-1 Houston conquest to split the four-game series. Altuve had two hits and stole three bases. Rasmus surprised the M's with a two-out, two-strike bunt RBI single in the third inning off Hisashi Iwakuma.

Cano homered for the only Seattle run. He took over the home run and RBI lead in the AL with 12 and 33, respectively. In the four-game series, Cano went 9-for-18 with three homers and seven RBI. In seven games against the Astros, Cano was 14 for 30 with five homers and 17 RBI. Hinch said he would have bought Cano a first class ticket out of town if necessary so he could terrorize other teams.

May 9---Mike Fiers and two relievers stopped Cleveland 7-1. Altuve's two-run double was one of the hitting highlights for the Astros, who knocked out former Cy Young winner Cory Kluber in the third with five runs as ten men batted. Kluber sported a career ERA of 1.98 against the Astros and he struck out the side in the first inning.

With Lance McCullers returning to Houston to throw a bullpen the next day, somebody in the rotation was about to lose his spot, it seemed.

May 10---Brady Castro entered the world at seven pounds. Maris and Jason Castro were parents for the first time, and Jason was on paternity leave. Max Stassi was called up from Fresno to replace him. Cleveland's Trevor Bauer warmed up with his usual long toss routine. He stood on the warning track in right center field, not far from the right field corner, and heaved the ball into the left field corner time after time to loosen his arm. He blew away the Houston hitters for seven shutout innings with 95 mph gas and a good changeup. The Indians won a 4-0 shutout.

May 11---The final game of the homestand wore on...and on...and on. It started at 1:10. Two hours before the game the players were in the clubhouse and some were playing video games. Their luggage had been dropped off at the equipment truck for a weeklong road trip to Boston and Chicago. There was no batting practice.

Doug Fister came into the game with a string of four straight quality starts. Danny Salazar brought great stuff and a 1.91 ERA into the game for Cleveland. The Astros loaded the bases against him in the first with nobody out. Then he buzzed 94 mph fastballs and 86 mph splitters past Rasmus, Gonzalez and Valbuena and struck them out to leave the bases loaded.

The Astros loaded the bases again in the second, but Salazar got Correa on a force play at second. The Astros left two men on in the third.

Jason Kipnis singled in a third inning run and Mike Napoli homered in the fourth to put Cleveland up 2-0.

Springer belted a 455-foot long ball in the Houston fourth. After five innings, Salazar had to leave with a 2-1 lead because his pitch count reached 106.

As the game moved through the middle innings, Correa tied it in the sixth and Terry Francona kept going to the Cleveland pen. He would wind up using 10 pitchers, including one of his starting pitchers in relief. Preston Tucker gave the Astros a 3-2 lead with a seventh inning single. Will Harris pitched a scoreless eighth. But when Luke Gregerson came in for the save, he didn't get it for the first time in 17 tries dating back to 2015. He gave up a Napoli double and a Carlos Santana triple as Cleveland tied the game at 3.

What followed was an extra inning extravaganza with a total of 489 pitches! The Astros didn't get a hit from the eighth through the 15th, being no-hit for 8 1/3 innings. But Marwin Gonzalez ripped a line drive homer in the 16th for his second career walkoff, giving the Astros a 5-3 win in 5:09. It was their first walkoff win of the year and it gave them their first winning homestand, 6-4. They headed to Boston exhausted but relieved because they didn't lose a game despite leaving 17 on base and whiffing 18 times. They got 10 hits and drew 12 walks but struggled to score. The 12 walks were the most by a Houston club since 2000. Gonzalez provided the latest walkoff hit for the Astros in a regular season game.

Topps created a digital baseball card of Marwin Gonzalez and sold it for $9.99. The cards sold out in a 24-hour period. A card of Jake Arrieta's second no-hitter produced sales of 1,808. Bartolo Colon's first career homer the previous Saturday was featured on a card with sales of 8,826. Colon was the oldest player at 42 to hit his first major league homer.

The best part of the game was the first major league win for Michael Feliz, who dominated the Indians for three innings, striking out five.

May 12---In the NBA playoffs, Russell Westbrook and Kevin Durant led the Oklahoma City Thunder to a 116-99 Game 6 win over San Antonio in the Western Conference semifinals. They moved on to face defending champion Golden State.

The seven-game road trip began in Boston with former Cy Young winners Dallas Keuchel and David Price opposing each other. George Springer was close to home. His family and friends arrived from New Britain, Connecticut to see him play at Fenway. In 2015 they had the same plans, but Springer was hit by a pitch by KC's Edinson Volquez, breaking his wrist in the final game before the Fenway series. "It was all in place and then I got hurt, and everybody flaked on me," said Springer. He went 2-for-4 in his first game at Fenway, where he attended games as a child. "It was all set up. My friends, my family still came," he recalled of his 2015 trip. "That was tough because I had just gotten hurt probably about five hours or so before the flight."

Price took the hill in Fenway Park with a 4-1 record but a horrendous 6.75 ERA. Altuve and Springer opened the game with singles off him. But he fanned the next three batters similar to the day before when Salazar whiffed the side after the first three reached base. Price struck out 12 and became the first pitcher since Sandy Koufax to fan ten or more Houston hitters four games in a row.

Keuchel allowed a Xander Bogaerts two-run homer in the first and a total of eight runs in six innings on the way to a resounding 11-1 loss. "I think I try to be too perfect on a lot of pitches, and that's not the way you go about it," said Keuchel.

"You work on the plate until you work off and expand, and sometimes I try to be too fine, and that works against me a lot more than it helps me." Keuchel mentioned a few days before the start that he was going to reduce his work between starts because he had felt at "about 75-80%" when he took the mound for his starts so far. "I'll get back to the drawing board, but I've been feeling good, man," he said. "It's going to be there, and when it does, we'll take off."

The eight runs were the second most allowed by Keuchel in 108 starts.

The Red Sox had swept Oakland with a hit fest, and this game marked their fourth straight scoring in double figures.

After the game, Lance McCullers was added to the roster for his Friday night 2016 debut. Josh Fields, who pitched two innings and allowed one earned run, was optioned to Fresno with a 7.24 ERA. Jason Castro returned from paternity leave and Max Stassi was optioned to Fresno.

In the minors, Joe Musgrove was promoted to Fresno after posting a 0.34 ERA for Corpus Christi over 26 1/3 innings, striking out 30 while walking three. Lefty reliever Reymin Guduan was also promoted to Fresno after allowing one run and seven hits in 13 innings at Corpus.

May 13---Carlos Gomez was at the plate in the top of the fifth at Fenway. The Astros had just rallied with four runs in the inning to tie the Red Sox 5-5 and Gomez was the ninth Astro to bat in the inning. There were runners at second and third and two outs. Knuckleballer Steven Wright was gone after blowing a 5-1 lead. Gomez was facing reliever Matt Barnes. Headed for free agency, hitting .196 at game time with five RBI and 0-for-2 in this game, Gomez had a chance for his first big hit of the season. Fans at home had been loudly booing him the last few games on the home stand when he failed to produce. But Barnes struck him out and the rally ended with the game still tied.

With Lance McCullers returning to the rotation, the Astros stayed with him despite a five-run Boston second. McCullers lasted 4 2/3 innings, leaving tied 5-5. Scott Feldman got the win in relief and the bullpen was excellent. George Springer gave his family and friends a thrill with his first Fenway home run, providing a 7-5 lead in the sixth. A few hours before the game, he and former University of Connecticut teammate Barnes sat in the stands for a TV interview. In the game, he victimized Barnes for the go-ahead and eventual winning homer. Springer and Altuve both had three hits in the game. The Astros squared the series at 1-1 with the 7-6 triumph, improving their record at Fenway to 4-12.

Major League Baseball suspended Rockies shortstop Jose Reyes until May 31 on domestic violence charges.

Reyes was on hold until this day while being paid until the charges could be investigated. No formal charges against him had been filed by the legal authorities in Hawaii.

Matt Bush was promoted to the Texas Rangers, a saga involving the former first draft choice in 2004 by San Diego. The 30-year-old Bush had served prison time for driving under the influence while injuring a bicyclist in 2012 in Florida. Bush was drafted as a shortstop but later converted to pitcher. He came up from AA Frisco to replace centerfielder Delino DeShields on the roster after Anthony Ranaudo was designated for assignment.

May 14---Luke Gregerson blew a save in the ninth when David Ortiz ripped a two-out triple to center field, tying the game. Then Boston beat Houston in the 11th, 6-5, when Ortiz struck again with a two-out game-winning double off Michael Feliz to touch off the Red Sox' celebration on the field. Ortiz had a milestone game, including a third inning homer off Collin McHugh. It was the first time he had a homer, triple and double in the same game. The homer was Big Papi's 512th, moving him past Eddie Mathews and Ernie Banks into 22nd place on the all-time list. The double was his 600th, making him the third player to have 500 homers and 600 doubles. Hank Aaron and Barry Bonds were the first two. It represented his 20th walkoff hit with the Red Sox.

A.J. Hinch was questioned about pitching to Ortiz in the ninth, but he never wavered from the decision not to walk him intentionally.

George Springer blasted a 455-foot grand slam over the legendary left field wall known as the Green Monster. It was his second slam of the year and his second straight four RBI game. After Springer's second-inning slam off Clay Buchholz gave the Astros a 5-1 lead, Houston never scored again. The Astros tried to push across a run in the eighth using small ball but it failed.

With runners at first and third and one out, Marwin Gonzalez broke from third on the pitch with Jason Castro batting. Castro took the pitch and Gonzalez was put out in a rundown, leading to speculation that Castro missed a sign for a squeeze bunt.

Altuve vs. Rose

Jose Altuve and Pete Rose both made their major league debuts at age 21. Through 38 games in 2016, Altuve was hitting .345 with an OPS of 1.079. He led the AL in runs (35), doubles (17) and steals (13). After 706 career games for both, Altuve had more hits (881-842), doubles (179-142) and steals (182-39) than Rose. His batting average was also higher (.307-.297). Rose went on to bang out a record 4,256 hits.

Altuve refined his pitch selection, swinging at 41.8 per cent of pitches compared to 52.2 per cent in 2015.

May 15---A bright, chilly day in Boston brought major problems to the Astros in the field. The day before, Carlos Correa lost a popup in the sun and it hit him in the shoulder. On this day, pitcher Chris Devenski caught a first-inning popup when the other infielders could not find the ball in the bright sky. Carlos Gomez lost a fly ball in the sun leading off the home second and it went for a double, leading to a four-run inning. For the hard-hitting Red Sox, who led the majors in batting average (.297) and runs (219), any extra assistance amounted to major trouble for the opposition.

In the seventh, a Ryan Hanigan fly ball fell between Springer and Gomez for an RBI single accounting for the tying run with two outs and leading to the winning run. Running across the third base line to back up the play, losing pitcher Scott Feldman watched the ball land uncaught in the outfield and reacted with despair. The play could have been made by Springer, who was closer to where the ball landed, but he pulled up as if expecting Gomez to catch it.

Gomez took responsibility. "I called it and I didn't catch it," said Gomez. "That's it. It's my fault. We lost the game because of me today."

The Red Sox won a slugfest 10-9.

Devenski came out of the game after two innings, trailing 6-3.

MAJOR OFFENSIVE PROBLEMS: Gomez began the day hitting .186 with no homers. His .486 OPS ranked 187th of 188 qualified major league hitters. His strikeout to walk ratio was 45:6. "I don't know what's wrong with me right now," said Gomez. "I get here, put in some work every day, come with a good attitude, do what I need to do every day to perform.

"I've been playing brutal. In everything. Defensively, Offensively, I'm not playing good." GM Jeff Luhnow acknowledged, "It's hard to continue to play a player that isn't helping you win ball games."

Gomez had company in the slumping brigade. Preston Tucker was starting the day at .185 through 81 at bats with a .370 slugging percentage. Jake Marisnick was hitting .100 in 30 at bats. Luis Valbuena was at .198 with one homer when the day started, although he belted a Sean O'Sullivan fastball far into the right field seats for a three-run shot and later added a two-run double that improved his .297 slugging percentage. With options at third in the minors, the Astros could call upon Colin Moran if they chose. He was hitting .281-2-21 at AAA Fresno.

Evan Gattis was about to return from the minors. His performance at Corpus Christi had been strong. He was hitting .360-3-6. The reports on his catching were good.

Alex Bregman played third base at Corpus Christi. "It went great. I felt great. I got some plays in the field and felt very comfortable. I played one summer at third base with the Team USA 18-year-old team, so it was not too crazy over there." The plans were for Bregman to play more third base. He was hitting .291-7-19. Going into an off day in Chicago, the Astros were 15-24, in last place and 7 ½ games out of first. After 39 games in 2015, they were 25-14 and had a 5 ½ game lead. On A.J. Hinch's 42nd birthday, the Astros' defensive play cost them the game. Frustration was running high, and changes were called for.

They seemed to be imminent.

After the game, the club announced the return of Gattis to replace Erik Kratz on Tuesday. Tucker was sent to Fresno and Tony Kemp was called up from Fresno. Kemp was not on the 40-man roster, so Kratz was removed from the roster to make room for him.

May 16---The economic crisis in Venezuela exploded into a public health emergency. There was a chronic shortage of antibiotics and the emergency was claiming untold lives. A surgeon in Caracas said, "The death of a baby is our daily bread."

Odorous Play

Much of the discussion May 16 was centered around the bench-clearing brawl between Texas and Toronto in Arlington the day before. There were six ejections after an eighth inning melee. Two more ejections later added up to a total of eight in the game. Jose Bautista was hit by a pitch from Matt Bush in the eighth inning with Toronto trailing by one run. Bush had been in prison when Bautista beat Texas in Game 5 of the ALCS. Joey Bats caused a stir with an emphatic bat flip after glaring at pitcher Sam Dyson. The bat flip had been discussed and dissected all winter.

In this seventh and final game of the season between the two teams, all had been calm with no repercussions from last October. Ian Desmond gave Texas a 7-6 lead in the seventh and he reveled in the moment with a bat flip. After Bautista was drilled in the rib cage, he was at first base when a grounder was hit to third. The throw went to Venezuelan-born Rougned Odor at second for the force play.

Bautista barreled close to him with a late, hard slide that carried him past the bag. Odor was dropping his arm angle low for the throw toward Bautista's head to make sure Bautista got down. Odor's throw was wild, past first base. When Bautista got up from his slide, Odor was squaring off with him waiting for a confrontation. Odor landed a haymaker to his jaw and the benches emptied.

The punch was replayed many times on highlight shows and a photo of it landed on the front page of *USA Today*.

"I was pretty surprised," said Bautista. "It shows at least the lack of leadership they have...when it comes to playing baseball the right way." Toronto manager John Gibbons added, "It was gutless. We've played them seven games. The other 29 teams...if they have an issue with you, they come at you right away." Sports network analysts waded into the episode the day after the game. It was assumed that Bush's pitch to Bautista was intentional. It also drew critical comments from analysts because of the timing of it.

They felt that Bautista was targeted in retaliation for his October bat flip, but strangely the Rangers waited until his final at bat of the final game of the season series.

A couple of veteran journalists suggested that the Rangers wanted to make Bautista worry about getting hit all through the series because it might affect his concentration at the plate. It might have worked that way, since he went 5 for 28 in the season series. Their opinion was that the Rangers should have hit Bautista the first game in Texas to settle the score and they felt that no brawls would have ensued had they chosen that time. But by waiting until the end of the series, as the opinions suggested, they stirred up more emotion from the Blue Jays. Bautista, his teammates and his manager probably agreed. Both managers were ejected. As they left the field, they had angry words.

This was at least the third manager-to-manager confrontation for Jeff Banister in his seven months as a big league manager. To compound the emotion of the moment, Banister left the field and banged his hands together, lifting them high while facing the fans behind his dugout. It was interpreted by some observers as a gesture to fire up the fans.

In the eighth, Jesse Chavez of Toronto retaliated by hitting Prince Fielder with a pitch and Chavez was ejected.

Matt Bush was not commenting on the pitch he threw to Bautista.

Odor was not available to the media. Odor was involved in a fight in a minor league game earlier in his career. In addition to sliding hard into Jose Altuve in 2015 and out of the baseline, he slid late and hard with spikes up into the leg of Johnny Giavotella of the Los Angeles Angels. Giavotella was on the left field side of second base when Odor made contact with him. Odor's behavior labeled him as an instigator with a hair-trigger temper. The Rangers won the game 7-6 and left town in first place with a 22-16 record. But they also faced the likelihood of some suspensions, especially a long one for Odor.

The next day, Odor answered a question about opposing teams being irritated by his style of play. "I just care about my team," he said. "I don't care about the other team. I just play the game how I play it. I play to win the game."

In the NBA playoffs, Oklahoma City surprised Golden State 108-102 in Game 1 of the Western Conference Finals at Oakland.

May 17---It was a hectic day for transactions involving the Astros. Evan Gattis rejoined the club from AA Corpus Christi. Erik Kratz was designated for assignment to make room for him. Kratz was removed from the roster because a non-roster player, Tony Kemp, was promoted. Another non-roster player, Colin Moran, was also promoted to take the place of Carlos Gomez, who went on the disabled list with sore ribs. In order to get Moran on the 40-man roster, AAA pitcher Asher Wojciechowski was also designated for assignment. The DFA moves gave the Astros 10 days to decide whether to keep these two players in the minor league system or release them. In some cases, players decide whether they want to leave the organization and take their chances as free agents.

"It's starting to become time to look at the internal options that we have to help us from the minor leagues," said Hinch.

"Gomez let us know on the plane on the way to Chicago that he wasn't feeling great. It's in the best interests of everybody to get him healthy, and he wasn't going to play in this series, based on the injury." Jeff Luhnow said, "He feels bad for the organization, the fans and his teammates. He knows he's not playing how he's capable and he's letting everybody down. We need this player to be good if we're going to be good this year."

Winners: Jake Marisnick would play more, Gattis was back with confidence to catch a little and be a bigger part of the club, Kemp and Moran got their first service time in the big leagues, and Tyler White was not demoted, although he probably had been worried about going down. Losers: Gomez was out for at least 15 days, Kratz and Wojo were off the roster, Stassi and Tucker were at Fresno. Marwin Gonzalez would lose playing time because Valbuena was going to play some first base when Colin Moran played third base.

Dallas Keuchel was perfect through 11 hitters before giving up three runs in 6 1/3 innings. Tyler White bashed two homers off Carlos Rodon. A Jose Altuve sacrifice fly in the eighth put the Astros ahead 4-3. After perfect relief by Ken Giles and Will Harris, Luke Gregerson blew a save in the ninth on a Tyler Saladino sacrifice fly. The game wore on to extra innings.

In the 11th, Gattis drilled an 0-2 pitch with two outs from former Astro and Houston native Matt Albers into the left field seats for a 6-4 lead. Tony Sipp gave up a run but saved it 6-5. Afterwards, Giles and Keuchel both drew rave reviews for their work and Harris extended his dynamic string to 16 straight scoreless outings.

The Astros reached the quarter pole with a 16-24 record, seven games out of first place. They could not afford another 40-game chunk of the season like that if they were going to be in contention.

But game number 40 had an old familiar 2015 feel to it.

Joe Garagiola Jr., in his role as senior vice president for Major League Baseball, announced discipline for 14 people involved in the Blue Jays-Rangers melee. Rougned Odor received an eight-game suspension. Jesse Chavez got three games for hitting Prince Fielder with a pitch after warnings. Jose Bautista and Elvis Andrus were handed one-game suspensions. Odor and Bautista announced their intentions to appeal. They were allowed to play until their appeals were heard. Odor's suspension was later reduced to seven games after his appeal.

The Atlanta Braves fired Manager Fredi Gonzalez and replaced him with Atlanta native Brian Snitker. Detroit skipper Brad Ausmus was rumored to be on thin ice, but he remained on the job with the exception of serving a one-game suspension for a tirade on the field.

In the NBA playoffs, Cleveland thumped Toronto 115-84 in Game 1 of the Eastern Conference finals to extend its postseason record to 9-0.

May 18---Economist Bill Gilmer projected a loss of 40,000 jobs in Houston through 2017 before a turnaround arrived.

At U.S. Cellular Field in Chicago, it was 57 degrees. But the Houston hitters were not deterred, banging out 13 hits in a 5-3 win over the White Sox. They tagged Mat Latos with his first loss, featuring a new lineup stacked with lefty hitters. Colby Rasmus and Jason Castro homered. Luis Valbuena started at first and chipped in with a single. Two new lefthanded hitters, Colin Moran and Tony Kemp, made their first major league starts. Moran reached once on a walk. Kemp tattooed the left field line with a single and a double and drew a walk. Kemp also made a big play, throwing out Adam Eaton trying to stretch a single for the first out for winning pitcher Doug Fister.

Fister won his fourth, registering his sixth straight quality start. The bullpen trio of Giles, Harris and Gregerson closed out the win. It was only the third time the Astros won back to back games. With 8-0 Chris Sale waiting for them the next night, it was reassuring to know they had clinched a series win.

Rasmus stopped at Shriners Hospital for Children on his way to the ballpark and met eight-year-old Owen Mahan, who was burned extensively in a 2009 accident. Owen attended the game and met some players, receiving a jersey from Rasmus. He also watched Rasmus crush a home run.

George Springer grounded into a 5-4-3 triple play. The Astros hadn't done that since 1989.

The Golden State Warriors rode the shooting of MVP Stephen Curry to a 118-91 thumping of the Oklahoma City Thunder to square their series at one game apiece.

Mike D'Antoni emerged as the favorite to become the Houston Rockets' choice for their next coach.

May 19---Chris Sale was on display, with his 8-0 record and his 1.67 ERA. Sale was only the fourth White Sox pitcher to win his first eight starts in a season. Ed Cicotte, John Whitehead and Jon Garland also did it.

Jon Garland

Jon Garland won his first eight starts in 2005, getting the Sox started on their World Series run. He faced the Astros in Game Three of the World Series at Minute Maid Park. Garland was 18-10 that year. In the first ever World Series game in the state of Texas, the Astros' players wanted the roof closed. They were 40-11 with the retractable roof closed, 4-1 in the postseason in 2005.

The players cited the noise level as a major part of their home field advantage. Major League baseball ordered the roof be open for the next two games, and the Astros lost both.

They played a marathon affair, lasting 5:41 in Game Three with the Sox winning 7-5 in 14 innings. Roy Oswalt was handed a 4-0 lead after four.

But after that, the Astros managed only one hit in the final 10 innings. Garland allowed four runs (two earned) in seven innings.

The Sox turned the game around in a five-run fifth.

But in the 14th, former Astro and future broadcaster Geoff Blum ripped a go-ahead home run off Ezequiel Astacio. For Blum, it was only his second at bat of the postseason. Ozzie Guillen called upon Game Two starter Mark Buehrle for the save in the 14th.

The game was the longest by time in Series history. The 14 innings tied a 1918 game for the longest World Series game as well.

Ed Cicotte

Cicotte's 1919 salary was $6,000. He had a bonus of $10,000 for winning 30 games. As the story went, tight-fisted owner Charles Comiskey ordered manager Kid Gleason to keep Cicotte out of his rotation for the final five games, depriving him of a chance to earn the bonus. According to legend, Cicotte resisted efforts by gambler Chick Gandil to pay him to lose games until it became apparent that Comiskey would not pay Cicotte even a portion of his bonus.

Cicotte lost the first game, allowing six earned runs in 3 2/3 innings. According to *Red Legs and Black Sox* by Susan Dellinger (*Emmis Books,* 2006), reporters and former players had heard the Series was fixed beforehand and they were suspicious about Cicotte's performance. He hesitated on a throw to second and cost his team a double play.

His catcher was furious with him, perhaps for disregarding signs. He also lost Game 4, making two errors and allowing two unearned runs in a 2-0 setback. He won Game 7 with a complete game, 4-1. But by then the White Sox trailed four games to two in the best of nine series. They lost five of eight. "I didn't care for the money after that," said Cicotte.

"I lost too many friends there at baseball, friends that look up to me, and everything depended on it and I couldn't stand it."

Later publications reported that the gamblers did not pay the White Sox players for throwing Game 1, leading to an angry hotel room meeting in which the players expressed their desire to win if they weren't getting paid to lose.

The winning pitcher of the final game, Cincinnati's Hod Eller, was confronted before the game by his manager, Pat Moran, because of the gambling rumors. Moran asked him if he had been confronted by gamblers. Eller said a gambler had offered him $10,000 to throw the game and Eller refused and threatened to punch the gambler. Satisfied that he was not in on a fix, Moran sent him out to pitch and Eller won the game.

Sale took the mound with no such problems as those experienced by Cicotte in 1919. He was highly motivated and performing at his career peak. Sale's salary was $6 million, a bargain by today's standards. He was 27 years old and a thin 6-6 and 180 pounds. His fastball averaged 92 and hitters were managing all of .176 against it. His slider, at 78, yielded a .145 average. He was throwing both of those pitches more often and his changeup less. His strikeouts were down, walks were down and innings were up. His goal was to pitch more innings.

The on base average against Sale was a puny .216. He had finished between third and sixth in the Cy Young balloting in each of the last four years, but never won the award. His arm angle was one of a kind. He slung the ball from a low angle nearer first base than anybody else.

His arm angle combined with his velocity gave the hitters fits. Sale was an absolute nightmare. And he had an edge to his approach. According to reports, Sale had a shouting match with White Sox President Kenny Williams in spring training regarding handling of the Adam LaRoche affair.

Sale came out of the bullpen dealing pellets. Jerry Sands drove in a run against Collin McHugh in the second and Alex Avila drove in a run with a fly ball in the seventh. McHugh was excellent. Evan Gattis belted an eighth inning homer off Sale, but Chicago won it 2-1. Sale's record went to 9-0 with a 1.58 ERA. "Sale came as advertised," said Hinch. "That's probably as good a stuff as we've seen all season."

Only Walter Johnson in 1913 and Sal Maglie in 1952 could match those numbers for their first nine games.

Gattis acquitted himself well at catcher. George Springer's glove went up above the right field wall to rob a homer from Jose Abreu in the first inning.

The Astros headed home from a 3-4 road trip, with five of the seven games decided by one run.

May 20---Phil Mickelson agreed to pay nearly $1 million in an insider trading SEC case.

On a beautiful day in Houston, there was a press conference in Arlington announcing plans for a new stadium with a retractable roof for the Rangers. The Rangers were in town with a 22-19 record to play the Astros in their second series of the season. Texas was in second place and preparing to regain the services of Yu Darvish in about a week. Colby Lewis, who was 9-1 with a 2.71 ERA against Houston, was set to start against Lance McCullers, who had lost both of his career starts to Lewis in Arlington.

McCullers was much better than in his Boston debut, allowing a two-run double to Prince Fielder in six good innings. He featured a sharp curve and his fastball started at 91 but reached the mid-90s. Lewis was better, winning 2-1 with seven shutout innings. Correa lined a ball off his head and it caromed into the air and was caught by Odor in shallow center field for an out. The loss dropped the Astros eight games behind Seattle.

May 21---After Exaggerator won the Preakness, the spiral continued for the Astros. They fell 2-1 again to the Rangers, losing by the same score for the third straight game. That had never happened in club history. Mike Fiers was the tough luck loser, Cesar Ramos the winner. The Astros managed only three hits. They sank to ten games under .500 at 17-27. Their improved starting pitching was not accompanied by timely hitting.

May 22---The Rangers left Houston after pushing the Astros into baseball's version of a drainage ditch. Cole Hamels won his 12th in a row, beating Dallas Keuchel 9-2. Keuchel retired the first six before running into a five-run third. The inning began with his first hit batsman of the season, on an 0-2 pitch.

"Just wasn't finishing my pitches, and that's the most frustrating part, because the first two innings were the same 'ol pitches: down-and-away sinker, good slider today, and just beating the ball into the ground," said Keuchel. He said getting some pitches up hurt him in the third inning.

"They've just beat the hell out of us," said Hinch. "They've come into our ballpark, at their ballpark, and they've just beat us. We have to find a new approach against them."

At the end of the day, the Rangers were 6-0 against the Astros and Houston was 17-28, 10 games behind Seattle. Since their 18-7 start in 2015, the Astros' record was 85-97.

May 23---The Astros had the day off. They were hitting .229 as a team. Jose Altuve was their only hitter above .254.

In the NBA Eastern Conference Finals, Toronto tied its series with Cleveland at two apiece with a 105-99 confidence-building win in Toronto.

May 24---A.J. Hinch made a change in the batting order. He promoted George Springer to the leadoff spot and moved Jose Altuve to second in the order. "We have to do something different." said Hinch.

"Springer is a rare talent who could hit in every one of the first five or six slots in the order." When Springer led off in 2015, his batting average and on base average were higher. He always referred to his objective of "just getting to first base" when he hit in the leadoff spot. As for his team's 445 strikeouts through 45 games, a major league high, Hinch said, "Since May 15, we've really gone outside the strike zone. Our chase rate has been almost 40 per cent."

The Baltimore Orioles, with the best winning percentage in the American League at .619, had their Opening Day pitcher ready. Chris Tillman brought a 6-1 record and a 2.61 ERA to Minute Maid Park, where he was 2-0 with a 1.32 ERA. Doug Fister took the mound after six straight quality starts. The two teams matched excellent pitching and home run hitting in a 2-2 tie through nine innings. Pedro Alvarez and Manny Machado homered for the Orioles, while Luis Valbuena hit a two-run shot for the Astros.

The game wore on to the 13th and passed the four-hour mark. The Astros tied a club record set in 1962 with 16 strikeouts by their bullpen in 7 1/3 innings. Six relievers kept the Birds at bay until the Astros won it in the 13th on a leadoff triple by Tony Kemp and a game winning single by Carlos Correa, snapping the four-game losing streak.

After the game, Oriole skipper Buck Showalter talked about HIS team expanding ITS strike zone. The Birds had fanned 40 times in their last three games.

In the NBA playoffs, Oklahoma City pushed Golden State into a 3-1 hole in the Western Conference finals with a triple double from Russell Westbrook in a 118-94 shellacking of the favorites.

May 25---Back to back doubles by Manny Machado and Jonathan Schoop put Collin McHugh behind 1-0 after just a few pitches. Of the 30 earned runs he had allowed, 12 were in the first inning. But he applied a tourniquet and the Astros came back to win a hard-fought one-run affair 4-3.

Another Valbuena long ball, this one a towering blast to left center field, snapped a 3-3 tie in the sixth. Evan Gattis supplied his second homer in three games earlier off loser Tyler Wilson. The bullpen nailed down the game, and the Astros' pitchers racked up 18 strikeouts, giving them 37 in two games to tie a club record.

The Cleveland Cavaliers took a 31-point halftime lead on their way to a 116-78 shellacking of Toronto to grab a 3-2 lead in their series.

May 26---The Houston Rockets hired Mike D'Antoni and signed him to a four-year contract to be their new coach.

With dark clouds outside and the roof closed, the Astros took the field behind Lance McCullers to shoot for their first three-game winning streak and their first sweep of a three-game series. The strikeout fest continued for the Orioles, who whiffed 15 more times in a 4-2 Houston win. McCullers struck out 10 in his five innings, surviving six walks. Ken Giles got his first save as an Astro. The Houston staff set a new major league record for strikeouts in a three-game series with 52, shattering the mark of 47 set in April by Washington in a three-game set against Minnesota.

George Springer led off the game with a home run off Kevin Gausman and hit a second homer in the fifth. Luis Valbuena added a two-run bomb. After the conclusion of a 3-3 homestand, the Astros headed for Anaheim and the start of a five-game road trip. Their next ten games would be against the Los Angeles Angels, Arizona Diamondbacks and Oakland Athletics, who had a combined winning percentage of .412. If they were going to make a move to get back into the race, it seemed that this had to be the time.

May 27---A new onslaught of torrential rains created rush hour havoc in Houston, with many motorists heading out of town for the Memorial Day weekend. Flooding was especially bad in Rosenberg and Humble.

The five-game road trip opened in Anaheim, and it opened poorly for the Astros. Mike Fiers was rocked for six runs in the third inning of a 7-2 loss. Winning pitcher Matt Shoemaker fanned 11 with no walks in 8 1/3 innings. Mike Trout drove in three with a double and Albert Pujols followed with his 570th career homer in the big third inning.

"They came out swinging from the start," said Fiers. "I've just got to make better pitches. I didn't show them any curveballs at all, and I think they really capitalized."

Chris Devenski helped the bullpen by working 4 1/3 innings in relief.

May 28---The Astros squared the series with a tidy come from behind 4-2 victory. The biggest story of the night was Dallas Keuchel turning around the game. After first inning blasts by Trout and Pujols, Keuchel slammed the door on the Halos, retiring 18 in a row and allowing his team to turn the tide on a two-run swing by Jason Castro in the sixth inning. It was Keuchel's first win since April 15. "I knew it was going to turn around, because I'm a pretty good competitor," Keuchel said. He added, "My breaking ball got a lot better. I was able to command it." The reasons for his slump? "At times I've tried to slow the game down too much, and that's not my game," said Keuchel. "It started with me pressing a little too much, trying to be too perfect."

In the NBA, Cleveland advanced to the NBA Finals by eliminating Toronto 113-87.

Golden State forced a seventh game in its Western Conference final series by winning at Oklahoma City.

May 29---At the end of a five-hour game, the Astros pulled Carlos Correa off the bench and Michael Feliz out of the bullpen. Correa ripped a pinch three-run homer to left field off Mike Morin for an 8-5 lead in the 13th. Feliz kept the Angels at bay and the 8-6 win gave the Astros a road series victory, their second of the season.

Correa was given the day off from starting for the only the second time all season. Correa's batting average had dropped below .250 at the start of the road trip and that was generating some questions. "It's about trying to be consistent, and I haven't been able to do that," he said. A.J. Hinch added: "I think he's a very selective hitter and sometimes might be too selective in trying to wait out the perfect pitch." Correa often took a hittable fastball on the first pitch. "His comfort with hitting at any point in the count has put him in some bad counts this season."

Correa, who was six years old the last time an Astro (Tony Eusebio) hit a pinch homer in extra innings, provided his second game-winner in the 13th inning in the span of a week.

After an 11th inning one-out triple by Kole Calhoun, Hinch ordered intentional walks to Trout and Pujols. Pat Neshek struck out Johnny Giavotella, hitting fifth, and retired Rafael Ortega to prolong the game.

American Alexander Rossi won the Indianapolis 500, running out of gas on the final lap because he stretched his final tank 90 miles while other drivers hit the pits for one more fuel splash so they could finish. The 66-1 long shot used a winning fuel strategy to outsmart drivers with much faster cars.

Texan Jordan Spieth secured his first golf tournament win in the Lone Star state, finishing at 17 under par at Colonial to win the Dean and Deluca Invitational.

In college baseball, Texas A & M won the SEC tournament. Sam Houston won the Southland Conference tourney. TCU took the Big 12.

May 30---American flags flew proudly all across the USA.

The Golden State Warriors rode the shooting of MVP Steph Curry to a Game 7 win over Oklahoma City 96-88 to cap a Western Conference comeback from a 3-1 deficit. Cleveland was waiting to start the NBA Finals.

Major league teams took the field wearing spiffy patriotic uniforms with their caps and uniforms dressed in camouflage.

For years, a common saying around baseball was, "The pennant races begin on Memorial Day." If so, the AL West and AL East had the tightest races from top to bottom. Only seven games separated AL East leader Boston from cellar dweller Tampa Bay. In the AL West, Oakland and Houston were tied for fourth and fifth, 7 ½ games behind new leader Texas, which took over the top spot Sunday by a half game over Seattle.

In Phoenix, the first of four straight games between the Arizona Diamondbacks and the Astros got under way at Chase Field. Collin McHugh was tagged by a first inning homer from Paul Goldschmidt. That was no indication of what was to come. McHugh wound up with the first complete game of his career in an 8-3 victory, giving the bullpen a long-awaited rest. It was the first time a Houston pitcher had gone the distance in 2016. The Astros peppered the Dbacks with 13 hits, opening an 8-1 lead after four and winning easily without a home run. The Astros took their sixth win in the last seven games.

MLB Veterans

When we use the term "veteran" about professional athletes, we use it in the context of a player who has spent years of experience honing his craft. In the military sense, there are few veterans playing pro sports now. In recent years, Pat Tillman performed one of the most heroic acts when he enlisted for military service at a time when the Arizona Cardinals were paying him millions of dollars. Tillman felt an obligation to serve his country, and he paid the ultimate price when he was killed by friendly fire on duty in Afghanistan.

During World War I and II and the Korean War, baseball players were among the many who enlisted to put their lives on the line in defense of their country. It was not uncommon for the best players in the sport to walk away from lucrative jobs in order to risk years of their lives and leave their families for a higher cause.

These are a few of those who served willingly and unselfishly:

Bob Feller

Bob Feller saw four years of military service during World War II. He was Chief Petty Officer aboard the *USS Alabama*. Feller enlisted in the U.S. Navy two days after the attack on Pearl Harbor. Feller became the first American professional athlete to enlist. He was visiting his terminally ill father when he got news of the attack. He saw direct combat during several naval battles. Feller was discharged in August 1945. He missed playing in the majors at ages 22-25 and most of his age 26 season. Like Ted Williams, he missed some of the potential prime seasons of his career.

Feller still pitched for 18 seasons and entered the Hall of Fame after a career with 266 wins and 279 complete games.

Ted Williams

Ted Williams was already an All-Star and in 1941 he had one of the best seasons in history, hitting .406 with 37 homers and 120 runs batted in. In 1942, he was drafted when his draft board classified him as I-A. His attorney objected to that classification because he was the sole supporter of his mother. Upon appeal to the Presidential draft board, he was reclassified 3-A. The public reaction was negative.

In 1942, Williams won the Triple Crown, hitting .356 with 36 home runs and 137 RBI. Despite winning the Triple Crown, Williams finished second to the Yankees' Joe Gordon in the MVP voting. He expressed his displeasure with the MVP voting, saying that he thought the draft board problems affected the voters.

Williams joined the Navy reserve after the 1942 season. He went on active duty in the Marine Corps in 1943, seeing many hours of combat as a fighter pilot. He was discharged in 1946.

But after returning to the major leagues to resume his hitting at the highest level, Williams was called from a list of inactive reserves to serve on active duty in the Korean War in 1952. He returned in August 1953 and rejoined the Boston Red Sox, hitting .407 in 110 at bats.

Williams missed more than four full seasons because of his military service. When he was asked what his favorite team was, he responded, "The U.S. Marines."

Williams became a Hall of Famer after winning six batting titles and two Triple Crowns.

Hank Greenberg

Hank Greenberg was initially classified 4-F by his draft board because of flat feet. Amid rumors that he bribed the draft board, Greenberg petitioned the draft board to re-examine him and he was reclassified fit for duty. He was inducted into the U.S. Army in May 1941 and was honorably discharged two days before Pearl Harbor in 1941. Greenberg re-enlisted in early 1942 and joined the Army Air Corps. He was discharged in June 1945. Greenberg served longer than any other major leaguer, 47 months.

Greenberg entered the Hall of Fame after winning two MVP awards and leading the American League in homers four times.

Yogi Berra

During World War II, Berra was a gunner's mate in the U.S. Navy on the attack transport *USS Bayfield* during the D-Day invasion of Normandy. Berra was part of a six-man crew on a Navy rocket boat. He fired machine guns and launched rockets at the German positions on Omaha Beach and Utah Beach. He was fired at but never hit. His service came before he reached the major leagues.

Berra became one of the greatest catchers of all time in a Hall of Fame career.

He was an 18-time All-Star who played on ten World Series championship teams.

Warren Spahn

Warren Spahn enlisted in the U.S. Army in 1942 when he was still in the minor leagues. He served with distinction and was awarded the Purple Heart. Spahn was involved in the Battle of the Bulge and at the battle of the Ludendorff Bridge as a combat engineer. He missed three full seasons and resumed his career at age 25 in the major leagues. He is the leading lefthander of all time in wins with 363.

Spahn played until age 44, entering the Hall of Fame after being named to 17 All-Star teams.

Jackie Robinson

Jackie Robinson was drafted in 1942 and assigned to a segregated U.S. Army unit. The armed forces had not yet been integrated at the time. After protests by heavyweight boxing champion Joe Louis and others, Robinson and other African-Americans were admitted into the Officer Candidate School. Robinson joined the "Black Panthers" tank battalion.

Robinson experienced racism in the Army when he was court-martialed after charges by an investigating duty officer after an incident on a bus in which he was told by the bus driver to move to the back of the bus. Robinson was acquitted by an all-white panel of nine officers. He was honorably discharged in 1944.

Robinson became a Hall of Famer after a career with an MVP award, six All-Star seasons and a Rookie of the Year award.

Ty Cobb

Ty Cobb enlisted in the Chemical Corps branch of the U.S. Army in 1918. He was sent to France and served 67 days before being discharged.

Cobb set the record for most hits in a career with 4,191 (later broken by Pete Rose). He also set 90 records while he was playing and hit .367 while winning 11 batting titles. He received the most votes of any player in the inaugural Hall of Fame balloting in 1936.

Christy Mathewson

Christy Mathewson, like Ty Cobb, served in World War I in the Chemical Corps branch of the U.S. Army. Mathewson was a captain in the unit. **George Sisler** was a lieutenant. Cobb, Mathewson and Sisler served under the command of Major **Branch Rickey.** Rickey was the president of the St. Louis Cardinals.

These players were assigned to the Gas and Flame division. They trained soldiers to prepare for chemical attacks by exposing them to gas chambers in a controlled environment. This work eventually was responsible for Mathewson contracting tuberculosis, which led to his premature death in 1925.

Mathewson won 373 games on his way to the Hall of Fame.

Willie Mays

Willie Mays was drafted into the U.S. Army in 1952 during the Korean War. He missed most of that season and all of 1953. He missed 266 games in the prime of his career. Mays spent most of his Army time playing baseball at Ft. Eustis, Virginia.

Mays played in 24 All-Star games in his Hall of Fame career.

Hoyt Wilhelm

Hoyt Wilhelm served in the U.S. Army. He was involved in the Battle of the Bulge in Europe, where he was wounded and received the Purple Heart. He played his entire career with a piece of shrapnel lodged in his back from that injury. His nickname was "Old Sarge," based on his military service. He was not called up to the majors until 1951, five years after returning from military service. He was in his late twenties at the time. Wilhelm pitched until he was nearly 50.

Grover Cleveland Alexander

Grover Cleveland Alexander was drafted in 1917 and spent most of 1918 as a sergeant with a field artillery unit in France. He was exposed to German mustard gas. A shell exploded while he saw action, causing him to lose hearing and experience epilepsy. When he returned from the war, he suffered seizures from epilepsy after returning to baseball. His physical problems caused him to drink heavily. Nonetheless, he was able to perform at the highest level in baseball.

Alexander won 373 games in a Hall of Fame career. Born during the first term of President Grover Cleveland, Alexander set a National League record with 90 shutouts.

Moe Berg

One of the most interesting stories about a ballplayer serving in the military was the story of catcher Moe Berg. He played for 15 major league seasons, mostly as a backup player. Berg worked for the United States government as a spy. Berg traveled to Japan, Yugoslavia and Italy to obtain information. Berg had degrees from Princeton University and Columbia law school.

May 31---With flooding continuing to cause problems in the Houston area, news crews captured footage of a dozen horses stranded on the front porch of a house in Simonton, southwest of the city. The weather forecast called for more rain later in the week, and worries were high about more loss of livestock and damage to homes.

In arid Arizona, the Astros rode their new leadoff hitter, George Springer, to an 8-5 win over the Dbacks.

Springer banged out three more hits and drove in four, three on an opposite field home run off Patrick Corbin. That made it seven wins in eight games and closed out a 4-1 road trip. As the club returned home for a five-game homestand, its May record of 17-12 had allowed it to stay almost as close to the leaders in the division as at the end of a horrible April. The AL West was the tightest division in the majors.

May Summary

The Astros' 17-12 May included a much improved ERA since April: 3.81.

Their top hitters were Jose Altuve (.345-3-18) and George Springer (.296-8-22).

Their top pitchers were Doug Fister (3-0, 2.84 ERA), Michael Feliz (3-1, 0.54 ERA, 1BB 26K in 16 2/3 innings) and Collin McHugh (3-1, 3.83 ERA). The Astros won all six of Fister's starts.

Noteworthy Achievements: The pitching staff struck out 52 in three consecutive games vs. Baltimore May 24-26 to set a new major league record. The staff set a club record for strikeouts in May with 267.

The bullpen compiled a 2.33 ERA to lead the major leagues.

May Standings in AL West

Texas 31-21 -

Seattle 30-21 -1/2

LAA 24-28 -7

Houston 24-29 -7 1/2

Oakland 24-29 -7 ½

7 June Monsoons

The heavy rains continued in the Houston area through early June. Undeterred with a stadium that prevented rainouts and delays, the Astros built on their 17-12 May by having their first June with 18 wins since 1989. Although the Texas Rangers increased their lead over Houston from 7 ½ to nine games, the Astros moved into the mix of contenders for a wild card playoff spot with plenty of time remaining to overtake Texas if they could avoid slumps.

Overcoming a 4-13 start against their divisional opponents, the Astros swept three three-game series against divisional foes, turning the trick twice against the Angels and once against Oakland.

With offensive turnarounds by several players and an airtight bullpen, they rebuilt their confidence. Carlos Gomez, Evan Gattis, Luis Valbuena and Marwin Gonzalez were offensive contributors to a more well-rounded attack. And Jose Altuve delivered the best month of his career, hitting .420. By the end of the month he had reached base in 32 consecutive games and was hitting .357, best in the majors.

June Game by Game Accounts

June 1---In the third game of the Arizona series, a 4-1 Houston lead disappeared in the ninth when Luke Gregerson allowed a tying, two-run homer by Jake Lamb to send the game to extra innings. George Springer hit a walkoff homer off Tyler Clippard in the 11th for the Astros' fifth straight win 5-4.

June 2---Zack Greinke halted the winning streak for Houston at five, beating Dallas Keuchel 5-0. Greinke fanned 11 and walked nobody.

June 3---In the opener of the weekend series with Oakland, Doug Fister blanked the Athletics for six innings and a seven-run Houston first put the game out of reach early, with the Astros winning 12-2. Tony Kemp hit a two-run triple in the first.

June 4---Former Astro Jed Lowrie ruined the night for Luke Gregerson with a two-out ninth inning homer to tie the game 5-5 and force extra innings. It was Gregerson's fifth blown save. Carlos Correa saved the day with a walkoff hit to right field, lifting Houston to a 6-5, 12-inning triumph. Gregerson was moved out of the closer's role after this game.

June 5---New Houston closer Will Harris picked up his first save by nailing down the final three outs in a 5-2 Lance McCullers win. Carlos Gomez blasted his first home run in 137 at bats and the Astros moved to within two games of .500 at 28-30.

June 6---On this date in 1944, U.S. troops invaded Normandy on D-Day. On the 72nd anniversary of the battle, veterans in their 90s and families of fallen soldiers commemorated the pivotal World War II moment with small ceremonies along French beaches.

At Globe Life Park in Arlington, A.J Hinch told the media about the way he uses his bullpen. "Everybody looks at the game from the ninth inning backwards," he said. "As the manager, I look at it from the middle of the innings where the starter starts to wobble or I've got to get him out of the game. I work that way. If I need any of those guys prior to the ninth inning, I would be foolish to name any of them a closer. This bullpen's made up of a versatile group able to handle any role I give them."

The Rangers' Colby Lewis took the mound on a sunny, 86-degree night in quest of his tenth straight win against the Astros, who countered with Mike Fiers. The Astros came unraveled in the first inning, with an error and a wild pitch as well as an infield hit when the pitcher did not cover first. The Rangers scored three runs. Houston tied the game on a Jose Altuve three-run opposite field home run. The Rangers set off a wild celebration on the field in the ninth when Rougned Odor lined a one-hop double off the left field wall to beat Ken Giles, 6-5. It was the 11th straight loss for the Astros at Globe Life Park.

After the game, Giles told the media about the frustration in the Houston clubhouse. "We have a better team than they do," he said.

"What we need to do tomorrow is put them to the ground." Those quotes were bulletin board material in the Rangers' clubhouse the next day.

On the team bus after the game, the only words spoken came from a player to the bus driver, informing him he should turn off the TV sets. The sets went blank, leaving only a memory of what had happened moments ago. Winning pitcher Sam Dyson was being interviewed while the screen showed stats from the game.

June 7---In the Kansas City-Baltimore game, Yordano Ventura hit Manny Machado with a pitch and Machado charged the mound, touching off a bench-clearing incident. Ventura was later suspended for nine games and Machado for four.

The Houston Minor League Player of the Month at AAA Fresno was Danny Worth, who won for the second consecutive month. Alex Bregman became a two-time winner in his second month at Corpus Christi.

The news of the betting line on the Astros-Rangers game came out in the late afternoon on Charlie Pallilo's sports talk show on Sports Talk 790. The Astros were favored in this game by the sports books. It was not apparent why.

Cole Hamels had an excellent career record against the Astros, while Dallas Keuchel had a number of rough starts against Texas and his Globe Life Park ERA was 6.75.

When Carlos Gomez belted a two-run homer in the second, the Astros were looking good to snap their losing streak against Texas. But Bobby Wilson tied it with his clout in the fifth and Ian Desmond's two-run shot in the eighth gave Texas a 4-2 lead. They held on to win 4-3 when Sam Dyson fanned George Springer for the final out with runners at first and third.

170

June 8--Tennis star Maria Sharapova was handed a two-year suspension for testing positive for banned substance meldonium at the Australian Open in January.

This was the anniversary date of Carlos Correa's arrival in the major leagues in 2015. A few days earlier, he reached 100 RBI for his career in fewer games than any Astro in team history.

Yu Darvish took the mound for Texas. He fell one out short of a perfect game against the Astros in 2013. In 2014 he pitched eight innings of one-hit shutout baseball against them. Doug Fister, the steadiest Houston starter, opposed him.

George Springer ripped Darvish's second pitch of the night for a leadoff home run. That was the only run Darvish allowed, but he left after five innings with tightness in his right shoulder. Jose Altuve clobbered a two-run double in the seventh off Tom Wilhelmsen for a 3-1 lead. The Astros protected the lead to halt their 12-game losing streak at Globe Life Park and their eight-game losing streak to the Rangers in 2016.

Fister was the dragon slayer. He gave up one run in six innings to win his sixth. He mastered the Texas lineup with his 86 mph fastball by executing an intelligent game plan the same way a boxer outsmarts his opponent. He showed the Rangers his fastball just outside the hitting zone and they couldn't hit it squarely. His most effective offering was his big, slow curve. It threw them off balance and their big swings were ineffective against it. In the fifth inning, he teased Rougned Odor with three pitches, all slow curves, and retired him on a fly ball to left field.

June 9---The Rangers dropped the Astros nine games behind them in the standings with a 5-3 win behind starting pitcher Martin Perez. Collin McHugh surrendered four runs in the loss. The Astros lost more than a game. Carlos Correa left the game with a sprained ankle, leading to Jose Altuve's first major league appearance at shortstop. Correa was day to day with the injury.

As the Astros boarded their plane for Tampa, their 1-9 record against Texas made it obvious that they were worlds away from the defending division champs. The underlying question centered around the makeup of the roster. It seemed necessary to institute some changes quickly.

After the game, the Astros selected 6-7 high school pitcher Forrest Whitley with their first choice, the 17th overall pick. His fastball had been clocked at 97 mph. Whitley was pitching in the Texas 5A State Semifinals at Round Rock when he was drafted. The 240-pound right-hander from San Antonio Alamo Heights struck out 11 and led the Mules to a win. He left the field to a standing ovation in the seventh inning.

June 10---Hockey legend Gordie Howe died at 88. He played for the Detroit Red Wings on four Stanley Cup champions and represented them more than 20 times as an All-Star. Howe also played for the Houston Aeros of the World Hockey Association.

Golden State took a 3-1 series lead over Cleveland with a 108-97 conquest of the Cavaliers. Draymond Green was suspended for one game for swiping his hand at LeBron James twice, connecting with James' groin after James stepped over him when Green was on the floor. Green was ruled guilty of a flagrant foul.

In St. Petersburg, Carlos Correa was not playing due to his sprained left ankle.

Tampa native Lance McCullers started for the second time in his career in his home area. He allowed four runs in the first two innings and the Astros left 11 on base, losing 4-3. Their record slipped to 29-34. Fans in Houston were turning their attention elsewhere.

June 11---Chris Archer mowed down the first nine Astros and took a 2-1 lead to the seventh on homers by Brad Miller and Evan Longoria. But Carlos Gomez ripped a two-out homer in the seventh. The go-ahead run scored in the eighth on a wild pitch by Erasmo Ramirez. Luis Valbuena homered off a lefty, Dana Eveland, in the ninth.

It was his first off a southpaw in 2016. But things got dicey for Will Harris in the ninth. His scoreless inning streak ended at 26 1/3 innings when the first three Tampa Bay Rays reached base. Harris was visibly upset behind the mound after his second walk of the inning loaded the bases. Jose Altuve came in to calm him down. Harris buckled down and limited the damage to one run on a sacrifice fly, ending the game on a double play ball to secure the 4-3 win.

Mike Fiers turned in seven solid innings and picked up his fourth win. The Astros began the day with the 11th best record in the American League. It seemed to be time to move in another direction, no longer assuming that this club could contend. Options? Danny Worth and A.J. Reed were hitting well at Fresno. Tyler White and Tony Kemp were limited in their roles in their first major league opportunities. Was it time to trade Valbuena, who was headed for free agency? Worth and Bregman both played third base.

Correa missed his second straight game with a sprained left ankle.

June 12---In hockey, Pittsburgh beat San Jose to clinch the Stanley Cup, four games to two.

On their 20th straight day of baseball, the Astros were blanked by Matt Moore and the Tampa Bay bullpen 5-0. The Rays scored all five runs in the fifth, with the help of an error and another defensive misplay. Dallas Keuchel lost for the ninth time.

His run support was the worst in the American League. But his 5.54 ERA spoke to the combination of good pitching, hitting and fielding that was missing for Keuchel in his 3-9 start. "It's major league baseball," Keuchel said. "Can't give extra outs. That's the way things are going." The Astros took a 30-35 record into their day off in St. Louis, trailing Texas by ten games.

June 13---On an off day for the Astros, the NBA wars continued with a Game 5 win for Cleveland over Golden State 112-97. Draymond Green's suspension cost the Warriors.

LeBron James and Kyrie Irving each scored 41 points.

June 14---On Flag Day, Doug Fister put together a symbolic flag-waving game for the Astros, pounding sinkers at the St. Louis Cardinals at Busch Stadium. Not only did Fister win his sixth in a row, but the Astros won his ninth straight start 5-2. And Fister drove in two runs with a single in the seventh against tough reliever Seung Hwan Oh.

Danny Worth was promoted from Fresno and he started at third base, delivering his first hit as an Astro. Luke Gregerson was placed on family medical leave status to create the opening for Worth.

June 15---On this date in 1964, the Cardinals traded pitcher Ernie Broglio to Chicago for Lou Brock. That deal changed baseball history and started Brock on a Hall of Fame path. Brock hit .348 for the Redbirds after the trade and stole 33 bases. He went on to become the career stolen base leader with 938 until Rickey Henderson broke his record in 1991.

Adam Wainwright took the mound in St. Louis with a career mark of 13-1 against Houston, including a 1.57 ERA. Collin McHugh was up to the challenge on a hot night.

The game was scoreless until the seventh, when Greg Garcia's pinch single off McHugh made it 1-0 St. Louis. Wainwright left after seven. George Springer ran hard to field a ball near the right field line in the fifth, pirouetted and fired a strike to Jason Castro at the plate to gun down Steven Piscotty. Springer blasted a two-run homer in the eighth off Kevin Siegrist.

A Carlos Gomez two-run single in the ninth gave the Astros a 4-1 lead and they won by that score. That concluded a long 4-5 road trip and the traveling party headed to Houston for a day off.

June 16---The Cleveland Cavaliers stormed out in front of Golden State early and thrilled their home crowd with a 115-101 victory to tie their series at three apiece.

They continued their quest to become the first team to win the championship after trailing 3-1 in the final series. They also kept Cleveland's hopes alive for a first title in any major sport in 52 years. Lebron James again scored 41 points.

Texan Andrew Landry was three under par in the first round of the U.S. Open when heavy rains halted play.

June 17---Dustin Johnson charged to the top of the U.S. Open leaderboard at four under par after two rounds, but not many of the golfers were able to finish the second round before darkness arrived at Oakmont.

The Cincinnati Reds spoiled Star Wars Night at Minute Maid Park, topping the Astros 4-2 in 11 innings. The Astros stranded 11 baserunners against the team with the worst ERA in the majors, 5.44. Tyler White was optioned to Fresno with the return of Luke Gregerson from the family medical emergency list.

June 18---At Oakmont, Shane Lowry moved to the top of the leader board at the U.S. Open. He made it through 13 holes of the third round before play was suspended by darkness.

At Minute Maid Park, a second straight 11-inning game was created by a two-out, two strike, two-run homer by Adam Duvall in the ninth inning off Ken Giles. Giles threw a hanging slider, and his blown save cost Dallas Keuchel a win. Will Harris was given the day off, and Luke Gregerson pitched the eighth. Some of the fans on Twitter referred to the Astros manager as "A.J. Hunch" when it came to using the bullpen. George Springer's walkoff single won the game.

June 19---On Father's Day, players around the majors took the field in special uniforms trimmed in light blue signifying a charity fund raiser for prostate cancer. The Reds had no red in their uniforms. Hinch said the Astros looked like the North Carolina Tar Heels with their light blue numerals and light blue socks. Mike Fiers and Chris Devenski teamed up on a five-hit 6-0 blanking.

The Astros won for the 17th time in 25 games and pulled to within two games of .500 at 34-36. The paid attendance for the three-game series passed 100,000.

Dustin Johnson tucked away the U.S. Open title at Oakmont for his first major title.

LeBron James led the Cavaliers to a surprise Game 7 victory over Golden State in Oakland 93-89. They became the first Cleveland team to win a title in a major sport since the 1964 Cleveland Browns. James scored 27 points with 11 rebounds and 11 assists.

June 20---The Astros jumped out to a 7-0 lead and survived a late grand slam to hold off the Los Angeles Angels 10-7. Doug Fister ran his record to 8-3.

June 21---Carlos Correa's walkoff two-run single in the ninth off Huston Street thrilled the crowd with a 3-2 Houston triumph. Correa drove in all three. Street took over in the ninth with a 2-1 lead. He walked George Springer. Before batting, Marwin Gonzalez asked A.J. Hinch if he should bunt Springer to second base. Hinch told him no, adding that Springer would steal second. He did. Gonzalez also asked if Springer stole second should he bunt him to third.

Hinch told him that his at bat needed to end with Springer on third, whatever he chose to do. Gonzalez also walked. Jose Altuve had asked Hinch if he should bunt both runners to second and third. Hinch told Altuve not to bunt because the Angels would then walk Correa intentionally. Altuve swung away and got a hit on a ground ball that hit third base. The bases were loaded when Correa drilled his game-winning hit.

The Astros drew 25,004 for the game, which evened their record at .500 for the first time since they were 1-1. "If you would have told me at the beginning of the season that we'd be at .500 on this date, we would have said, 'We should be better,'" Hinch said.

"I want to keep it in proper perspective. Yes, I'm happy with how we've continued to grind and continued to play. We've shown some personality and are pretty tough. We've done everything we can to inch back to relevance, but this isn't going to accomplish anything. We've shown good resiliency because of how the season started."

At NRG Stadium in the Astrodome neighborhood, Argentina blitzed the USA 4-0 in a soccer game prior to the Olympic Games.

June 22---At a noon press conference, first round draft choice Forrest Whitley, a 6-7 righthander from Alamo Heights High School in San Antonio, was introduced to the Houston media after signing for a $3.148 million bonus from the Astros. He was the 17th overall choice, and he dreaded calling Florida State to break his commitment to play college baseball. Nolan Ryan scouted him when he pitched a no-hitter.

In a day game, Lance McCullers needed relief help in the sixth trailing 1-0. The rested Houston bullpen kept the Angels at bay for another 3-2 Houston last at bat win. Marwin Gonzalez snapped a 1-1 tie in the eighth with an RBI triple on Tal's Hill. The 5-1 homestand pulled the Astros over .500 for the first time since they were 1-0.

After this game, the Astros trailed Kansas City by just two games for the second wild card berth.

June 23---The Supreme Court deadlocked at 4-4 on a decision regarding illegal immigrants, blocking President Obama's executive order to grant amnesty to millions. The case was returned to a federal judge in Brownsville to consider the legality of the full case.

On an off day, the Astros traveling party left for Kansas City at mid-afternoon. The players were geared for extreme heat at both stops on the road trip. Missouri and Southern California were hot boxes.

In the NBA draft in the evening, LSU's Ben Simmons was the first pick, by Philadelphia. The Houston Rockets took big men Chinanu Onuaku from Louisville and Zhou Qi of China with their first two choices.

June 24---Harris County officials rolled out a plan to spend $105 million to raise the floor of the Astrodome for two new levels of parking beneath it. The 51-year-old structure would be repurposed for events or an indoor park. Commissioners would be presented with the plan publicly in a few days and could vote to authorize it as early as September.

As the series opened in torrid Kansas City, the Royals had the best home record in the AL at 20-8. The Royals were two games ahead of the Astros in the race for the second wild card spot. Toronto was 2 ½ games ahead of Houston.

Dallas Keuchel and Edinson Volquez squared off in a rematch of their Game 3 pairing in the ALDS. The Royals were 3-1 against the Astros in the regular season in 2016. Keuchel's ERA of 5.32 was the second highest for a Cy Young Award winner through 15 starts the year after winning the award. Keuchel's statistics made it clear that his major problems involved pitching from the stretch. He was mowing down hitters from the windup, but when men reached base his ERA soared and the batting average against him was much higher. He was tucking his head and his arm was not in the same position when he released the ball from the stretch. The lower arm slot was causing his pitches to flatten out and the hitters were teeing off on pitches up in the zone.

The Houston bullpen ERA was the second best in the American League since May 1.

The relievers had a spectacularly low walk rate of 5.5%, lowest in the majors since 1947.

Jeff Luhnow's remark of May 2 looked prophetic. "This is too good of a team to stay at this level," he had said. "So we'll have a shot at it at some point in the summer." The tweaking of the roster led to improvement. Carlos Gomez started hitting after a stay on the disabled list. Evan Gattis contributed more after he became the backup catcher, replacing Erik Kratz.

Tyler White was at Fresno, while Marwin Gonzalez was making his presence known as the first baseman and number two hitter. Preston Tucker was at Fresno and Tony Kemp was a contributor in infrequent roles. George Springer was an impact player as the leadoff hitter. Will Harris and Luke Gregerson were excellent in their new roles.

In the minors, A.J. Reed was ready for the majors after getting hot. James Hoyt was ready to help the bullpen and Brady Rodgers stood in line to join the rotation, but there was no room for any of them.

George Springer began the game with a triple off the center field wall. Later in that nine-run first, Springer belted his third grand slam of the year! Springer became the first player in modern baseball history to hit a triple and a grand slam in the first inning. He helped make the night miserable for Volquez, who hit him with a pitch to put him on the disabled list for weeks in 2015. The Astros' nine-run first inning was their best since July 10, 2003.

Colby Rasmus had four hits, including a home run. Keuchel, who had the worst run support in the majors, 2.66 per nine innings coming into the game, got the win despite allowing 11 hits and four runs in 6 1/3 innings.

After the game, the club announced the promotion of first baseman A.J. Reed to the majors. Tony Kemp was optioned to Fresno. Reed would make his debut as the DH Saturday and play first base quite a bit. Since Reed was not on the 40-man roster, catcher Alfredo Gonzalez was removed to make room for him.

June 25---On another sizzling night in Missouri, the Royals wore "Los Reales" and the Astros "Los Astros" on their chests as they took the field.

The Astros blasted another Kansas City starter early in the game. This time it was Chris Young. The 6-7 righthander ran into a seven-run second inning, including a Jose Altuve three-run homer followed immediately by a Carlos Correa blast.

Altuve wound up with four hits, missing the cycle when he fell before he got to second on what would have been a triple to complete the cycle. He piled up 102 hits in the first 75 games, taking over the American League batting lead with a .348 average.

Mike Fiers failed to get through the fifth to qualify for the win. But the Astros handed the Royals their first back to back losses at home all season. Royals' skipper Ned Yost flew the white flag in the ninth, using backup catcher Drew Butera to pitch. For the second straight night the Astros scored 13 times, winning 13-5.

A.J. Reed drew two walks, scored twice and drove in a run in his major league debut as the DH.

June 26---The Panama Canal opened for bigger ships with a deeper and wider channel to accommodate super freighters from the Far East. Eventually the Houston Ship Channel was in line to benefit from additional traffic because it had been dredged deeper to handle ships with more tonnage.

Simone Biles, a 19-year-old native of Spring, Texas, won her fourth straight women's all-around U.S. Gymnastics title.

Naval Academy graduate Billy Hurley III won his first PGA tour title at Congressional Country Club.

The Royals snapped their four-game losing streak and the Astros' seven-game winning streak behind Ian Kennedy 6-1. Kennedy stopped the Astros on three hits and fanned 11 in seven innings, beating Doug Fister for the second time in 2016 and halting the Astros' ten-game winning streak in Fister's starts.

June 27---In Anaheim, Matt Shoemaker shut out the Astros for six innings. Mike Trout golfed a low Collin McHugh curve for a home run and the Angels led 2-0 after six. The Astros got two in the seventh to tie and won with two in the ninth 4-2.

Carlos Correa, who was named American League Player of the Week earlier in the day for the first time in his career, snapped a 2-2 tie in the ninth with a sacrifice fly. Correa hit .333 the previous week with three homers and nine RBI. He became the youngest Astro to win a league player of the week award. Ken Giles, Luke Gregerson and Will Harris kept the Angels scoreless for the last three innings, although Harris had to escape a bases-loaded no out jam in the ninth for his seventh straight save.

June 28---Pat Summitt died of early onset Alzheimers disease at age 64. She coached Tennessee to eight women's NCAA basketball titles.

Buddy Ryan died at 85 after coaching in the NFL from 1968-95, including 1993 as the Houston Oilers defensive coordinator.

In a night game at Anaheim, Scott Feldman started in place of Lance McCullers, who had a blister on his pitching hand. Feldman got run support early from a Carlos Correa three-run homer and went five innings to qualify for the win in a 7-1 Houston shellacking of Tim Lincecum.

In the minors, 2015 first round draft choice Alex Bregman ripped a homer in the Texas League All-Star Game in Springfield, Missouri. Bregman and Joe Musgrove were chosen to play in the All-Star Futures Game in San Diego.

Bregman hit 14 homers in 236 at bats for Corpus Christi, helping the Hooks win a first half title in their division in the Texas League. Word leaked out that Bregman and outfielder Teoscar Hernandez were being promoted to Fresno later in the week.

June 29---In an afternoon finale of the road trip, Dallas Keuchel beat Jered Weaver 10-4 with four hits from Jose Altuve. Altuve ended the 5-1 road trip hitting .357, best in the American League. The Astros headed into a day off with a 42-37 record after an 18-8 June which had them squarely in contention in the wild card race.

June 30-Coastal Carolina won the College World Series with a victory over Arizona.

San Francisco's Madison Bumgarner ripped a double in his first at bat against Oakland. Bumgarner became the first pitcher to be in the starting batting order when his manager elected not to use the designated hitter since 1976, when Ken Brett batted for the White Sox.

June Summary

A solid 18-8 record in June included a 9-2 record at home. The Astros had a run differential of 135-88 and their ERA was an excellent 3.11.

Sizzling Jose Altuve led the club with a .420 batting average. Altuve had the best June in club history. He ended the month reaching base for the 32nd consecutive game. His OPS for the month was 1.004. He took American League Player of the Month honors. Altuve led the majors with a .357 average at the end of the month.

The top pitchers were Will Harris (0-0, 1.64, 7 saves) and Doug Fister (4-1, 2.45).

June Standings in AL West

Texas 51-29   —

Houston 42-37 -8.5

Seattle 40-39 -10.5

Oakland 35-44 -15.5

LAA   32-47 -18.5

8 July Heat

The Texas Rangers went into a freefall in July, giving the Astros a chance to cut into their lead. Houston slashed the lead to 2 ½ games by July 23, but then hit a cold spot at the end of the month, losing five of their last six games to fall six games behind the frontrunners. With three-game sweeps of Seattle and the Los Angeles Angels, the Astros moved into the playoff hunt.

As the month came to a close, the question for the front office was whether to part with prospects for a frontline starting pitcher. Having signed Yuliesky Gurriel and expecting his arrival in mid-August, the Astros had added Alex Bregman to their lineup already.

Despite good stretches of starts, the five-man rotation was lacking an ace. Dallas Keuchel ended July with a 4.86 ERA. Collin McHugh was at 4.75. If Chris Sale was available, the Astros would need to part with maybe four or five talented young players. Jose Quintana, like his teammate Sale, would probably extract about the same price in a deal. Another target could be Chris Archer of Tampa Bay. With a few hours left in the trade deadline, there were no media reports suggesting any serious talks involving these pitchers. The common knowledge among reporters was that in 2016 a number two starter would bring a price equal to a number one starter's return in a previous year. That was very steep. With an unappealing free agent market looming over the winter, did the Astros think they could provide a major pitching upgrade from the farm system? Joe Musgrove? Frances Martes? Or would they be better off trading one or both of them to get an established starter? Those questions were central to the organization's plan for 2017. It seemed sensible to talk trade with clubs about players under affordable contracts for the next few years if the price was so high in prospects. Sale, Quintana and Archer all fit into that category.

July Game by Game Accounts

July 1---The Astros began a ten-game homestand with a 5-0 blanking of the Chicago White Sox. Mike Fiers and three relievers collaborated on a five-hitter, with a two-run homer by Carlos Gomez. The Astros moved into the second wild card position with their 11th win in 12 games. A.J. Reed collected his first major league hit after an 0-for-16 start with a single off Miguel Gonzalez.

July 2---Chris Sale survived a three-run fourth to win his 14th game 7-6. The White Sox pounded Doug Fister for nine hits and totaled 13 in the game.

Jose Altuve, named American League Player of the Month for June, ripped a homer and drove in three. Altuve became the first Astro since Lance Berkman in 2008 to win a player of the month award. His .420 average was the highest in June in club history. He was the first Houston second baseman to win the award!

A.J. Reed connected for his first major league homer as a pinch hitter in the ninth off White Sox closer David Robertson.

The Astros signed 12 players on the first day of the international signing period. The most prominent was 16-year-old Freudis Nova from the Dominican Republic, ranked by Baseball America as the fifth best player in the international class. He received a reported $1.2 million signing bonus.

July 3---The Astros got a leadoff home run from George Springer in the first off Jose Quintana, but Quintana halted his seven-game losing streak in a 4-1 White Sox series clinching win. That halted the Astros' series winning streak at five. A.J. Hinch was ejected in the seventh inning after Quintana threw a pitch behind Evan Gattis. In the top of that inning, Astros reliever Chris Devenski hit Jose Abreu with a pitch.

Home plate umpire Ryan Blackney tossed Hinch when he stepped on the field after Blackney issued warnings to both teams.

The Astros were incensed that Blackney did not eject Quintana, who missed Gattis with an inside pitch earlier in the at bat.

July 4---A NASA spacecraft reached Jupiter after a five-year voyage.

Kevin Durant sent shock waves through the NBA by announcing he would sign a two-year contract with Golden State.

The Seattle Mariners opened a three-game series tied with the Astros for second place, 8 ½ games behind Texas. All teams wore specially designed July 4 patriotic uniforms and caps. Special pregame ceremonies involved veterans bearing flags of all the service branches. Gymnast Simone Biles threw out the first pitch in a special way after performing a side aerial. Shortly afterwards, Leonys Martin crushed a 2-2 Lance McCullers changeup for a triple to the top of Tal's Hill in center field. But McCullers, pitching for the first time since June 22 because of a blister, escaped by striking out two and tagging out Martin at home plate. Robinson Cano swung at a pitch in the dirt and had to be thrown out at first. Martin tried to score on the play and was thrown out.

In the seventh, McCullers led 2-1 when the Mariners loaded the bases with nobody out. McCullers started a double play on a comebacker and retired Adam Lind. He walked away with a 2-1 win when Luke Gregerson and Will Harris got the final six outs. The Astros gained a game on the Rangers, trailing by 7 ½ games.

McCullers, who struck out 10, came in for high praise on the MLB Network from Hall of Famer John Smoltz the next morning for his electric stuff.

The losing pitcher, Wade Miley, presented more problems for the Astros' righthanded hitters. Before the game, the Astros were 9-15 when facing a lefthanded starter. They were hitting .226 against southpaws.

It was puzzling that a lineup with righthanders Jose Altuve, George Springer, Carlos Correa, Evan Gattis and Carlos Gomez could not manage more than a .390 slugging percentage against lefties. Another lefty would face them Wednesday, Wade LeBlanc. Miley, with a 55-50 career record and a 4.09 ERA, was slightly above the average lefty starter. But with a 91 mph fastball, he presented the latest case in point for the Astros' struggles against lefties. Altuve was the only hitter with an average better than .268 against lefthanders.

"It's a little uncharacteristic for us, given how good our righthanded hitters are," said skipper A.J. Hinch. "I think sometimes we can get a little anxious with the guys that front-back us a little bit with speed and change our timing." He was referring to lefties with good changeups. Hinch pointed out the schedule before the All-Star break would bring a few more lefties against his hitters.

Shortstop Alex Bregman hit two more homers for AAA Fresno, giving him a .476 average with four homers and 11 RBI in five games since his promotion.

July 5---FBI Director James Comey announced that no criminal charges would be recommended against Hillary Clinton for using a private email system while Secretary of State. He called the email practices "extremely careless" and said the investigation revealed that 110 emails involved classified information. In late October, the investigation was reopened based on new information.

At Minute Maid Park, Jose Altuve was named an All-Star starting second baseman for the second straight year. It was his fourth overall selection to the team. Reliever Will Harris was named to the team as a replacement for injured Kansas City reliever Wade Davis. George Springer was one of five players in the American League named in a final vote by fans which would take three days.

With the temperature reaching 96 degrees, a blown circuit breaker at a power station a few blocks from the stadium caused the air conditioning system to be out of order. Fans were feeling the heat inside. Seattle's Tijuan Walker also felt some heat on the mound after being tagged for long home runs by Luis Valbuena, Colby Rasmus and A.J. Reed.

Dallas Keuchel continued his turnaround by going six innings in a 5-2 Houston win. "I don't feel like I'm on a roll," said Keuchel. "I just feel like I'm coming out in every start and giving the team a chance to win now, and that's a good feeling."

July 6---The Astros blew out to a 5-0 lead after three, but Mike Fiers was roughed up for three Seattle long balls in the fourth and the game turned into a donnybrook. Houston stayed on the attack and built a 7-4 lead, only to lose it when Seth Smith ripped a three-run homer off Michael Feliz in the seventh to tie it 7-7. Valbuena belted his second upper deck homer in two games for a 9-7 lead in the eighth. It then got dicey in the ninth with Will Harris being rested.

Luke Gregerson, in his first save situation in the ninth since June 4, surrendered an RBI double to Robinson Cano and dodged three walks to strike out Nelson Cruz and Dae-Ho Lee in a wild ninth. Gregerson got Lee with the bases loaded on a slider to cap a 9-8 win, giving the Astros a sweep of the series and a 29-11 record over the last 40 games, the top winning percentage in the majors during that time.

July 7---The horrific events in Dallas, Texas seized the attention of the nation and the world. A sniper targeted white police officers, killing five and wounding seven in downtown Dallas. Police killed the sniper. Memories of sniper Lee Harvey Oswald assassinating President John Kennedy in 1963 in Dallas flooded back for people who were alive at that time. Parkland Memorial Hospital, where President Kennedy was pronounced dead, was again the scene of shocking tragedy. Some of the shooting victims were in surgery at Parkland.

Sports was meaningless on this night. Oakland opened a four-game series at Minute Maid Park with a 3-1 win behind the strong pitching of lefty Rich Hill.

July 8---All-Star voting for the final spot on each team came to a close. Voters cast their ballots on social media sites and the announcement of the final totals came late in the afternoon. George Springer finished second in the AL voting behind Michael Saunders of Toronto. Saunders, a native of Canada, had an entire nation voting for him.

The Astros built a 6-3 lead through five against Houston native and Athletics starter Daniel Mengden, with Carlos Correa driving in three. It was 7-4 going to the ninth. The wildest ninth inning of the season then began to unfold. With All-Star Will Harris beginning the ninth, his string of 37 games without allowing an extra base hit was snapped quickly by a Billy Butler double and a Yonder Alonso home run. Harris allowed two more hits and left with a 7-6 lead, one out and runners at second and third. Michael Feliz allowed a two-run double to Khris Davis and a run-scoring single to Josh Reddick to give Oakland the upper hand 9-7. Ryan Madson came in to close the game. Jose Altuve got a hit with one out. Correa swung at a wild pitch and struck out but reached first when the pitch skipped past Oakland catcher Stephen Vogt. Luis Valbuena blasted a three-run walkoff homer for a 10-9 Astros triumph and the Friday night crowd went crazy.

July 9---At Wimbledon, Serena Williams won the women's singles and doubles titles. Williams beat Angelique Kerber to win her 22nd grand slam singles title, tying Steffi Graf for the most championships in the Open era. She teamed with her sister Venus to win their 14th grand slam doubles title.

On another oppressively hot day in Houston, fans were lined up early to be among the 10,000 to get a navy blue Jose Altuve jersey.

Lance McCullers was off his game, with Stephen Vogt reaching the Crawford Boxes with a second inning home run and driving in a third inning run with a single. Home plate umpire Kerwin Danley missed some calls on McCullers' curve. Four walks caused McCullers extra trouble and he was out of the game after four innings.

Kendall Graveman was throwing nothing but fastballs in the strike zone, handcuffing the Astros through eight and leaving in the ninth. Ryan Dull closed out a 3-2 Oakland win after the Astros got two in the ninth. The crowd of 35,312 cheered loudly in the Houston ninth, but the loss left the Astros with a 5-4 record on the homestand.

July 10---At Wimbledon, Andy Murray won his second men's singles title, beating Milos Raonic.

With Sahara dust invading Houston, the day was cloudy but still extremely hot with a game time temperature of 93 degrees. The Astros' offense stayed in a deep freeze, trailing 1-0 heading into the bottom of the ninth. Dallas Keuchel gave up a sixth inning run but looked as good as he did in most of 2015. Evan Gattis doubled into the left field corner with two outs in the ninth for a 1-1 tie. Carlos Correa was safe on a throwing error with two outs in the tenth for a 2-1 Houston win, its eighth walk off win to lead the majors.

At the All-Star break, the Astros were 48-41. They were also seven games over .500 in 2015 at the break. They trailed Texas by 5 ½ games in 2016. In 2015, they trailed by ½ game at the break. Their .539 winning percentage was their best at the break since 2001, when they played .558 baseball to that point of the season.

In the evening, Alex Bregman ripped three hits in the All-Star Futures Game in San Diego. He tripled to right center field, doubled to left center and lined a single off the shortstop's glove. Joe Musgrove threw a perfect first inning in 11 pitches, just 20 minutes from where he grew up in El Cajon.

The performances by Bregman and Musgrove were part of a broader question for the front office over the break. Were these two players part of a plan to improve the team? Would they get a shot in the majors before decisions about making trades for the stretch drive?

"I feel like I'm (close to) accomplishing one of my goals, and that was to get to the big leagues this year," said Bregman. Asked if he felt major league ready, Bregman said, "Yeah, I do. I feel ready to go. I feel like I can help up there and help win games."

Bregman was regarded as the Minor League Player of the half season by one publication. He was the only minor leaguer in a full season league with an OPS above 1.000 at 1.019. His wRC+ was 183, with 100 being the average. That statistic factors in ballpark effects and league statistics. His number was the highest in the minors. He had 19 home runs. "Versatility on the field is a big part of my game," said Bregman. "If I can play third base and help this team win and go to the playoffs and hopefully win in the playoffs, that would be a dream come true." Mike Elias, Houston's director of scouting when Bregman was drafted, said, "I really think the selling factor on Alex was his makeup. He exudes a confidence and a work ethic and a competitive focus that is special."

All-Star Break Analysis

Over the 31-13 stretch from May 24 to July 10, the Astros turned around their season. Could this continue over a longer period of time or did the front office need to make changes?

Luis Valbuena was one of the catalysts in the offensive resurgence. Headed for free agency, he had made himself indispensable with his lefthanded power. Colby Rasmus and A.J. Reed were the other lefthanded power hitters. They had combined for 13 homers in more than 300 at bats. Valbuena's bat was the only dependable one among the three.

The Astros struck out 825 times in 89 games, most in the American League. Their team batting average was a low .244. Their 401 runs was in the bottom half of the American League. Their primary need was another contact hitter. They had some very low on base averages on the team: Carlos Gomez .282, Marwin Gonzalez .295, Evan Gattis .281, Jake Marisnick .248, Danny Worth .219.

Carlos Gonzalez of the Colorado Rockies was having a good season and there were rumors that he wanted out of the Mile High City for a chance to play on a playoff team as Troy Tulowitzki had done in 2015. Gonzalez would make $10 million in 2017. The Astros would be needing at least one outfielder for 2017 and maybe two, with Rasmus and Gomez headed for free agency. Would they be interested in giving up prospects for Gonzalez?

If they promoted Alex Bregman, how would they use him? He had played shortstop and third base in the minors. Carlos Correa was the shortstop. Luis Valbuena could move to first base to open up third base for Bregman. A.J. Reed, under that scenario, could be the DH and Marwin Gonzalez would go back to utilityman and play much less. Worth would be sent back to the minors. Gattis would play less at DH and remain the backup catcher. That scenario would not involve taking on salary or losing prospects. It seemed to be an option worth strong consideration, based on an assumption that Bregman was ready to hit well in the majors.

Keuchel's recent starts were encouraging. The bullpen was very strong except for Tony Sipp. Another front line starting pitcher would be desirable. One option would be to send Michael Feliz to the minors to start and insert him into the rotation once he was ready. Another would be to promote Joe Musgrove or Brady Rodgers. These options, like the Bregman plan, would not impact payroll or prospect load. They also seemed to be worth strong consideration.

While the players who weren't All-Stars were resting, the front office was grinding away on how to proceed.

July 11--- Giancarlo Stanton, who was not on the All-Star roster, hit a record 61 home runs at Petco Park to win the Home Run Derby.

Tim Duncan quietly announced his retirement from the NBA.

Jordan Spieth withdrew from the Olympics, the fourth top golfer to decline the Rio Games.

July 12---In Dallas, President Obama and former President George W. Bush spoke at a memorial for the five police offers who were killed by a sniper. "When the bullets started flying, the men and women of the Dallas police, they did not flinch, and they did not act recklessly," said Obama.

In San Diego at the All-Star Game, Jose Altuve led off for the American League in the bottom of the first. Altuve went 0-for-3 and made an error. Will Harris came in from the bullpen with the bases loaded and two outs in the eighth, striking out Aledmys Diaz with a 4-2 lead. The American League won, clinching home field advantage for the World Series for the 14th time in 17 years since that format was adopted. Defending World Series champion Kansas City Royals Eric Hosmer and Salvador Perez homered in the second inning off their former teammate Johnny Cueto.

"It was great," said Harris. "I was excited that Ned (Yost) wanted me to get up in that situation with obviously all of the talented guys we have down there. It meant a lot."

The American League team was the first in All-Star Game history to start all nine fielders who were 27 or younger. Major league baseball announced that future batting championships will be named after the late Tony Gwynn in the National League and Rod Carew in the American League.

Commissioner Rob Manfred answered a question about the surge in home runs. Home runs were up .3 per cent over 2015 and .6 per cent over 2014. The average was 2.32 homers per game in 2016.

Manfred recited the figure of 22,000 drug tests per year. He told the media that the baseball had been tested as well as the players. The operative theory for the increase, Manfred said, involved the way the game was being played as opposed to other influences. With batting averages dropping and teams emphasizing putting home run hitters at the top of the lineup so they could get more plate appearances, home runs had become a more prominent way to score runs.

Leaders at the All-Star Break

Abbreviated Standings

AL West	AL Central	AL East
Texas 54-36 –	Cleveland 52-36 -	Baltimore 51-36 -
Houston 48-41 -5.5	Detroit 46-43 -6.5	Boston 49-38 -2
Seattle 45-44 -8.5	Kansas City 45-43 -7	Toronto 51-40 -2
	Chicago 45-43 -7	

NL West	NL Central	NL East
San Fran 57-33 –	Chicago 53-35 -	Washington 54-36 -
LA 51-44 -6.5	St. Louis 46-42 -7	New York 47-41 -6
	Pittsburgh 46-43 -7.5	Miami 47-41 -6

Batting average: AL: Jose Altuve, .341   David Ortiz .332   Xander Bogaerts .329

NL: Daniel Murphy .348 D.J. LeMahieu .334 Wilson Ramos .330

Home runs: AL: Mark Trumbo, 28

NL: Kris Bryant, 25

RBI: AL: Edwin Encarnacion, 80

NL: Nolan Arenado, 70

Hits: AL: Jose Altuve, 119

NL: Daniel Murphy, 117

Pitchers won-lost : AL: Chris Sale, 14-3

NL: Johnny Cueto, 13-1

ERA: AL: Steven Wright, 2.68

NL: Clayton Kershaw, 1.79

Saves: AL: Zach Britton, 27

NL: Jeurys Familia, 31

July 14---The British Open began at Royal Troon in Scotland under mild conditions. The golfers took advantage with a bundle of birdies. Phil Mickelson took the lead with a 63, one off the course record.

A federal court rejected Tom Brady's appeal of a four-game suspension. Brady would be missing a game against the Houston Texans September 22.

Baylor hired Missouri's Mack Rhoades, the former AD at the University of Houston, to become its athletic director.

The Astros resumed play after the All-Star Game at Seattle. The scramble for wild card spots in both leagues involved 18 teams within five games of playoff spots.

The Boston Red Sox traded a prospect for San Diego pitcher Drew Pomeranz.

July 15---Donald Trump named his running mate, Governor Mike Pence of Indiana.

At Royal Troon, the winds came up to 20 mph and the golfers were playing in rain suits. Phil Mickelson held on to his lead but the scores were higher.

As the Astros prepared to open play after the break, word leaked out that they had signed 32-year-old Cuban Yuliesky Gurriel to a five-year, $47.5 million free agent contract. Gurriel defected from Cuba after the Caribbean Series in February along with his younger brother, outfielder Lourdes Gurriel, Jr. In June Yuliesky was declared a free agent. He had worked out for the Mets, Yankees, Dodgers and Padres as well as the Astros.

Gurriel had been working out in Miami. Estimates were circulating that he would need 50 or 60 minor league at bats. The thought was that he could join the Astros in August. The Astros had not yet announced the deal and they were not commenting. Gurriel could play third base, second base or possibly left field.

Yuliesky Gurriel was an Olympian in 2004 and he had played in all three World Baseball Classics. Some experts projected that he could hit about .285 in the majors with maybe 15-18 homers and 85 RBI over a full season. If reports of this signing were accurate, this signing was one of the most significant in Houston history.

Carlos Lee signed a six-year, $100 million deal in 2005, but the Astros had never signed an international free agent for anything close to what was reported as this package.

George Springer led off the night game in Seattle with a home run off James Paxton, starting the Astros on a 7-3 win. Doug Fister ran his record to 9-6 and the bullpen backed him with four scoreless innings. The Texas Rangers lost to the Cubs, moving Houston to within 4 ½ games of Texas.

July 16---At Royal Troon, 40-year-old Swede Henrik Stenson overtook Phil Mickelson by one to grab the third round lead for the first time in his career in a major grand slam event.

In Seattle, the Mariners blanked the Astros 1-0 behind Hisashi Iwakuma and two relievers. Lance McCullers took the loss.

A few hours before the game started, the Astros announced the signing of Gurriel at Minute Maid Park.

Yuliesky Gurriel

Yuliesky Gurriel was introduced to the Houston media at Minute Maid Park. There was a buzz on social media, with Astros fans weighing in on the value of the signing. This kind of signing was rare for the Astros, especially in July. "We're delighted to be adding a talent of this caliber," said Jeff Luhnow. "This player has had an incredible history of success." Luhnow told of his plans to send Gurriel to Florida for some workouts and to obtain a work visa before sending him to play with a team, possibly Corpus Christi. Luhnow indicated that an August timetable for his addition to the major league club was reasonable.

Gurriel had hit .335 with 250 home runs and 1,018 RBI during a 15-year career in Cuba and with the Central League of Japan. Gurriel, 6-0 and 190, said he became a fan of the Astros during their postseason run in 2015. "The spirit these guys bring is the spirit of playing great baseball," said Gurriel.

"Clearly, the goal is to get him in uniform and get him playing at Minute Maid Park as soon as possible," Luhnow said.

"One of the reasons why (agent Adam Katz) and I worked so hard to get this deal done as timely as we could was that I want and Yulie wants to be part of a playoff run this year."

Luhnow said the Astros planned to pursue Yuliesky's younger brother Lourdes as well when he became a free agent in the fall. The brothers had expressed a desire to play on the same team. (Lourdes signed in November with Toronto for $22 million over seven years.)

The Astros players reacted favorably to the signing. They had been checking out videos of Gurriel and were looking forward to welcoming him as a teammate soon. A.J. Hinch was embracing the hitting credentials of Gurriel and said it was his job to decide where Gurriel played. "I don't have a favorite position and I have no trouble moving around," said Gurriel. The options Hinch mentioned were third base, second base and the outfield. Second base was an option because Jose Altuve could get a rest for his legs and act as the DH occasionally.

Matt Duffy, last year's Pacific Coast League MVP, was taken off the 40-man roster to make room for Gurriel.

Cuban players had been making an impact in the majors for years. There were good Cuban players in the majors in the 1950s and earlier. Pitcher Camilo Pascual won 174 games from 1954-71. Hall of Famer Tony Perez and top pitcher Luis Tiant were some of the best players of the 1970s. Shortstop Bert Campaneris and second baseman Tony Taylor each played for 19 seasons. Catcher Joe Azcue was one of the top throwing receivers for his 11 seasons. Tony Gonzalez was an excellent centerfielder in the '70s. Zoilo Versalles was a good shortstop for 12 years and the 1965 AL MVP. Cookie Rojas played infield for 16 years and later managed. Perez also managed, as well as Preston Gomez. Fredi Gonzalez of Atlanta was in his tenth season as a major league manager.

Rafael Palmeiro probably would have joined Perez in the Hall of Fame had he not been suspended for using performance enhancing drugs and accused of lying to Congress.

Livan Hernandez and his half-brother Orlando were among the defectors who achieved success in their careers in the majors, including remarkable postseason performances. Another who defected and played in the U.S. was Rey Ordonez. He was a little shortstop who was a regular for the New York Mets.

Of the current sizable crop of Cuban defectors, Aroldis Chapman was considered the top closer in the game. The big lefty, now a Cub, was a strikeout machine. Known as the Cuban Missile, Chapman had 182 saves in seven seasons. He whiffed 636 in 377 innings for the best strikeout rate in history. Jose Abreu was an elite slugger playing first base for the Chicago White Sox. Abreu has 91 homers and 308 RBI in three seasons.

Outfielder Yasiel Puig had a legendary arm and tremendous offensive tools, but his undisciplined style had created many problems for him with the Los Angeles Dodgers. The 26-year-old with the nickname "Wild Horse" has a career .833 OPS. In August, Puig was demoted to the minor leagues. He got into more trouble by posting videos of himself and his teammates singing, dancing and using profanity after a loss by Oklahoma City.

Yoenis Cespedes, Yunel Escobar, Leonys Martin and Kendrys Morales are other well-known Cubans in the majors. Pitcher Jose Fernandez was an elite performer when healthy before his untimely death in 2016. Jorge Soler of the Cubs was a rising young talent. There were 42 Cuban players on major league rosters at this time in 2016. In baseball history, 198 Cubans had played in the majors.

When Gurriel arrived in Kissimmee, Florida the Astros realized that there would be a delay in getting his work visa, preventing him from playing for any of their minor league teams for some time.

July 17---Henrik Stenson held off Phil Mickelson in a duel for the British Open, firing a 63 to Mickelson's 65 for a three-shot triumph for his first career major at age 40. Stenson finished 20 under par at 264, the lowest 72-hole score in a major.

In Seattle, the Astros rode a four-hit performance by Jose Altuve including his 15th homer and a Carlos Gomez grand slam to an 8-1 drubbing of the Mariners. Collin McHugh squared his record at 6-6, dealing with two bases loaded jams, and the Astros pulled eight games over .500 for the first time at 50-42. The Mariners committed four errors and hit into five double plays.

July 18---The Republican National Convention opened in Cleveland.

The World Anti-Doping Agency issued a report detailing widespread cheating by Russia on more than 300 positive drug tests.

The Chris Correa Case

In Houston, 35-year-old Chris Correa stood before U.S. District Judge Lynn Hughes for sentencing in the computer hacking case. Correa, the former director of baseball development for the St. Louis Cardinals, was sentenced to 46 months for hacking into the Astros' database some 60 times between March 2013 and June 2014.

Correa, no relation to Carlos Correa, pleaded guilty earlier in the year. He also was sentenced to pay $279,000 in restitution. The maximum penalty was not more than five years in federal prison. Correa stated in January during his guilty plea that he believed the Astros had stolen proprietary information from the Cardinals. He said he believed he had discovered that same information in the Houston database after gaining illegal entry.

His suspicion was based on the employment by the Cardinals of Jeff Luhnow and Sig Megdal, both of whom took jobs with the Astros when they left the Cardinals.

The Astros then refuted that information and Judge Hughes refused to allow Correa to subpoena documents from the Astros. Hughes said the actions of Correa were "intentionally, over a long period of time, stupidly" directed.

Prosecutors charged that Correa obtained the Astros' rankings of draft-eligible players in 2013 and 2014. Correa also obtained information regarding trade discussions. Some of the information appeared publicly on Deadspin.com. Correa also broke into the Houston database during the June 2013 amateur draft. The judge called his actions pure unadulterated theft. This case was the first of its kind involving professional sports and as such attracted widespread attention. The next phase of this story involved what if any additional punishment would be levied by Commissioner Rob Manfred on the Cardinals. Federal prosecutors charged that the information on potential draft choices cost the Astros $1.7 million. Manfred had admitted to the media that major league baseball did not possess the investigative capabilities of the FBI. He had indicated that he hoped there would be cooperation between the investigative agencies and major league baseball so he could reach a decision based on all of the facts that had been uncovered for the trial.

In the night game at Oakland, Mike Fiers and A.J. Hinch had words in the dugout after Hinch took Fiers out of the game in the fourth inning. Fiers took a 2-1 lead to the fourth in his first outing in 11 days. He retired the first two batters and had an 0-2 count on Stephen Vogt before Vogt doubled. Five straight batters reached and Fiers was lifted trailing 4-2 with the bases loaded. Those two runners later scored and they were charged to him, leaving him with six earned runs allowed. Fiers was clinging to his spot in the rotation because he had not been going deep enough into games to avoid taxing the bullpen. He exploded at Hinch when he left the mound.

"They were battling and I needed to get it done and I needed to make that pitch and get out of that inning," Fiers said. "Just really a meltdown of an inning for me, and I needed to be better for this team. A.J.'s got to do his job and I wasn't doing my job. He had to take me out and I'm never going to be happy with being taken out of a game, so we had a couple of words here and there and we smoothed it over."

Scott Feldman finished with four innings in relief to hold the bullpen together. Jose Altuve stepped between Fiers and Hinch in the dugout. Later Hinch and Fiers talked on the bench, but Fiers may have contributed to his fate by contesting the manager's decision. The Athletics beat the Astros 7-4.

July 19---The Republican National Convention nominated the Donald Trump-Mike Pence ticket.

In Oakland, Dallas Keuchel was a bit rusty after a nine-day layoff, but he did not allow a run while he was in the game. Two runners left on base were charged to him after his 6 1/3 innings. Oakland won the battle of the bullpens 4-3 in 10 innings on a walk off hit by Josh Reddick off Tony Sipp. The Astros got four hits from Altuve, who raised his average to .354. But rookie lefty Dillon Overton became the latest in a long string of southpaws without strong credentials to hold the Houston offense at bay. Texas also lost, leaving Houston at 50-44 and still trailing by 4 ½ games.

July 20---"Houston" was the first word spoken 47 years ago on this date from the moon by NASA astronaut Neil Armstrong.

In a day game at Oakland, Doug Fister blanked the Athletics for seven innings and collaborated with Chris Devenski on a four-hit shutout, winning 7-0. Carlos Correa drove in three runs and Jose Altuve reached base four times. Altuve extended his road hitting streak to 19 games and reached base for the 35th straight road game. "He absolutely demolished us this series," A's catcher Stephen Vogt said.

"Altuve is some kind of special hitter. He's got a magic wand, and there's no way to get him out. He has to get himself out."

The Astros finished the road trip with a 3-3 record. In a late night game, the Los Angeles Angels jumped on the Texas Rangers early and completed a sweep, 7-4. The Rangers got bad news earlier in the day regarding Prince Fielder and Shin Soo Choo. Choo went back on the 15-day disabled list with back problems. For Fielder, the news was even worse. He would be out for the season with two herniated discs in his neck. By the end of the game in Anaheim, the Rangers' lead had been sliced to 3 1/2 games.

July 21---The Astros and Angels both had the day off before opening their three-game series. Altuve led the majors in hitting with a .357 average.

Alex Bregman led off and played left field in the final game of a four-game series at Round Rock. Some Houston reporters were at the game 165 miles west of Houston. A.J. Reed was optioned to Fresno, but Bregman did not replace him on the roster. Instead, Preston Tucker was promoted to the Astros.

July 22---Hillary Clinton chose Virginia Senator Tim Kaine as her running mate.

The Los Angeles Angels brought a six-game winning streak into the series, with several torrid hitters in a lineup that produced the most runs in the majors in July. With an excellent crowd of 36,453 stoked for Friday night fireworks and wearing giveaway Carlos Correa fedoras, Lance McCullers quieted the hot Halos, whiffing 10 in eight innings and leaving with a 2-0 lead. Will Harris nailed down the 2-1 win after allowing an RBI single. Preston Tucker contributed a triple as the DH. The Astros pulled to within 2 ½ games of the Rangers, who lost at Kansas City.

July 23---With 10,000 fans opening boxes containing giveaway Evan Gattis gnomes, Gattis exploded for two home runs and four RBI in a 7-2 Houston win.

Gattis was in the original lineup as the DH, but was switched to starting catcher a few hours before game time because Jason Castro had a bruised hand from a foul ball the night before.

Gattis threw out Yunel Escobar trying to steal second base in the first inning with Collin McHugh on the mound. He went to work with the bat in the second with a three-run homer off Jered Weaver. "Today was Gatty Day, " McHugh said after lowering his ERA to a season low 4.18. Gattis had a much higher career OPS as a catcher than he had as a DH. "He's got a lot of responsibility as a catcher," said A.J. Hinch. "He takes it very seriously. In essence, it (catching) lifts his mind a little bit from some of the mental grind of being a hitter." The Astros were 14-7 with Gattis as their starting catcher.

Carlos Correa ripped his 36th career home run, taking over the CAREER leadership for a Houston shortstop at age 21!

In Chicago, Chris Sale erupted during batting practice over the throwback uniforms the White Sox were going to wear for that night's game against Detroit. He was due to be the starting pitcher. Sale took scissors to the 1976 throwback shorts selected by the front office.

He cut into several uniforms and ruined so many that the club changed to different throwbacks for the game. Sale was sent home after his tirade and had to be replaced by an emergency starter, Matt Albers, the former Astro. Albers, making his only start of the season, lasted just two innings, but the White Sox won 4-3. The next day, Sale was suspended for five days.

July 24---The Astros belted five home runs and knocked Tim Lincecum out of the game in the second inning of a 13-3 rout, their 11th straight win over the Angels. Jose Altuve hit two homers and drove in six, raising his average to .360.

After the game, A.J. Hinch announced the promotion of Alex Bregman to the majors and Danny Worth was designated for assignment.

July 25---During the day, the Cubs and Yankees worked out a trade. The Yankees agreed to send their closer, Aroldis Chapman, to Chicago in return for four players. The experts felt this trade would be the biggest of the week. "Every chance to win is sacred," said Cubs President Theo Epstein. "So if you don't do it now, when?"

The Astros held a press conference to introduce Alex Bregman to the media. He was in the lineup at third base, batting sixth. With his parents and many friends in the stands, Bregman made some dazzling plays at third base and came up about three feet short of a grand slam, going 0-for-4 in his debut. The Astros lost to the Yankees 2-1 on a six-hitter by Michael Pineda, Dellin Betances and new closer Andrew Miller.

After the Astros-Yankees game ended, Adrian Beltre hit a walkoff homer in Arlington to give Texas a win over Oakland, adding a game to its lead. It was now a 3 ½ game difference between the two.

July 26---Hillary Clinton became the first female to be nominated presidential candidate by a major political party. Former President Bill Clinton addressed the Democratic National Convention.

The Yankees beat the Astros 6-3 behind C.C. Sabathia, who defeated Doug Fister. Marwin Gonzalez blasted two homers, one from each side of the plate. The last Astro to deliver switch hit long balls in the same game was Lance Berkman in 2006. Luis Valbuena fell running to first base on a grounder, straining his right hamstring. He came out of the game immediately. Later he said he did not think the injury would sideline him for much time.

San Diego traded Melvin Upton, Jr. to Toronto. Toronto also traded Drew Storen to Seattle for Joaquin Benoit.

July 27---President Obama and Vice President Biden addressed the Democratic National Convention.

With the Yankees going for a sweep of the series at Minute Maid Park, they ran into a brick wall named Lance McCullers.

McCullers struck out 10 in six innings, winning 4-1. His strikeout rate for the season improved to 11.79 per nine innings, tops among American League starters. Of his 100 strikeouts, 84 came on curve balls. Network analysts talked about his devastating fastball-curveball combination, with both pitches delivered from the same arm slot. McCullers was emerging as the number one starter for the club. "He's got one of the better curveballs you're gonna see, and out of 90 pitches, it seemed like he threw 89 of them," said Yankees catcher Brian McCann, who homered off a fastball.

With Chris Sale trade rumors swirling, the Rangers and Astros were both weighing the steep price of acquiring the White Sox ace. The Rangers traded infield prospect Travis Demeritte to Atlanta for former Astro starter Lucas Harrell and lefty reliever Dario Alvarez. They announced that Harrell would start for them Sunday and Alvarez would join their bullpen. Reporters described these acquisitions as "sticking a finger in the dam" until the Rangers could acquire better pitching. Harrell had been a revelation for Atlanta despite not being in the big leagues before May. Alvarez was acquired on waivers by the Braves. But he, too, had been very effective.

Carlos Gomez left the game with a right hamstring strain. Colby Rasmus snapped an 0-for-29 slump with a two-run homer. Rasmus was diagnosed the day before with cholesteatoma, a growth of skin cells behind the eardrum that causes damage to the eardrum itself. "My ear had a little bit to do with it and kind of got me down those few days there," said Rasmus of his July slump.

He said he would eventually need surgery.

July 28---Jimmy Walker shot 65 for the first round lead in the PGA Championship at Baltusrol.

As a much needed rain fell on parts of Houston, the traveling party took off for Detroit. Sometimes George Springer helped the flight attendants by passing out snacks early in the flight.

The manager and coaches typically sit in first class, with the radio and TV broadcast teams and staff members in the middle and the players in the back. On the United charter flight, about 45 travelers spread out on a full sized aircraft, which was normal. Each row of three seats usually had at least one vacant seat.

Texas beat Kansas City 3-2 behind Cole Hamels to pull three games ahead of Houston. In a 27-game span for the Rangers, Hamels was their only starting pitcher to win. It was his fourth win in that stretch.

July 29---Robert Streb fired a second round 63 to tie Jimmy Walker for the lead in the PGA Championship.

Minnesota traded All-Star Eduardo Nunez to San Francisco for Adalberto Mejia. The Giants needed infield help due to injuries to Matt Duffy and Joe Panik.

Miami traded former Astros starter Jarred Cosart, Carter Capps, number two prospect Josh Naylor and Luis Castillo to San Diego for Andrew Cashner, Colin Rea and Tayron Guerrero. The Rangers had been pursuing Cashner, whose 97 mph fastball belied his high ERA of 4.76. The Rangers continued to pursue Chris Sale. The price might include Nomar Mazara, Joey Gallo and two or three other top young players.

The extremely high price for a staff ace like Sale gave a general manager pause. Wrote Jake Kaplan in the *Houston Chronicle*: "But in one of the worst starting pitching markets in memory, the cost in prospects could very well prove too steep for a team like the Astros, whose 48-29 record since May 1 is the best in the American League."

In the opener at Detroit, Jose Altuve homered in the first to extend his road hitting streak to 20 games. But the Tigers jumped on Collin McHugh for 10 hits and eight runs in 1 2/3 innings.

McHugh joined Shane Reynolds as the two Astros with the worst starts of less than two innings. The Tigers pounded the Astros 14-6 and Texas won to pull four games ahead of Houston in the AL West.

Tyler White joined the Astros from Fresno, replacing Luis Valbuena. Valbuena was placed on the disabled list with a right hamstring strain.

The *Houston Chronicle* named its five best and worst deadline deals for the Astros. The five best were the trades for Jeff Bagwell in 1990, Randy Johnson in 1998, Kevin Bass in 1982, Dan Wheeler in 2004 and Danny Darwin in 1986. The five worst involved dealing Ben Zobrist in 2006, Hunter Pence in 2011, Michael Bourn in 2011, Carlos Gomez and Mike Fiers in 2015 for four young players, and Roy Oswalt in 2010.

July 30---Strong and steady rain prevented the third round of the PGA from being played in New Jersey.

Detroit's Justin Verlander retired 16 straight in a 3-2 thriller. Verlander and Mike Fiers traded zeroes until Detroit got an unearned run in the sixth. An uncharacteristic Jose Altuve error on a popup with two outs allowed the run to score. Verlander, who walked one and fanned 11, pitched the ninth but lost the lead. Carlos Correa's RBI single tied it and Colby Rasmus gave Houston a 2-1 lead on a force play. Will Harris came in to try for the save. But the Tigers staged a two-out rally on singles by James McCann and Jose Iglesias to win it.

Injuries rendering players unavailable hurt A.J. Hinch. With Carlos Gomez unavailable with his hamstring injury and Marwin Gonzalez hurting with a painful right hand, Hinch used Evan Gattis as a pinch hitter and left him in to catch, moving Jason Castro to first base. Starting first baseman Tyler White moved to third and Alex Bregman moved from third base to left field. Bregman made a throwing error, which factored in the second unearned run of the night. The winning hit came on a grounder to Castro, whose throw to Harris covering first was a split second too late. The Tigers moved ahead of the Astros in the wild card standings.

Doug Fister, who stayed in Houston with his wife Ashley due to deliver their first child, was to start Monday at home against Toronto.

Since the baby had not yet arrived, the Astros were making plans for another starter for that game. Fresno's scheduled starter, Joe Musgrove, was scratched for this game and was rumored to be in line as Fister's replacement if needed.

Cuban infielder Yuliesky Gurriel got his work visa and played for the Gulf Coast League Astros.

The Washington Nationals traded two players to Pittsburgh for closer Mark Melancon, another former Astro.

The Atlanta Braves traded Hector Olivera to San Diego for Matt Kemp.

Kansas City traded Brett Eibner to Oakland for Billy Burns.

Milwaukee held catcher Jonathan Lucroy out of the lineup because of trade talks.

July 31---Despite temperatures in the mid 90s, fans arrived early to see the opening of Houston Texans training camp. DeAndre Hopkins was a holdout, but by the end of the day he planned to end his holdout with no renegotiation of his contract.

The Sunday morning headlines told of a trade sending lefty closer Andrew Miller from the Yankees to Cleveland for a package including two of the Indians' top three prospects. This deal stamped the Indians as the team to beat in the American League. Furthermore, the Tribe attempted to add Milwaukee catcher Jonathan Lucroy in another deal. In what was reported to include a package of four prospects, the Brewers submitted the deal to Lucroy for his approval according to the terms of his contract. The Indians were one of eight teams on his no trade list. He and his agent reportedly asked Cleveland to drop his $5.25 million option for 2017 in return for his approval of the deal.

Lucroy wanted playing time guarantees for 2017 which Cleveland would not provide, according to reports. Cleveland had Yan Gomes on a multiyear contract and Lucroy wanted to make sure he was not relegated to the bench during his free agent year.

The deal fell apart. But other teams renewed talks about Lucroy.

The Andrew Miller deal was a difference maker for the Tribe. Miller was 4-0 with a 1.55 ERA in 26 games for Cleveland after the trade, finishing 10-1 with a 1.45 ERA during the regular season. He blazed through the first two rounds of the playoffs with a 0.00 ERA for six games, striking out 21 in 11 2/3 innings.

The St. Louis Cardinals traded for White Sox lefty reliever Zach Duke.

Baltimore traded a top prospect to Seattle for lefthander Wade Miley.

The Yankees traded a prospect to Arizona for reliever Tyler Clippard.

In the game at Detroit, the Tigers pounced on Dallas Keuchel in a six-run first, winning an 11-0 blowout game. One of the few bright spots was Alex Bregman's first major league hit, snapping an 0-for-18 start to his career. It came off Mike Pelfrey. When Bregman got to first base, Miguel Cabrera wrapped his arm around Bregman and said, "Congrats. 2,999 more. Let's go." The one-sided affair sent the Astros home with five losses in six games.

Their slump at the end of the month left them 2 ½ games back in the wild card race and six games behind Texas. With the trade deadline approaching the next day, they would open a seven-game homestand against Toronto and Texas. It appeared to be as big a week as any they had faced all season.

Jimmy Walker won the PGA Championship by one stroke over Jason Day.

July Summary

The Astros' 13-12 July included a 10-6 record at home.

They outscored their opponents, 110-97 and had a 3.76 ERA.

Their top hitters were Jose Altuve (.362, 5 HR, 16 RBI), Carlos Correa (.276, 2 HR, 18 RBI) and Luis Valbuena (.264, 4, HR 13 RBI).

Altuve went on a road rampage, hitting in 21 straight road games with a .512 average.

Their top pitchers were Ken Giles (1-0, 0.00 ERA for 9 games), Luke Gregerson (0-0, 0.87 in 10 games), and Lance McCullers (3-2, 2.08 ERA)

July Standings in AL West

Texas   62-44 -

Houston 55-49 -6

Seattle   52-51 -8.5

Oakland 47-58 -14.5

LAA   47-58 -14.5

---

9 August Angst

The month began with six losses in eight games to Toronto, Texas and Minnesota. But the Astros rebounded to win the last three games of the series in Minnesota. They fell into another five-game losing streak, falling to 61-59 in their first 120 games. After that 13-5 thumping at Baltimore, they sprang to life and finished the month on a 10-2 run.

With many fans turning their attention to football and the start of the school year, the third youngest team in the American League went through the end of August with eight rookies, moving into the thick of the wild card race.

As they left town for a critical stretch, they were only one game out of a playoff spot.

August Game by Game Accounts

August 1---With the trade deadline at 3 p.m. CDT, the morning was quiet regarding any announcements. But the texts were flying back and forth around front offices. Then the 18 trades came in machine gun fashion. Here is the approximate timeline on the most significant deals as the deadline loomed:

1 p.m. EDT: Cincinnati traded outfielder Jay Bruce to New York for Dilson Herrera and Max Wotel.

1:01   : Oakland traded pitcher Rich Hill and outfielder Josh Reddick to the Los Angeles Dodgers for three right-handed pitching prospects: Jharel Cotton, Frankie Montas and Grant Holmes. Hill would provide the Dodgers with a large reward, help their injury-riddled rotation to win the National League West and pitch a key shutout in the playoffs against the Chicago Cubs. Reddick also helped the Dodger cause with solid play in the outfield.

1:10   : Minnesota dealt reliever Fernando Abad to Boston.

2:06   : Tampa Bay traded Brandon Guyer to Cleveland for two minor leaguers.

2:28   : San Francisco acquired lefty reliever Will Smith from Milwaukee for Andrew Susac and Phil Bickford.

2:55   : The Yankees traded Carlos Beltran to Texas for Dillon Tate and two other prospects. Tate was the fourth overall pick in the 2015 draft.

2:56   : Houston traded Scott Feldman to Toronto for 18-year-old pitcher Lupe Chavez.

2:57   : The Angels traded Joe Smith to the Cubs for Jesus Castillo.

2:59   : Milwaukee traded Jonathan Lucroy and Jeremy Jeffress to Texas for Lewis Brinson and Luis Ortiz

2:59   : The Angels traded Hector Santiago to Minnesota for Ricky Nolasco and Alex Meyer

2:59   : Matt Moore was traded by Tampa Bay to San Francisco.

2:59   : Miami traded Colin Rea to San Diego for Luis Castillo

2:59   : The Yankees traded Ivan Nova to Pittsburgh for prospects

2:59   : Tampa Bay traded Steve Pearce to Baltimore

2:59   : The Los Angeles Dodgers acquired Jesse Chavez from Toronto for Mike Bolsinger

2:59   : Pittsburgh dealt Jonathon Niese to the New York Mets for Antonio Bastardo

During batting practice, Astros GM Jeff Luhnow answered questions near the batting cage for a large media group. "Almost every player that got moved, we were involved in the discussions in one way, shape or form over the last couple weeks," Luhnow said. "We just made the decision that the cost for us relative to what we would be gaining was too high at this point in time." Scott Feldman walked down the hallway to the Toronto clubhouse after being traded for 18-year-old Lupe Chavez. In another deal, Josh Fields went to the Dodgers for 19-year-old Cuban first baseman/outfielder Yordan Alvarez.

"Texas took three of their top five prospects out of their system to improve today, and that's a decision that they made for their own benefit," added Luhnow. "We are not prepared to do that for our organization at this point in time. I feel like we've got a young team that's going to be here for a while. We don't have any windows closing. We're just getting into our window, if you want to call it that, and we want to keep it open for as long as possible and have as many shots to go to the playoffs as possible."

"This stretch of the season is going to let us know if we're for real or if we have to go (into) the offseason and kind of figure out next year," said Lance McCullers.

Doug Fister took the mound for the 7:10 game with Joe Musgrove in the bullpen. Fister's wife was not going to give birth on this night according to doctors. He and Toronto righthander Marcus Stroman learned quickly that home plate umpire Ryan Blackney owned the night. Blackney was giving the pitchers a generously wide strike zone. It set the tone for a 40-strikeout game in 14 innings! Fister struck out eight in six innings. Stroman set a career high with 13 in seven frames. Jose Altuve's sixth inning homer was the only run until Russell Martin blasted a tying homer off Will Harris leading off the ninth.

Former Astro Scott Feldman, the 14th pitcher to work in the game, gave up an Altuve single and a game winning double by Carlos Correa in the 14th.

It was Correa's sixth go ahead RBI in the ninth inning or later, the most by an Astro since Jeff Bagwell had seven in 1992.

August 2---Christopher Russo, the host of High Heat on the MLB Network, predicted the Chicago Cubs would meet the Texas Rangers in the World Series based on the trades and their status as division leaders.

Jim Duquette, former New York Mets general manager, wrote an article for MLB.com ranking the four most improved teams through trade deadline deals as: 1. San Francisco 2. Los Angeles 3. Texas 4. The New York Yankees.

In his daily media briefing on the bench, A.J. Hinch said Ken Giles would replace Will Harris as the closer. "As always, these roles in the bullpen evolve over time, and the ebbs and flow of the season sometimes create change," said Hinch.

"All my work is paying off right now," said Giles. "I'm always finding a way to get better. I'm trying to be smarter on the mound and trying to be a complete pitcher right now, and I think that's what has really been helping me lately."

Luke Gregerson was placed on the disabled list with a left oblique strain. A.J. Reed replaced him on the roster. James Hoyt was in the clubhouse and spoke with the media, but he would not be joining the active roster for another day. Doug Fister would be placed on the paternity list the next day and Hoyt, the closer at Fresno, would replace him. Marwin Gonzalez was still sidelined with a sore right hand, but Carlos Gomez was back in the lineup with a wrapped right hamstring.

Gomez took his position in center field behind Lance McCullers as the game got under way.

McCullers threw a high dosage of fastballs early, keeping his trademark devastating curve out of the mix to a degree. Jose Bautista ripped his 300th career homer off a fastball in the third.

Edwin Encarnacion drilled a curve for a long home run, rounding the bases for his usual home run trot with his right elbow raised as if holding his imaginary parrot on his shoulder. By the fifth, McCullers left the game with a right elbow injury.

Knuckleballer R.A. Dickey kept the Astros at bay until the seventh, when Evan Gattis singled in a run.

Joe Musgrove came out of the Houston bullpen when McCullers was injured and started making history. Musgrove retired the first ten hitters in his major league debut. He finished with eight strikeouts, setting a club record in relief and tying a major league record for a reliever making his debut. In Musgrove's 4 1/3 innings he allowed one hit and no runs. But the Blue Jays won 2-1. The negatives kept piling up. First a slump at the end of July. Then no major trades by the deadline. Now, for the first time all season, injuries were hitting the club in the solar plexus. Valbuena was on the DL. Gonzalez and Gomez were active but not at full strength. Now McCullers apparently was headed for the DL. Prior to the game, the Astros had the fewest days on the DL in the majors, 105 days. The next closest team was the Marlins, with 305 days.

August 3---Lance McCullers was placed on the 15-day disabled list with a sprained right elbow. He was told not to pick up a ball for two weeks. The unspoken and underlying concern was that his elbow injury would lead to Tommy John surgery. McCullers said he had felt fine during the game up to his final few pitches before leaving. Brad Peacock was promoted from Fresno to fill the roster vacancy. James Hoyt made a good major league debut in the game with a scoreless inning. Joe Musgrove was named the starter for Sunday against Texas in McCullers' rotation spot.

On Pokemon Night, fans were wandering around on the field before batting practice looking at their phones for directions to Pokemon. Collin McHugh and Marco Estrada needed no guidance to find home plate. McHugh walked only one in six innings, while Estrada and the Toronto bullpen did not issue a walk.

The Blue Jays won 3-1 on three solo homers, two by Josh Donaldson. All six of their runs in the series were on solo home runs. The strikeout fest continued. In the first three games of the four-game series there were 84 strikeouts, 50 by Houston pitchers.

The Texas Rangers also lost, keeping their margin over Houston at 5 ½ games. The Astros fell to three games back in the wild card race.

August 4---The club strikeout record for a series fell in this one. Mike Fiers and three relievers fanned 11 Blue Jays in a 4-1 loss to former Astro J.A. Happ. That gave the Astros' pitchers a club record 61 strikeouts for a four-game series. But a bigger story was the continued failure of the offense. The Astros had scored 21 runs in 10 games. Their league high strikeout count for the season reached 997. The loss knocked them 6 ½ games behind the Rangers, who were coming to town the next night.

August 5--- The 2016 Olympic Games opened with ceremonies in Rio de Janeiro. Supermodel Gisele Bundchen, Tom Brady's wife, took her final runway walk before retiring to the song "Girl from Ipanema." Team USA sent 554 athletes to Rio to compete for medals. Swimmer Michael Phelps was the flagbearer.

The AL West race came to Minute Maid Park with the Texas Rangers bringing a 9-1 record in head-to-head play against the Astros. Dallas Keuchel set a different tone, blanking them on three hits 5-0. It was Legends Weekend. While former Astro slugger Glenn Davis joined the Root Sports telecast, he lent some karma to the slumping hitters and they broke out with a four-run inning against loser Martin Perez. Former Astro Carlos Beltran continued to be booed lustily.

He went 1 for 4 while new catcher Jonathan Lucroy rested.

August 6---Team USA won its first gold medal in Rio when 19-year-old Ginny Thrasher captured the women's 10-meter air rifle title.

On a 96-degree day in Houston, fans lined up hours before the game at Minute Maid Park to be among the first 10,000 to receive a Mike Scott 1986 rainbow jersey as a part of Legends Weekend. Scott threw out the first pitch to Dallas Keuchel in a Cy Young battery. Several of the 1986 Astros took part in activities before the game. The 2016 Astros took the field in rainbow uniforms looking like the 1986 Astros, who won the NL West and lost one of the best playoff series ever to the New York Mets in six games.

Doug Fister threw out the first pitch of the actual game. The new father gave the Astros a good chance to win, allowing just one run in six innings. Former Astro Lucas Harrell was on the ropes early, walking in a run in the first before striking out A.J. Reed with the bases loaded. Again he dodged a bullet in the third, getting Jake Marisnick with the bases full. He lasted only 3 2/3 innings, but the bullpen pitched scoreless baseball for 5 1/3 frames in a 3-2 Texas win. New catcher Jonathan Lucroy, with family and friends in attendance from his home in Louisiana, ripped two home runs. One came off loser Chris Devenski.

August 7---Swimmer Katie Ledecky won the 400-meter freestyle for a gold medal in Rio, breaking a world record. Michael Phelps won his 19th gold medal in the 4x100 meter freestyle relay.

Golfer Jim Furyk set a PGA Tour record with a final round 58 in the Travelers Championship in Connecticut.

Tony Kemp arrived in Houston on a red eye flight from Las Vegas. Colby Rasmus was placed on the disabled list with a cyst in his right ear. Kemp had not been able to see a dentist in Las Vegas to do some necessary work, but the Astros found a dentist in Houston on Sunday morning. He arrived at Minute Maid Park about game time.

There were other concerns for A.J. Hinch. Marwin Gonzalez was unable to start, rendering him a bench player.

Tyler White was getting treatment for inflammation in his left knee, which had caused the manager to shy away from using him as a pinch hitter against lefty Jake Diekman the night before. Carlos Gomez was ill.

Joe Musgrove was strong in his first major league start. Yu Darvish answered his scoreless innings. The Rangers scored in the fifth on a Jonathan Lucroy double. Will Harris gave up two runs in the eighth and Texas led 3-0. Alex Bregman and Jose Altuve knocked in runs in the eighth. Kemp came off the bench with a tying RBI single in the ninth, his third hit after the seventh inning. But the Rangers got two in the 11th off Chris Devenski and won 5-3, dropping the Astros 7 ½ games behind them and leaving them in awful shape for a playoff spot.

The team left for a week long road trip to Minnesota and Toronto, needing to make a big run in the win column.

In Denver, Ichiro Suzuki became the 30th player to reach 3,000 hits in the majors with two hits against the Rockies. He banged a triple at Coors Field, joining Minnesota manager Paul Molitor as the only players with triples as their 3,000th hits. Including his years in Japan, Suzuki had 4,278 hits professionally. Of the 30 players with 3,000 hits, Alex Rodriguez and Rafael Palmeiro were tainted in the public eye because of association with performance enhancing drugs.

Rodriguez and the Yankees announced that in a few days he would be released as a player but retained as a special advisor and instructor, with his employment guaranteed through 2017 to complete his 10-year, $275 million contract. Rodriguez did not completely close the door on playing for another team. He had 696 home runs. Some were speculating that he might wind up playing for Tampa Bay, which could get an attendance pop from Rodriguez. Rodriguez said, "Of course, I think I can play baseball."

The three-time American League most valuable player made it clear that the Yankees made the decision not to use him as a player.

Few thought he would be elected to the Hall of Fame because of his involvement with performance enhancing drugs. He admitted to using illegal substances from 2001 to 2003 with the Texas Rangers.

He also served a one-year suspension in 2014 for his role in the Biogenesis doping scandal in 2013. Rodriguez was a 14-time All-Star whose career earnings were $392 million. The 41-year-old finished third on the alltime RBI list with 2,084.

Barry Bonds received 44.3% of the Hall of Fame vote in his fourth year on the ballot in 2015, well short of the 75% needed for induction. Roger Clemens received 45.2% in 2015. Neither acknowledged using steroids as Rodriguez had done. Some of those who voted for Bonds and Clemens did so on the basis that they felt those two players were two of the greatest even before they started using banned substances.

August 8---In Rio, gold medalist Ryan Murphy and 30-year-old David Plummer, who won the bronze, made headlines in the 100-meter backstroke. American Lilly King won the gold medal in the 100-meter breaststroke, edging Russia's Yuia Efimova. Efimova, like many of the Russian athletes, was booed by the fans because she was allowed to compete despite serving a previous 16-month suspension for doping and testing positive again in 2016. Possible sanctions were put on hold for the Russians while more research was done on the drug meldonium, which was discovered in her system in the drug test. King said of her gold medal, "It just proves you can compete clean and still come out on top with all the hard work you put in behind the scenes."

On a beautiful night in Minneapolis, the Astros opened a seven-game road trip needing a quick turnaround after their 2-5 homestand. They got more of the same: a 3-1 loss. Twins starter Tyler Duffey, a Houston native who pitched at Rice, stopped them on one run through six innings despite his 6.21 ERA. Jose Altuve was resting after playing 202 consecutive games. Marwin Gonzalez played second base.

Tony Kemp led off and George Springer batted third.

The Twins scored all three of the runs in the third inning off Collin McHugh. Jorge Polanco lined a single past Carlos Gomez, who hustled over to play it but failed to pick it up on one bounce and allowed Polanco to reach third on the two-base error.

Two pitches later, Juan Centeno hit a routine fly ball to left center, but it went for a triple when Gomez lost the ball in the twilight sky above Target Field. Centeno came home on a single by Danny Santana.

"It's something you don't feel good about, and we lost the game because of that," Gomez said of his misplays. "I feel worse than anybody in this clubhouse. I have nothing to say. I don't feel good in this situation."

The fan reaction on Twitter regarding Gomez had been negative for weeks and he was being booed in Houston. His .594 OPS was the worst among all American League regular outfielders. A.J. Hinch was asked if Gomez would play the next night and he answered in the negative. "We've been pretty beat up in a lot of ways and you keep trying to hang in there with guys," said Hinch. "You want to encourage more than anything. Clearly it's been a rough patch for him for a while. I'll take a look and see how it comes out tomorrow."

August 9---The Zika virus claimed the life of a Texas baby born in Harris County to a woman who had traveled to Latin America during her pregnancy.

Michael Phelps collected two more gold medals, his 20th and 21st, in the Rio Olympics. He won the 200-meter butterfly and anchored the 4x200-meter freestyle relay. Simone Biles of Houston and the U.S gymnasts took the gold in the team competition.

Hector Santiago took the mound at Target Field for the first time as a Twin. He had come there in a trade with the Angels.

Carlos Correa ripped a two-run homer off him in the first and a two-run single in the sixth in a 7-5 Houston win.

Jose Altuve returned after his first day off to bang out four hits and improve his average to .361. He would be hitting .300 even if he went 0-for-90. The bullpen protected the lead for winner Mike Fiers with Ken Giles getting his second save.

Yuliesky Gurriel made his AA debut at Corpus Christi and went 0-for-3.

August 10---In the Games of the XXXI Olympiad, Katie Ledecky anchored the gold medal winning 4x200-meter freestyle relay team. Kristin Armstrong took a gold medal a day before her 43rd birthday in road cycling.

Longtime ESPN anchor John Saunders died at the age of 61.

In warm, muggy Minneapolis weather concerns were moving into the picture for the Astros-Twins series. A major storm was approaching, due to hit late this night and stay through the next day. Heavy rains were expected. Storm clouds were hanging over Carlos Gomez as well. Rumors circulated throughout the day that he would be designated for assignment. General Manager Jeff Luhnow announced to the media before the game that the Astros were doing just that, giving them ten days to trade him or release him. To replace him on the 25-man roster, 22-year-old rookie reliever Jandel Gustave arrived from Fresno.

Gomez left the clubhouse and apologized for his poor performance, wishing the players and organization all the best.

"We really wanted to start playing the guys who we felt were going to help us on a nightly basis," said A.J. Hinch. "That's not a knock on Carlos Gomez. He brought his best every single day that he could to try to help us win. But the roster construction is going to change over the next week to ten days, and he was starting to be on the outside looking in." It was a difficult move for Luhnow, who traded a strong prospect group to Milwaukee for Gomez and Fiers. Gomez would have been a free agent in October, however. The Astros decided to cut ties with him six weeks earlier than they planned.

"I know he carried the burden of being a big acquisition," said Hinch. "He often spoke of feeling responsible to try to play better, knowing he was our big addition last July. I think he put a lot of pressure on himself to be perfect. The more he tried, the harder it became."

When the game started, Ervin Santana escaped first inning trouble. Brian Dozier led off the bottom of the first with a home run off Dallas Keuchel. The Twins cashed in on a second inning error by Alex Bregman and another by Carlos Correa, piling up a 5-0 lead by the time the inning ended. Then a downpour hit Target Field hours earlier than expected, driving everybody for cover as the grounds crew covered the infield with the tarpaulin. Thousands of white umbrellas with red baseball-like seams popped open in the stands. The Twins, with providence on their side, had given out the umbrellas before the game as their giveaway item for that night. A lengthy rain delay ensued with no breaks in the heavy downpour. As the rain delay wore on, it became more and more likely that the game could not be resumed, making a Thursday doubleheader more and more probable. Two innings did not constitute an official game, and the game would have to be restarted if the rain did not halt.

August 11---In Rio de Janeiro, Houstonian Simone Biles easily captured the Olympic all-around gold medal. Martha Karolyi, the legendary coach who lives in the Houston area, declared her the greatest gymnast ever.

Sugar Land's Simone Manuel tied for first in the women's 100-meter freestyle, becoming the first African-American woman to claim a gold medal in an individual swimming event.

In the Twin Cities, the day dawned gloomy and rainy. But the clouds cleared and by game time at 12:10 for the opener of the day-night doubleheader it was a sunny, 77 degree day with plenty of humidity. The players got on the team bus smiling after avoiding a loss the night before due to the rainout.

In the first inning they went right to work, scoring twice off Jose Berrios. It was the beginning of a 19-hit onslaught in a 15-7 blowout win for Doug Fister, with Jose Altuve and Marwin Gonzalez contributing four-hit games. Altuve's average climbed to .366 with eight hits in his last nine at bats.

The game lasted three hours and two minutes, leaving the players three hours to rest before the start of the night game at 6:10. The crowd from the first game left the stadium and the stadium was cleaned before the gates were reopened at 5 p.m. The Twins would get revenues from two separate games, a much more lucrative practice than combining both games of the doubleheader into one ticket price as in years ago.

In the nightcap, both managers pulled pitchers out of their bullpens to start. The Twins used lefty Tommy Milone, and the Astros torched him for five runs in three innings. Evan Gattis cracked a three-run homer and Carlos Correa ripped a solo shot to right center field into the seats, a 445-footer. Chris Devenski threw five shutout innings and earned his first major league win 10-2. George Springer made his first start in center field and powered a homer and two doubles. The doubleheader sweep was the first for the Astros in the American League. They scored 25 runs in the two games, second most runs in team history in a twinbill.

After the game, they boarded a bus for the Minneapolis airport and headed for Toronto, filling out customs forms and taking their luggage through the Toronto airport. Customs officials in Toronto gave sports teams more expedited treatment than decades ago in Montreal. With a 60-55 record, they had breathed life into their playoff chances. Their chances still were not strong, but they gained a game and half on Texas and now trailed by 7 ½ games. They were now two games out in the wild card race. The series with the Blue Jays took on added importance in their pursuit of postseason play.

August 12---Louisiana was hit hard with a "monsoon depression," dumping more than 20 inches of rain. Baton Rouge and Lafayette were hit with massive flooding. Eleven people died.

In Rio, Katie Ledecky and Michael Phelps were the headliners. Ledecky completed a sweep of the 200, 400 and 800-meter freestyle events. She blew away the field in the 800, winning by more than 11 seconds. Phelps finished in a three-way tie for silver in the 100-meter butterfly. It was his fifth medal at Rio.

At Yankee Stadium, Alex Rodriguez played his final game for the Yankees. He doubled in a run in his first at bat and took the field at third base briefly for the first time all season, leaving the field to a big ovation.

In Toronto, the Astros woke up from a 3 a.m. arrival for the opener of a meaningful series with the first place Blue Jays. It was the start of a 12-game stretch against contending clubs. With the temperature in the mid-eighties, more roster moves were announced. Preston Tucker was placed on the disabled list with a right shoulder strain. He was replaced by Teoscar Hernandez. Hernandez woke up at 4 a.m. to travel from Fresno to Toronto. He was held up at the Toronto airport for three hours getting through customs and did not arrive at Rogers Center until about an hour before game time, taking the field with no batting practice on his first day in Canada. Luke Gregerson was returned to the 25-man roster, replacing Ken Giles. Giles was in Houston on the paternity list. A.J. Hinch was not sure who his closer would be, naming three options. Gregerson was not ready to pitch after his 15 days on the DL. He did not have a minor league rehab assignment. He would need another bullpen session before he was pronounced fit to return to game action.

A huge crowd of 46,330 packed into the stadium. Former Toronto farmhand Joe Musgrove started for Houston. Carlos Correa gave him a 2-0 lead in the third with a single off Francisco Liriano.

Musgrove was on target for his first major league win, exiting with a 5-2 lead after seven innings. His former minor league teammate, Hernandez made a memorable major league debut with a home run in the sixth. He was known more for his speed and defensive play than his power. Musgrove and Hernandez were joined in the 5-3 Houston win by three other rookies for a total of five. "It means a a lot to me," Hernandez said of his homer off Liriano.

"Liriano's one of the best pitchers in the major leagues, and to get my first hit and first home run off him is so exciting for me."

There were 10 rookies on the Houston roster. Pat Neshek and Will Harris finished the win to give the Astros consecutive victories by rookie starting pitchers.

August 13---In Rio, Michael Phelps won his fifth gold medal in 2016 and 23rd of his career in the 4x100 individual medley relay.

Light rain fell in Toronto, ruining tourists' plans to visit the CN Tower for beautiful views of Toronto. There would not be a good view of the city on this cloudy, muggy day.

With Toronto on fire for baseball, another sellout crowd of 47,505 got quiet when Aaron Sanchez was tagged for three straight opposite field line drive hits in the first, including Carlos Correa's two-run double. Sanchez turned off the spigot after that and the Astros did not score again. Collin McHugh led 2-1 when he was removed in the sixth with two men on base. James Hoyt retired Troy Tulowitzki but hung a 3-2 slider to Russell Martin. Martin ripped the pitch over the center field wall for a three-run homer and Toronto won 4-2.

August 14---The showcase continued at Rio for Simone Biles. She won her third gold medal in the women's vault, giving her an all time 17 world or Olympic medals. She broke Shannon Miller's world record and still had two events remaining.

Usain Bolt of Jamaica easily took the gold medal in the 100-meter sprint. Andy Murray won the gold in men's tennis and Justin Rose took gold in golf.

The Houston Texans beat San Francisco in their preseason opener.

A beautiful, sunny morning in Toronto brought long lines to Rogers Center. The fans arrived early to collect giveaway bobbleheads of former Toronto pitchers Pat Hentgen, Dave Stieb and Roy Halladay.

A pregame ceremony brought some of the club's top pitchers to the infield. It was part of the 40th anniversary celebration of the team, created as an expansion club. The Blue Jays won the World Series in 1992 and 1993. The crowds were in the spirit of those top teams as they cheered for the 2016 club. The Blue Jays took the field in first place, leading Baltimore by ½ game and Boston by two games.

Young Marcus Stroman had a quick first inning. Mike Fiers gave up a Troy Tulowitzki RBI single in the bottom of the first, and the crowd ramped up its support. Not only did the Astros lose 9-2, they suffered three more injuries. Jose Altuve, who went 0-for-4 to snap his 43-game on base streak on the road, fouled a ball off his left ankle in the first. He also tweaked his left quadriceps muscle with his first swing of the day. He was not moving well after the first inning. In his final at bat he scorched a line drive to third. In the second, Marwin Gonzalez was hit by a pitch on the left kneecap and fell to the ground. He had to be replaced by a pinch runner. Jason Castro fouled a ball off his left knee, marking the second time a ball hit him on the left knee in three days. Despite a winning 4-3 road trip, the team limped home for an off day.

The injured made their way through customs in Toronto, producing passports and clearing security screenings. In a line alongside them, the Toronto Blue Jays went through the same process for their flight to New York. On their United charter, the Astros waited about an hour for the equipment truck to unload its cargo into the airplane's cargo compartment.

ESPN's Sunday Night Baseball featured the Cardinals and Cubs. The Cardinals were next up for the Astros, and the Cubs were about three weeks from a series in Houston. The Cardinals were strapped for healthy players also. The Cardinals staged a rousing late inning comeback to win 6-4.

Yuliesky Gurriel, 2-for-17 at Corpus Christi, would not be joining the Astros Tuesday after all. He was heading to Fresno for perhaps a week of games at the AAA level.

"I think defensively, he's got his legs under him," said Jeff Luhnow. "But right now, the timing isn't quite there." Houston had only 11 homers and 43 RBI from the DH position all season. The club needed a lift from somebody offensively other than Altuve, Correa and Springer. Whether Fiers could stay in the rotation and be effective or Chris Devenski should replace him was also debatable.

August 15---In Rio, Ryan Lochte and three other U.S. swimmers were in trouble after a night of carousing. The ongoing saga in the next few weeks involved Lochte's corporate sponsors ending their contractural agreements with him. The other swimmers paid severe fines just to recover their passports so they could leave the country. Lochte was charged with falsely reporting a crime.

Rain fell lightly on an off day for the Astros in Houston. There was a good chance for rain all week. The Astros would be moving on to Baltimore after Wednesday afternoon's game. Ken Giles was activated off the Paternity List. His wife Estella had given birth to Brody Robert Giles, who weighed 6 pounds and 3 ounces and measured 20 inches. To make room for Giles on the active roster, Jandel Gustave was optioned to Fresno.

Carlos Correa was named American League Player of the Week. It was the second time he won the award in 2016. He hit safely in all seven games August 8-14, hitting .429 with three homers, 12 RBI and a 1.324 OPS. He led all major league shortstops in RBI with 82.

It was the fifth Player of the Week award for an Astro in 2016.

Carlos Gomez might be putting on a Miami Marlins uniform soon, Miami's top run producer, Giancarlo Stanton, was down for the rest of the regular season. He had a severely pulled groin muscle. The Marlins were in the wild card race and they needed help quickly. They also discussed signing free agent Alex Rodriguez. But Rodriguez' publicist made it clear in a statement that Alex would not be playing again in 2016.

The Astros were facing some long odds to make the playoffs. Fangraphs predicted they would finish 23-21 for an 84-78 final record. Fangraphs projected seven teams would finish ahead of them in the American League, with Baltimore projected to nail down 90 wins for the final AL wild card playoff spot. Another statistical service rated their playoff chances at about 25%. They were in need of an unexpected finish. That's what they got in 2004 from this date to the end of the season.

2004 Astros

From August 15 to the end of the regular season, the 36-10 finish was the hot topic in the National League. It was the second best finishing kick over that span of time in the National League in 55 years. Only the 1951 Giants had done it better. From August 27 through September 8, the Astros' 12-game winning streak got the attention of baseball observers everywhere.

They reeled off 18 straight wins at home to set a club record. Even months later, reasons for the turnaround were as elusive as reasons for the lack of success earlier. The players did not see it coming. Was it the midseason managerial change from Jimy Williams to Phil Garner? Perhaps over the long haul. But when Garner took over a 44-44 club at the All-Star Break, the Astros went 12-16 in his first 28 games. Hitting coach Gary Gaetti and pitching coach Jim Hickey came in with Garner.

Garner had assessed the team when he took over as manager. "What I really thought was that there was a bit of uneasiness in the bullpen," he said. "I came in and the first thing I did was to say, 'Look, we're just gonna run Lidge out there and he's gonna be the guy.' I'm gonna use the bullpen frantically."

During an August series, Garner and General Manager Gerry Hunsicker had lunch in Philadelphia. "I told Gerry at lunch that day that for my money, the team wasn't responding for whatever reason," said Garner.

"If it were my team, I'd blow up the team. I'd trade guys and I'd get myself a pile of cash and I'd start all over the next year. And that was my assessment. And to Gerry's credit he listened. And he said, 'Well, I want to give these guys every chance I can, so we'll hold the line.' And I went off to the ballpark and Roger Clemens was starting that night and I'm thinking, 'Well, we'll continue doing what we're doing because it's the right thing to do. And hopefully we'll catch fire.' Well, that night we're down two runs with the bases loaded and there's a 3-1 or 3-0 count and I give a take sign to Clemens, who's hitting. And he misses the take sign and hits the ball and it's a double down the right field line unloading the bases and from that point we take off."

Lance Berkman broke out with seven August home runs and six more in September on his way to his third team MVP award. From August 15 on during the 36-10 run, the Big Puma drilled 12 long balls in the 46 games to finish with 30. Many of them were difference makers.

Berkman hit .354 in August and September combined with 13 homers and 41 RBI. "It just seemed like every one of those games like that coming down the stretch was a playoff game," he said. "I think that actually played in our favor because once we got to the postseason it was really like well, here we are, it's just another game like we've been playing. Especially in '04 in this building. No one could beat us."

With three games to go, it came down to a three-game season for Houston, Chicago and San Francisco.

Fans again packed into Minute Maid Park with high anxiety for the final day of the regular season. The Astros needed only to win to make their eighth trip to the playoffs.

The lineup card on the clubhouse wall that Sunday morning had Clemens in the ninth spot for Houston. But by late Sunday morning, word circulated in the press box that Brandon Backe was going to start the game because Clemens had been attacked at midnight Saturday by a stomach virus. Backe dialed up a gem and the Astros cinched a playoff spot.

Brad Lidge struck out the final four, making him the National League's all time season strikeout leader among relievers, breaking Dick Selma's record set in 1970. Lidge, who whiffed 157, had piled up 80 appearances and 94 2/3 innings, a monstrous pace for a closer.

When Lidge whiffed Colorado's Aaron Miles for the final out of the final game of the regular season, the Astros mobbed each other on the field while the fans went delirious.

The end result was a one-game margin over San Francisco, with Chicago falling three lengths behind.

August 16---Simone Biles made more history.The 4-8 gymnast landed her fourth gold medal in the floor exercise, the most in a single Olympics for a U.S. gymnast. The 19-year-old Houston native was now a major sports figure.

On a rainy night at Minute Maid Park, the St. Louis Cardinals took a 2-0 lead. The Astros answered with Alex Bregman's first major league home run, sailing into the right field stands to tie the game. Jose Altuve's second hit of the game in the fourth made it 4-2 Houston. But after retiring 12 straight, Dallas Keuchel gave up a tying home run to Tommy Pham. He left the game with two men on base and was tagged with the 8-5 loss when Jed Gyorko ripped a three-run bomb off Pat Neshek.

"This is probably the most frustrating loss of the season because of the way we bounced back and got four runs off Jaime (Garcia) and had a lead at home," said Keuchel. "I just have to be better than that."

The memorable moment for Astros fans came in the ninth, when Altuve lined a high pitch from Seung Hwan Oh to left field for his third hit. It was number 1,000 of Altuve's career. It took him 786 games to reach the milestone, at age 26 in his sixth season. Cesar Cedeno made it to 1,000 hits in 889 games, the previous club record. It took Jeff Bagwell 890 games. Bob Watson needed 952 games.

Craig Biggio picked up number 1,000 in his 971st game in his seventh season.

Ichiro Suzuki, who started playing major league baseball at age 27 after years in Japan, banged out his 1,000th hit in his 696th game. Among active players, Ichiro was the fastest to that mark. Pete Rose, also in his sixth season, reached 1,000 in his 831st game. Among the players on baseball's all-time top ten list for hits, only five reached their 1,000th hit in fewer games than Altuve. Four were Hall of Famers Ty Cobb, Hank Aaron, Stan Musial and Honus Wagner. The other was Derek Jeter, who would be entering the Hall of Fame when he was eligible. The others on the top ten list who needed more than Altuve's 786 games were Rose, Tris Speaker, Carl Yastrzemski, Paul Molitor and Eddie Collins. Altuve was the ninth youngest player to reach 1,000 hits. The younger players all reached 3,000 hits. They were Ty Cobb, Al Kaline, Alex Rodriguez, Robin Yount, Hank Aaron, Tris Speaker, George Brett and Derek Jeter.

In the Astros clubhouse after the game, the media surrounded Keuchel in front of the "interview wall," while Altuve sat quietly at his locker checking his cell phone. Carlos Correa's locker was on one side, Marwin Gonzalez' on the other. Altuve smiled and accepted congratulations from a well-wisher before he went in front of the media. He looked tired but relieved. There would be no time to rest on his laurels. Tomorrow's game was at 1:10, and the players would be traveling to Baltimore afterwards.

"I don't want to stop," said Altuve. "I want to keep going. I want to keep getting better and helping my team, and I'm not going to be good until I take my team to the World Series." With the home fans cheering him on, Altuve got the milestone in one of only two games on the abbreviated homestand. "All the games that it took me to get all the 1,000 hits, they were here for me," he said. "Rooting for me, pushing me, encouraging me. And I have to say thank you for everything that the fans, my teammates and everybody has done for me."

"The coolest thing about it is he's the youngest to get to 1,000 hits in Astros history and he's not satisfied," said Alex Bregman. "He's trying to get better every single day. He's constantly just working, working, working. He's pretty spectacular. He's got to be the best player in baseball."

Where would Altuve's career take him? He seemed destined for greatness at this stage. But Edgar Renteria had 1,235 hits through age 26 before his career tapered off. Ruben Sierra's career total was 1,160 through age 26. He, too, failed to keep up that pace and fell short of greatness.

August 17---Swimmer Simone Manuel arrived at George Bush Intercontinental Airport with her two gold and two silver medals from the Olympics. She was greeted by the Fort Bend Austin High School drum line and dance team. The 20-year-old swimmer said she was humbled by the reaction to her performance.

With more rain falling, the players brought their luggage to Minute Maid Park for another travel day. This 48-hour stopover at home seemed like part of a longer road trip except for spending two nights in their own beds. The Cardinals scored three in the third off Doug Fister and their starter, Carlos Martinez threw five no-hit innings. The Cardinals won 8-2 to keep their spot in the wild card standings. After the game, a hard rain fell and the team buses left for Bush Intercontinental Airport for the flight to Baltimore.

Brian T. Smith wrote a column in the Houston Chronicle about the Astros. "This is a critical time for a thinned-out club that's just 7-15 in its last 22 games and still hasn't recovered from doing nothing at the trade deadline."

"This is yet another test for us," said A.J. Hinch. "We have to play better if we expect to make a push here. This is a different team than what everybody expected it to be in August. That doesn't mean that it has to be a crutch or it has to be an excuse."

The Astros released 22-year-old Corpus Christi outfielder Danry Vazquez. Vazquez was suspended indefinitely as a result of his arrest for an alleged domestic violence incident.

August 18---In Rio, Usain Bolt won his eighth career Olympic gold medal, grinding out a win in the 200 meters. News broke that Brazilian authorities found American swimmer Ryan Lochte's story about being robbed at gunpoint to be a fabrication. Security footage was uncovered showing Lochte and three other swimmers starting an altercation at a gas station and doing some damage. *San Francisco Chronicle* columnist Ann Killion wrote: "It doesn't matter what else Lochte has done in his Olympic career. This cemented his legacy: most embarrassing Olympic athlete." Lochte had won 12 medals. The next day Lochte apologized for his behavior and his untruthfulness.

With more rain falling in Houston, the black cloud seemed to be following the Astros to Baltimore. The game was at Oriole Park at Camden Yards, near the boyhood home of Babe Ruth. Baltimore began the night two games behind Toronto for the AL East lead. Kevin Gausman of Baltimore set a strong tone by striking out three of the first four batters. But Joe Musgrove was attacked by the AL's home run leaders. Mark Trumbo ripped a three-run first inning "Trumbomb" to trigger an explosion of six homers by the Orioles. Chris Davis and J.J. Hardy each homered twice and the Orioles waltzed to a 13-5 win. The Houston bullpen was taxed, so first baseman Tyler White pitched the eighth inning and surrendered a home run.

The Orioles ran their league-leading total to 183 home runs.

Major league baseball owners, meeting in Houston, were considering changes to the game on the field. Commissioner Rob Manfred mentioned the possibility of adding a 20-second clock on the field to speed up the game. "I would because there's no temporal assigned to that," said Manfred if he would want a 20-second time clock. He also discussed limiting pitching changes and altering the strike zone. All of those ideas would be in play, he said, in negotiations on a new basic agreement with the players' association.

August 19---As the game started in Baltimore, George Springer belted his sixth leadoff homer of the season. Jose Altuve also had hit six, giving the club 12 leadoff homers. Home run balls cascaded down on the fans at Camden Yards – a total of nine of them! For the first time in major league history, a team hit four home runs from the first five batters in the game. Baltimore tattooed Collin McHugh in a five-run first. Adam Jones led off by going deep. Hyun-Soo Kim followed with a single. Then Manny Machado, Chris Davis and Mark Trumbo all homered for a 5-1 lead with nobody out! The five-game Houston losing streak made this a huge hill to climb.

What followed was even more spectacular. The Astros got up off the canvas and became the first Houston team in history to win while allowing five homers. They banged out five runs on five hits in the second off Wade Miley. Miley was removed for Ubaldo Jimenez. With the Astros leading 7-6 in the fourth, McHugh gave way to Chris Devenski. "The Dragon" saved the day and became the winning pitcher, giving up one run in four innings. It was his ninth relief outing of three innings or more.

Jose Altuve reached a major milestone with his 20th home run in the sixth inning. He became a member of the "20-20 Club" for home runs and steals in the same season. Carlos Beltran was the last Astro to do it in 2004. He was traded by Kansas City to Houston that year but he reached 20-20 status during his games with Houston.

Altuve also reached 80 RBI. During the game, a throw from catcher Evan Gattis to Altuve between innings hit him on the collarbone when he failed to catch it. He smiled after the game on a TV interview and said he was fine when asked about the incident. "I know this game is going to create some momentum and we're going to keep winning games," said Altuve.

Hack Wilson was the only other player 5-6 or shorter to have a 20-home run season. The last time he did it came in 1932 for the Chicago Cubs. Wilson had a much thicker build and was listed at 190 pounds. Altuve was listed at 165. Wilson leads all 5-6 or shorter players in career home runs with 244. Altuve now has 60 to rank second.

"For anybody, hitting 20 homers is obviously great, but he's doing it hitting .368 or whatever it is, so that's impressive," said George Springer.

"He is every bit of what we're all about," said A.J. Hinch. "He's got a good supporting cast when we're at our best, but it doesn't shock me when he finds his way into the middle of it."

August 20---Baltimore brought 15-game winner Chris Tillman to the mound after scratching him from a scheduled start a few days earlier. Tillman's arm was the subject of speculation at this point. George Springer led off with a single and Alex Bregman blasted a home run off Tillman to get Houston started.

Tillman did not leave until allowing six runs in two innings. Springer banged a two-run homer in a 14-hit Houston attack. The Astros, with Mike Fiers the winner, put Baltimore away 12-2. "I needed it," said Fiers. "The team needed it. I think everybody needed it. We need to get rolling here and put a bunch of wins together. We know it's going to come down to the end and one game could be the difference like it was last year."

After the game, A.J. Hinch announced the promotion of Yuliesky Gurriel to the major league club effective the next day.

"He got up to 50 at bats with us in the minor leagues," said Hinch. "That's a normal spring training for him. We've bounced him around the country. But from a baseball standpoint, he's ready and he's ready for this challenge." Tyler White was optioned to Fresno. The Astros trailed by 4 ½ games in the race for the second wild card spot, tied for fourth place in that race.

Luis Valbuena was sent home after a setback with his hamstring injury following a workout Friday. "So as the limp got worse and he tried to push through it, we shut it down and took it inside," said Hinch. "The more he rested and the more he cooled down, the worse he felt. He was pretty upset, so we decided to send him home."

The Texas Rangers signed free agent outfielder Carlos Gomez. He would need a few minor league games before joining them.

August 21---Closing Olympic ceremonies in Rio highlighted a day including a U.S. men's basketball gold medal winning game. Kevin Durant led the way to the win over Serbia. The U.S. won the most medals and the most gold medals.

There was rain in Houston and in Baltimore. The Astros-Orioles game was delayed four hours at the outset and another half hour during the game. Dallas Keuchel was angry at the way the weather situation was handled, not being told about the initial delay. He came out to warm up and noticed his mound opponent, Yovani Gallardo, was not on the field. Then, after the four-hour delay, the game started only to be stopped after a half hour by more rain. Keuchel said he channeled his anger into performing well and wound up with his best fastball of the season. He stopped the hard-hitting Birds on five hits and two runs in eight innings and beat them 5-3.

"Major league baseball is not meant to be played like that," said Keuchel. "I don't really condone that type of setup before the game. We're kind of sitting around for four hours, and then all of a sudden, we have a 30-minute window to play.

"If we want good, professional baseball, that can't happen. Then we get one inning in and another rain delay. I don't know who makes the calls around here, but that was pretty subpar."

Carlos Correa lined a two-run double to right in the win. The Astros left for Pittsburgh much later than scheduled but happy with taking three of four from Baltimore. The losses knocked Baltimore into the second wild card spot. The Astros climbed to 64-60, 3 ½ games behind Baltimore for that wild card spot.

Yuliesky Gurriel got a hit in his first major league plate appearance, batting sixth at the DH spot against the Orioles. He also walked and grounded out.

But he left the game after tweaking his hamstring and A.J. Hinch did not plan to play him Monday night in Pittsburgh. "This is a dream of mine for years," said Gurriel. "Not only for me to make it but a Cuban player to make it to the big leagues is a big deal."

The Astros struck out only five times in this game. They bunched three of their nine hits in their three-run fifth. If Alex Bregman, Gurriel and Teoscar Hernandez could add contact hitting to the others in the lineup, including A.J. Reed, the attack could be much more consistent. And if Keuchel went on a hot streak, things would be looking up.

August 22---A federal judge in Texas struck down the Obama administration's directive on transgender bathrooms, effective blocking the change on the first day of school in Texas.

At PNC Park in Pittsburgh, The Woodlands' Jamieson Taillon took the mound for Pittsburgh against his hometown team. The second overall pick in the 2010 draft, Taillon had missed the two previous seasons recovering from Tommy John surgery. He bounced back well in 2016. Taillon continued his resurgence by retiring the first 11 Astros, fanning five of the first seven batters. Doug Fister matched him with hitless baseball in the first three innings.

In the fifth, A.J. Reed led off with a walk. Teoscar Hernandez ripped a 3-1 inside fastball for a two-run home run to left field. The 2-0 lead held up, with both clubs scoring a run in the ninth for a 3-1 Houston win. Winners of six of their last nine road series, the Astros grabbed a leg up in this three-game set. Alex Bregman added a ninth inning home run. Houston still trailed by 3 ½ games in the race for the second wild card spot.

August 23---Before the game in Pittsburgh, A.J. Hinch announced that Luis Valbuena would be having surgery on his right hamstring tendon in the next few days. "He tried to play through it and see if he could rehab it," Hinch said. "Turns out he couldn't. Surgery is the next consideration, and he'll miss the remainder of the season."

Pittsburgh's Ivan Nova handcuffed Houston on six hits in a 7-1 complete game win. Joe Musgrove allowed hits to the first six batters, trailing 4-0 before he got an out. His ERA rose to 5.20 in the loss. "I throw a lot of strikes, and that's been a strength for me," said Musgrove. "Up here, guys don't miss pitches as much, so I'm going to have to learn to throw more quality balls in certain counts. I just made bad pitches tonight, and they took advantage of it."

Jose Altuve went 1-for-4 with an RBI double in the ninth. He lined to right field in the first and was robbed by David Freese at third with a lunging stab in the sixth. Altuve now had 37 doubles and 83 RBI. Altuve already had enough plate appearances (502) to qualify for the batting title. With a .363 batting average, Altuve was 42 points ahead of David Ortiz. If he did not play another game, he would undoubtedly win the batting title!

August 24---The most decorated U.S. female gymnast in history, Simone Biles, arrived home and was honored with a parade in Spring, Texas.

Faced with a 12:30 start time in Pittsburgh, A.J. Hinch was still without Yuliesky Gurriel in his lineup.

He chose not to play Gurriel in the spacious PNC Park left field to avoid reinjuring his hamstring. Marwin Gonzalez was in left field. Carlos Correa was taken out the night before after the seventh inning because he was affected by the illness that had invaded the Astros' clubhouse.

With the Astros 4 ½ games out of the second wild card spot, this game was critical. Five teams were ahead of them in the race for the final playoff spot. Pittsburgh ace Gerrit Cole and a rested Pirate bullpen were waiting for them. But Cole continued his August struggles. Correa lined a single between his legs into center field. The ball left Correa's bat at 107 mph. Evan Gattis ripped a two-run homer into the shrubs above the center field wall. Gattis hit his 20th home run for his fourth consecutive season as a major leaguer. "It means a lot to me, hitting 20 for four years," Gattis said. "It's definitely a milestone. I'm glad it happened."

The Houston lead grew to 5-1 in the fifth before the Pirates closed the gap against Collin McHugh to 5-3. Then the managers began to make moves in this game in a National League park.

Chris Devenski entered the game in the sixth. A.J. Hinch triggered several moves, inserting Devenski into the seventh spot in the batting order and removing A.J. Reed. He moved Marwin Gonzalez from left field to first base to replace Reed, moved Teoscar Hernandez from center field to left field, inserting Jake Marisnick in the ninth spot playing center field. In the eighth, he called on Gurriel as a pinch hitter. A concoction of four relievers worked under pressure, with Ken Giles nailing down the save in a ten-pitch ninth. Giles seemed to have regained his swagger, jumping up and down while looking to the outfield after a strikeout of Gregory Polanco to end the game. It was his most important outing as an Astro.

The Pirates were involved in the NL wild card scramble, and this game was meaningful for both teams. Houston put the final touches on a 5-2 road trip to two contending clubs' home parks. The players loaded onto buses for a trip home for a day off.

"I'm really proud of our guys," said Hinch. "We have a small margin for error these days, and our guys are responding by playing well. The schedule's running out, so we need as many wins as we can get. We play this kind of baseball where we deliver a big blow, we pitch well, we have some situational hitting, then we feel like we can find some wins. But again, there will be a one-game mentality for us. We've got to show up on Friday after the day off ready to play."

In the MVP race, Boston's David Ortiz belted his 30th homer at Tampa Bay, becoming the oldest player to have a 30-home run season at age 40 years, 280 days. Texas' Adrian Beltre lined a winning ninth inning double and made a spectacular play to end a 6-5 win at Cincinnati. Detroit's Miguel Cabrera had four hits, including his 28th homer to lead the Tigers to a 9-4 win. The MVP race was every bit as hot as the wild card race.

August 25---On an off day for the Astros, Carlos Gomez hit a home run in his first at bat for the Texas Rangers. The Rangers beat Cleveland 8-0. Boston, Toronto, Baltimore and Seattle all lost. The idle Astros gained a half game on all of them in the wild card race and now trailed by four games.

Marc Rzepcynski was traded from Oakland to Washington. Jeff Francouer was dealt by Atlanta to Miami.

Philadelphia's Carlos Ruiz exchanged uniforms with A.J. Ellis of the Dodgers in another move involving backup catchers. The Dodgers benefitted from the trade in a major way when Ruiz provided the go-ahead hit in the seventh inning in Game 5 of the NLDS October 14, sending them to a 4-3 win over Washington. Ruiz caught Clayton Kershaw, who finished the game in relief.

August 26---With Tampa Bay at Minute Maid Park to open a six-game home stand, the Astros were trying to shake off seven losses in their last eight home games. The Rays had a 22-8 record against the Astros since 2010.

The Astros took a 3-0 lead off Drew Smyly after two innings, but the Rays came back to tie it 3-3 after Mike Fiers left on Corey Dickerson's third double of the night.

The ninth inning was packed with drama. With two outs, Mikie Mahtook ripped a Ken Giles fastball onto the railroad tracks in left field for a 4-3 Rays lead. With Alex Colome shooting for his 29th save in 30 attempts, Carlos Correa led off the home ninth with a tying home run to right field. Evan Gattis worked the count to 3-2 before tomahawking a neck-high fastball for a walk off home run, sending the crowd into a frenzy. Gattis got to home plate and his teammates ripped his jersey open, exposing his bare chest. It was the first time in Houston club history the Astros won a game on a walk off homer back-to-back with a tying homer. The Astros sliced a game off the Rangers' lead and trailed by 7 ½ games. They also moved a game closer in the wild card standings, trailing by three.

"It was one of the best at bats all year," Correa said of Gattis' winner. Even the pitch he hit was a ball up in the zone and he was able to zing it up top and drive it out of the ballpark, so that was pretty amazing."

"I don't think any of us know how Gattis hit that pitch out," Marisnick said. "That pitch was at his neck. The excitement in the stadium and in the dugout, that was awesome."

"Emotional wins can lift a team," said A.J. Hinch. "The clubhouse is screaming. We got to watch Gattis strip his clothes off. That was entertaining, and we get to walk out of here with a nice walk off for the fans."

Colin Kaepernick

San Francisco 49ers backup quarterback Colin Kaepernick sat during the playing of the national anthem before a preseason contest. "I am not going to stand up to show pride in a flag for a country that opposes black people and people of color," said the biracial QB who started the 2012 Super Bowl loss to Baltimore.

"To me, this is bigger than football and it would be selfish on my part to look the other way. There are bodies in the street and people getting paid leave and getting away with murder." Kaepernick was referencing shootings of blacks by police leading to the Black Lives Matter movement.

Arizona Diamondbacks chief baseball officer Tony LaRussa, a Hall of Fame manager, expressed his sentiments on a national radio show. "I would tell (a player protesting the anthem) to sit inside the clubhouse," he said. "You're not going to be out there representing our team and our organization by disrespecting the flag. No sir, I would not allow it...If you want to make your statement you make it in the clubhouse, but not out there, you're not going to show it that way publicly and disrespectfully."

The chancellor of the University of Texas, retired U.S. Navy four-star admiral William McRaven, told system presidents and athletic directors that sitting during the national anthem to protest the U.S. flag is "disrespecting everyone who sacrificed to make this country what it is today – as imperfect as it might be." McRaven wrote in a memo: "Those that believe the flag represents oppression should remember all the Americans who fought to eliminate bigotry, racism, sexism, imperialism, communism and terrorism."

Kaepernick said he would continue to protest until he feels "the flag represents what it's supposed to represent. Nothing has ever been done without criticism. Every great change, whether it is revolution or evolution of things there is always criticism and there is always that 'I don't like change' kind of mentality. In the long run they will see what is going on, they will see what is right, and they will understand."

What is the flag supposed to represent? According to Wikipedia, the modern meaning of the flag changed in 1860. Before that year, it served mostly as a convenient marking of American territory.

But in the weeks after the U.S. garrison was moved to Fort Sumter in Charleston Harbor, the flag was used to symbolize American nationalism and the rejection of secession by Southern states. The flag turned into a powerful symbol of Americanism. The Bill of Rights as stated in the U.S. Constitution protects free speech and the right to demonstrate as Kaepernick did. But many objected to Kaepernick's chosen method of protest. Should a person refuse to pay tribute to the flag, which represents the freedoms that allow him to refuse to honor it? Or should he protest police brutality in a different place than a football stadium? Jacksonville Jaguars defensive end Jared Odrick wrote a column in *Sports Illustrated.*

"Exercising a First Amendment right isn't an affront to our military," wrote Odrick. "The notion that the flag is sacred and untouchable – or that it has pledged the same allegiance to everyone – is one of the great hypocrisies of our time."

The protest triggered a national conversation about how an athlete should call attention to a cause. The 49ers and the National Football League issued statements asserting the rights of players to participate or fail to participate in the celebration of the national anthem. Police and first responders reacted swiftly against Kaepernick's form of protest. Veterans groups also expressed their outrage at this form of social protest. As a result of a conversation with former NFL player and U.S. military veteran Nate Boyer, Kaepernick changed his form of making a statement. He decided to kneel rather than sit during the anthem as he had for previous games. He mentioned his decision to switch tactics was an attempt to show more respect to veterans while still protesting the anthem.

His teammate Eric Reid joined him the second time he protested, this time by kneeling. "We are respectfully taking up this issue with the national anthem in order to raise awareness," said Reid. "It's not meant to disrespect the military. We have the utmost respect for the people who serve and put their lives on the line for this country. We love this country so much, we just want it to be better."

Reid mentioned supporting veterans groups, standing up against police brutality and supporting equal pay for women.

Kaepernick was brought up with a church background. His touchdown pose, nicknamed "Kaepernicking," involved kissing his right bicep where he had tattoos with "Faith," "To God the Glory," and Psalm 18:39. He had said earlier in his life, "God has brought me this far. He has laid out a phenomenal path for me. And I can't do anything but thank Him."

As the sporting events flashed by quickly just as storefronts flash by the window of a passing taxicab, Kaepernick's actions and comments brought some pause for sports fans. Is it proper and necessary for an athlete to involve himself in a social cause? Jim Brown had done it many times after retiring from the NFL. Others, including Olympians John Carlos and Tommie Smith in 1968, had risked their popularity and reputations by taking public stances against what they felt were injustices.

Was it essential for athletes to repeat commentary made by others in different arenas of the workforce? Did the publicity given to athletes unfairly afford them a platform to take their arguments to a deeper public consciousness? All of these questions were in play.

At Crosby (Texas) High School football coach and athletic director Jeff Riordan talked to his student-athletes and warned them to stand for the anthem or be sent to the locker room. Some team members complained and that decision was reversed days later. Players decided to kneel during the coin toss and stand for the anthem. An entire youth football team in Beaumont, Texas knelt for the anthem. An education law professor, Joe Dryden, said students' rights not to stand for the anthem at extracurricular activities is a gray area not protected by the 1943 Supreme Court ruling giving students those rights. A sporting event falls under a different category because it involves voluntary participation outside the classroom.

In an interview days later, Adam Jones of the Baltimore Orioles said baseball players had not joined Kaepernick in his national anthem protest because "Baseball is a white man's sport. We already have two strikes against us." African Americans make up about eight percent of major league rosters. "So you might as well not kick yourself out of the game," said Jones. "In football, you can't kick them out. You need those players. In baseball, they don't need us." This was a separate issue Jones was raising. Jones said he'd never consider not standing for the anthem. His father spent 22 years in the Navy and his brother also served in the military. In 1975 there were 27 per cent of blacks on rosters.

Baseball was integrated in 1947 when Jackie Robinson joined the Brooklyn Dodgers. The U.S. Army had not been integrated at that time. In the past five years, 20 per cent of first round draft choices were African American. Major league baseball had planted six urban youth academies around the country and they involved 20,000 inner city players. MLB's RBI (Reviving Baseball in Inner Cities) program involved 230,000 participants. And the sport had never been so diverse, with 36 per cent of rosters including black and foreign born players.

The Astros' Tony Sipp talked about his family's roots in slavery in Mississippi. "I look at it different," said Sipp. "When I look at what I overcame, it makes me even more proud of where I am now than to be bitter about it. I take pride that it was a little harder for me to get to where I am right now, because it means more." On the Kaepernick issue Sipp added, "If I had any advice, be a little more specific about what it is that you want to stand for."

New York Times columnist David Brooks wrote: "I hear you when you say you are unhappy with the way things are going in America. But the answer to what's wrong in America is America – the aspirations passed down generation after generation and sung in unison week by week.

"We have a crisis of solidarity. That makes it hard to solve every other problem we have.

"When you stand and sing the national anthem, you are building a little solidarity, and you're singing a radical song about a radical place."

Brooks also pointed out in his column that Martin Luther King sang the national anthem before his "I Have a Dream" speech and then quoted the Declaration of Independence within it. "When we sing the national anthem, we're not commenting on the state of America," wrote King. "We're fortifying our foundational creed. We're expressing gratitude for our ancestors and what they left us. We're expressing commitment to the nation's ideals, which we have not yet fulfilled."

August 27---Fans lined up early for Jose Altuve bobbleheads. The bobblehead featured a gold glove and a silver slugger as part of the Altuve likeness.

Dallas Keuchel, 0-4 with a 5.11 career ERA against Tampa Bay, worked around two Alex Bregman errors in the first two innings. He escaped a bases-loaded, one-out jam in the second with a Corey Dickerson double play ball.

Then the Astros went to work on Tampa Bay lefty Blake Snell, with three straight doubles from Carlos Correa, Evan Gattis and Yuliesky Gurriel. Gurriel picked up a pair of doubles in the game and drove in his first two runs as a major leaguer. Bregman ripped a two-run homer in the 6-2 Houston win, pulling the Astros to within two games of Baltimore for the second wild card spot. Baltimore, Detroit, Seattle and Kansas City all lost, allowing the Astros a rare opportunity to pick up a game on four contenders in the same day. Seattle fell into a second place tie with Houston.

August 28---In South Williamsport, Pennsylvania, George and Laura Springer were honored as George and Barbara Bush Little League Parents of the Year. The Springers raised three Little Leaguers - not only their son George III, the right fielder for the Astros, but their daughters Lena and Nicole, who were softball standouts.

In downtown Houston, a small ceremony marked the 180th anniversary of the founding of the city by the Allen brothers from New York. The Allens banked their boat on a sandbar where White Oak and Buffalo bayous converge and named the area Houston. It was plagued by mosquitoes August 30, 1836. The native Karankawa smeared gator fat and dirt on themselves to keep the insect swarms away and avoid devastating epidemics.

Dog owners led their pets around the warning track on "Bark in the Park" day before the game. Tampa Bay ace Chris Archer fired his unhittable slider many times in seven innings, fanning 10 Astros in a 10-4 Rays win. The loss dropped the Astros three games back in the wild card race. When Archer fanned Springer for his 10th strikeout, Springer yelled at Archer, "Act like you've struck out somebody before." Archer had pumped his fist when he got the final out of the seventh leading 4-3. Archer yelled back at Springer. "I'm just having fun. This is a game." They smoothed over the exchange later and parted on amicable terms.

On Sunday Night Baseball on ESPN, Boston blew a 4-2 lead when Kansas City exploded for eight runs in the sixth in a 10-4 KC win.

Boston and Baltimore were the wild card leaders with Detroit two games behind and Houston in a three-way tie three games out. The ESPN broadcasters agreed that the AL MVP race was wide open with about a month remaining.

Patrick Reed of Spring, Texas qualified for the Ryder Cup golf team by winning The Barclays at Bethpage Black in New York.

August 29---A smallish crowd of 18,615 watched Joe Musgrove take the mound with a different mindset than in his last start, a 7-1 loss at Pittsburgh. Musgrove was determined to pitch with more intensity early in the game rather than trying to preserve his energy some and stay in the game longer. Mixing up his offerings and hitting the edges of the strike zone, Musgrove held Oakland scoreless and left with a 2-0 lead in the sixth and two men on base.

"That's the kind of pitcher I am," Musgrove said. "I've got to be the guy that goes as hard as I can as long as I can, and the past couple of outings I kind of got away from that."

Luke Gregerson came in from the bullpen for the first time in 11 days. Recovering from an ankle sprain from stepping in a hole on the field in Baltimore, Gregerson induced a double play on his second pitch. Pat Neshek and Brad Peacock collaborated on the four-pitcher 6-0 shutout win. "Just trying to get my feet back in there and do what I normally do and it just happened to work out that way," Gregerson said. "It was nice." With Gregerson, Neshek, Will Harris and Ken Giles the Astros had a fighting chance to hold leads in the final month.

Jose Altuve hit a low breaking pitch into the Crawford Boxes for his second home run in two days. Carlos Correa drove in a run to tie Miguel Tejada's club record RBI total of 86 for a shortstop from 2009.

With Baltimore losing to Toronto, the Astros moved to within two games of the second wild card spot. They had gained four games in the wild card chase since August 19.

August 30---The team photo was taken before batting practice with players situated on risers around the home plate area. If the photo had been taken in July, it would have looked quite different. It would not have included Yuliesky Gurriel, Tony Kemp, Teoscar Hernandez or Alex Bregman.

Around the batting cage before the game, Jose Altuve and Bregman wore each others' jerseys.

Colby Rasmus returned from the disabled list without any minor league injury rehab time. Rasmus told reporters he had done the same thing in 2013 with Toronto and he had hit four homers in his first four games back. After his surgery to remove a cyst in his right ear, Rasmus regained his strength and had some strenuous workouts. He and his manager were convinced he did not need at bats in the minor leagues.

A.J. Hinch needed him against righthander Kendall Graveman, who had pitched two strong games against the Astros. Hinch referred to the loss of lefthanded hitter Luis Valbuena and how the Astros needed another lefthanded hitter in their lineup. Rasmus was in left field, batting sixth. He came to the plate in the second inning, saddled with an 0-for-23 slump. His last big league hit was July 29. On a 1-2 pitch, he swung and unleashed a Colby Jack, a soaring home run into the right field seats for a 1-0 lead. Collin McHugh stopped Oakland for six shutout innings and the Astros carved out a 3-1 win, keeping them two games out in the wild card race.

August 31---Baltimore traded for outfielder Michael Bourn so he would be eligible for a postseason roster.

Brian McTaggart wrote at MLB.com: "As far as rallies go, this was about as improbable as they get for Houston, though manager A.J. Hinch joked it happened just the way he drew it up. After sleepwalking offensively for 7 2/3 innings Wednesday afternoon, the Astros pulled off perhaps their most unlikely rally of the year by scoring three times with two outs in the eighth to stun the A's 4-3 and sweep the series at Minute Maid Park."

Mike Fiers stumbled through five innings, allowing eight hits and three runs. The unearned runs came in the second after Carlos Correa was charged with an error on Joey Wendle's hard ground ball. Many balls were hit hard off Fiers, who trailed 3-0 after three innings.

Lefty Ross Detwiler kept the Astros off balance through seven, leaving with a 3-1 lead. Liam Henricks got the first two outs in the ninth. George Springer ripped a triple to right center. With the count 2-2 on Alex Bregman, he swung and missed at a pitch in the dirt. Rookie catcher Bruce Maxwell failed to block the pitch, allowing Bregman to reach first base on the strikeout and Springer to score from third. Jose Altuve ripped a 1-2 fastball for a triple, scoring Bregman to tie the game 3-3. After an intentional walk to Correa, Evan Gattis lined an RBI single to left for his second winning hit in the final at bat on the homestand.

The small crowd of 20,033 came to life during the stirring three-run eighth and witnessed a 4-3 thriller. "We didn't play extraordinarily well today until the very end," said A.J. Hinch. "We had two really big hits with the two triples, and then Gattis after the intentional walk. That inning was about the only offense we brought to the table today. It was enough to get the win. Just proud of our guys for being resilient and keep coming back to win some games."

The 5-1 homestand equaled the team's best of the season and added win number 71. With Baltimore losing to Toronto, the Astros moved to within one game of the second wild card spot. Detroit also won and moved into a tie with Baltimore for that second wild card position.

August ended with a 16-13 record for Houston, its fourth straight winning month. A brutal stretch was next, with the next 13 games against first place teams. The players headed for home before departing for North Texas the next day, which was a day off.

Brian T. Smith wrote in the *Houston Chronicle*: "These super-streaky, sometimes frustrating, randomly thrilling 2016 Astros? They're fun again as September begins."

Jake Kaplan wrote, "The streakiest team in baseball capped its streakiest month with perhaps its most important come-from-behind win of the season."

August statistics

The Astros record of 16-13 included 138 runs scored to their opponents' 125. Their ERA was 4.00.

The club's top hitters were Jose Altuve (.333-4-27). Carlos Correa (.304-4-23), Evan Gattis (.311-5-14) and Alex Bregman (.274-5-20).

The top pitchers were Dallas Keuchel (3-1, 3.10 ERA). Chris Devenski (2-2, 1.85 ERA), Doug Fister (2-2, 3.15 ERA) and Ken Giles (1-0, 2.31 ERA, 6 saves)

August Standings in AL West

Texas   80-54 -

Houston 71-62 -8.5

Seattle   68-65 -11.5

LAA   59-74 -20.5

Oakland   57-76 -22.5

---

10 September: Shuffle of Wild Cards

Beginning September with a 70-62 record, the Astros were two games out of the second wild card position.

As the month evolved, the team was unable to gain ground in a string of 13 straight games against first-place teams. The 5-8 record against Texas, Cleveland and the Chicago Cubs cost the Astros dearly. They were without their top two starting pitchers, Dallas Keuchel and Lance McCullers, for the entire month. That led to rookies and minor league callups starting 10 games and the bullpen being overtaxed. The staff ERA for September was 4.85.

The biggest backbreakers were three consecutive losses at home to the Los Angeles Angels. In two of those losses the Astros lost leads in the late innings. The final record of 84-78 was two games short of the team's 2015 finish.

September Game by Game Accounts

September 1---Florida braced for Hurricane Hermine, the first hurricane to hit the state in over a decade. It was tracking toward North Carolina as well.

A SpaceX rocket exploded on the launch pad at Cape Canaveral, destroying a $200 million communications satellite that would have extended Facebook's territory across Africa. An impact could be felt later on NASA's cargo deliveries to the space station.

The Houston Texans beat the Dallas Cowboys in Dallas to complete a 4-0 preseason.

Sadly, cancer patient Dylan Tindall-Heathcock passed away. Jose Altuve, Carlos Correa and other players spent some time with him earlier in the season and Altuve hit a home run after the youngster requested it. Coincidentally, major league players wore yellow wristbands in support of Childhood Cancer Awareness Month.

On this date, major league rosters can be expanded from 25 to 40. Most teams call up a few minor leaguers and their rosters swell to 32 or 33. The Astros planned two waves of promotions but did not announce them yet. They took a late afternoon charter flight to Dallas on the day off.

With only a few teams scheduled to play, some media attention went to the AL MVP race. September would decide the winner, and how the teams fared would play into the voting as well. These were the top five contenders, in no particular order, and their statistics in batting average, home runs and RBI:

Mike Trout, LAA: .319-25-84 Josh Donaldson, Toronto: .296-34-92 Jose Altuve, Houston .351-22-89 Mookie Betts, Boston: .320-30-96 Manny Machado, Baltimore: .305-32-83

David Ortiz of Boston was having a fantastic offensive year, but since he was a DH the voters could not in conscience give him consideration equal to the others.

September 2---Houston's September callups included James Hoyt, Jandel Gustave, Tyler White and Brady Rodgers. Rodgers was spending his first day in the majors, taking photos with his family during batting practice at Globe Life Park. He grew up in the Houston area rooting for the Astros. Rodgers was voted the Pacific Coast League Pitcher of the Year, finishing 12-4 with a 2.86 ERA, walking 23 and striking out 116.

A number of Astros fans made the trip to Arlington for the big series. The Astros were 2-11 against Texas, 1-6 at Globe Life Park.

Texas had outscored them 53-38. The Rangers led them by 8 ½ games.

Alex Bregman homered in the first off A.J. Griffin and Evan Gattis made it 2-0 on a sacrifice fly. But Texas countered with two off Doug Fister in the second after an error by Bregman.

Fister was moving into Dallas Keuchel's spot in the rotation because Keuchel was experiencing soreness in his left shoulder. Fister was working on four days rest. Keuchel was being pushed back four more days for his next start, which would be against Cleveland.

"We're just going to give it as much time as possible," Hinch said. "He's not responding to the in-between starts as well as we wanted him to."

The Rangers sent ten men to the plate in the seven-run fourth, belting three home runs. That headed them off to a 10-8 win. The Astros fought back from a 9-2 deficit but could not overcome the fourth inning.

September 3---On the first college football weekend of the season, the Houston Cougars upset Oklahoma at NRG Stadium 33-23. Texas A&M beat UCLA in overtime. LSU was upset by Wisconsin in Green Bay.

Playing in 87 degree heat in a 3:10 start for network television, Joe Musgrove and Derek Holland both had quick first innings. The Rangers mounted another middle inning onslaught, banging out a 12-4 whipping of the Astros to build a 10 ½ game margin over their in-state rivals. This was the most lopsided score of the season between the two.

To make matters worse, Jose Altuve pulled up limping on the ending double play ball with discomfort in his right calf. The Astros seemed undermanned and lacking fight. Their pitchers were not moving the Rangers hitters away from home plate.

September 4---Pope Francis named Mother Teresa a saint. "She bowed down before those who were spent, left to die on the side of the road, seeing in them their God-given dignity," said the Pope.

"Must win" was not a term baseball teams used in early September. But it applied to this game. The Astros were outscored 22-12 in the first two games of the series at Globe Life Park and they lost two games in two days to Baltimore in the wild card race. They were now 2-12 against Texas and 1-8 in Arlington. Texas had won 21 of 25 from Houston.

What was the biggest issue? Starting pitching was at the forefront. The Astros were hitting only .213 against Rangers' starters with a .347 slugging percentage in the 14 games. The heart of the Houston lineup had been stopped. In the season series, Texas had outscored Houston 75-50. After this game, the trio of George Springer-Jose Altuve-Carlos Correa was hitting a combined .205 against Texas this season.

Yu Darvish, who had allowed one run in 12 innings against Houston in 2016, was greeted by George Springer's seventh leadoff home run of the season. Yuli Gurriel also drove in a run in the first.

Jose Altuve was in the lineup as the DH, with his calf muscle getting some relief from the cramping that caused the problem Saturday. But his slump continued after an 0-for-3 day. Pitchers were throwing slow curves at the bottom of his strike zone and borderline fastballs. After this game, Altuve had dropped 20 points since game one of the August 11 twinbill, from .366 to .346. He was hitting .289 on offspeed pitches since the All-Star break, compared to .321 before the break. His walk rate was down and his strikeout rate was up in that six-week period of time. "I'm seeing a little anxiousness," Hinch said of Altuve. "As you get towards this time of year, guys always want to carry the team and he knows he's a central figure of our offense. So he gets a little bit anxious at the plate. I see him a little more pull-conscious than when he's at his best."

Collin McHugh was starting several of the Rangers with slow curve balls. He kept them at bay for three innings until Rougned Odor ripped a two-run homer off him. Houston had built a 5-0 lead. After five it was 6-5 Astros. "I made some good pitches and some bad pitches, and all the bad pitches got hit," said McHugh. "Not a whole lot you can do about it other than tip your hat to them for making good swings."

In the sixth, a critical error by Odor allowed the seventh and final Houston run to score. The Rangers made it close but lost 7-6.

In the sixth inning, Carlos Gomez, now with the Rangers, bunted for a hit and stole second. Carlos Correa dropped the throw from Evan Gattis to second base, which allowed Gomez to slide in headfirst safely. But Gomez' batting helmet fell off his head and bounced off the ground, gashing his left eyebrow. Play was stopped while he got a bandage and the streaming blood was wiped off. As he led off second base, Chris Devenski used an inside spin move to his right for a pickoff throw, but Gomez was safe. Devenski then tried a different move, turning to his left. This time he picked off Gomez. Astros fans enjoyed the turn of events for Gomez, who was on base six times in the series to their chagrin.

Devenski got the win in relief with a clutch performance. Will Harris, Luke Gregerson and Ken Giles each worked an inning to nail down a one-run win against the best team in the majors in one-run games. Giles registered seven pitches 100 mph or better, two more than he had all season entering the game, according to Statcast. With Baltimore losing and Detroit winning, the Astros headed for a four-game series at Cleveland trailing both of those wild card contenders by two games.

Texas beat Notre Dame in a Sunday night college football game in double overtime. The new Texas quarterback, Shane Buechele, debuted on the big stage on network television and played extremely well.

September 5---Labor Day brought cookouts, outings and plenty of sporting events to the U.S. To baseball fans, it marked the start of the final stage of the pennant races. In 2016, they were in for a treat. Of 30 teams, 18 were within five games of a playoff spot. Mark Whicker wrote capsules of each team in *Sports Weekly*: "A 3-13 record against the Rangers has stunted Houston's chances of winning the division, as has a 24-23 record in the second half."

An injury to Lance McCullers and a drop-off by Cy Young Award winner Dallas Keuchel didn't help either. "Jose Altuve has pretty much defined MVP by his amazing season, and the Astros have hung in there despite a game of musical closers.

"This is still a team of the future, but it's probably not now," wrote Whicker.

In Cleveland, the Astros had no chance to pause and celebrate what the labor movement had meant in this land of plenty. They were busy getting ready to play a night game against one of the hottest teams in baseball, the Cleveland Indians.

The pregame news was a blow. Dallas Keuchel was in Houston for examinations on his inflamed left shoulder. Not only would he not be starting the next night; he also would miss his next start over the weekend in Houston against the Chicago Cubs. "We tried to give him some gaps in time in giving him some rest periods," said A.J. Hinch. "That hasn't solved it. He's going to go see the doctors he needs to see, and until he's pain free he's not throwing."

Brad Peacock would rejoin the team as a September callup to take Keuchel's start the next night. Catcher Max Stassi and reliever Kevin Chapman were in Cleveland as two more September reinforcements.

Cleveland manager Terry Francona, with his club in first place with a five-game lead over Detroit, decided to skip Josh Tomlin in his rotation. Tomlin was the only struggling Indians starter in their five-man rotation. Francona said he would use his deep bullpen to get through this game, with September reinforcements a key part of his plan.

Francona chose rookie Mike Clevinger as his starter, with a brief outing in mind. Clevinger allowed a Jose Altuve RBI double in the first. Altuve was hitting .125 in his previous ten games. Alex Bregman ripped a two-run homer in the third off Jeff Manship. The Tribe got to Houston starter Mike Fiers on a long Mike Napoli blast in the fifth and trailed 3-2.

The parade of Cleveland pitchers continued, with three of them seeing action in the three-run Houston eighth.

George Springer's mad dash home on a short sacrifice fly by Yuli Gurriel was a highlight.

Bill Brown

Springer stabbed home plate with his left hand a fraction of a second ahead of Roberto Perez' tag on his back for the fourth run for Houston.

Baltimore and Detroit won to remain two games ahead of the Astros. Toronto and Boston lost.

The 6-2 win played well in the clubhouse. But there were ominous signs from recent games. Although the Astros were 3-2 in their last five games, here were the innings pitched by the starters: Fiers 5, McHugh 4 1/3. Musgrove 4 1/3, Fister 3 2/3, Fiers 5. Fiers needed 92 pitches in his five innings this night.

September 6---*USA Today* announced in the morning that Alex Bregman was its minor league player of the year. The award was created in 1988 and Bregman was the first Astro to win it. In 80 games in the minors between AA Corpus Christi (62 games) and AAA Fresno (18 games), Bregman hit .306 with 20 homers, 61 RBI and a .986 OPS. Of the 27 prior winners of the award, 18 became major league All-Stars.

Bregman was a factor again in the game at Cleveland with an RBI triple. That gave him 27 RBI for Houston. Corey Kluber was the Indians starter, with a 15-8 record and 10 consecutive quality starts. Kluber mowed down the Astros in the first. His mound opponent, Brad Peacock, was not in line for a long night on the mound because he had pitched in relief for Fresno three days ago, throwing about 45 pitches. Peacock was in immediate trouble with runners at second and third and no outs in the first but retired the Tribe's 3-4-5 hitters without a run scoring. Kluber got the first two outs in the second but walked the next two and then surrendered a three-run homer to Marwin Gonzalez on an 0-2 pitch. It was the first time in 193 batters faced that Kluber allowed a home run on an 0-2 count, dating back to early in 2015. Houston led 4-1 in the fourth when A.J. Hinch removed Peacock after 72 pitches with a man on base and two outs. James Hoyt started the parade of five Houston relievers.

The Tribe scored in the eighth and ninth to create a 4-3 game, but Ken Giles got the final two outs under pressure for his ninth save in the 4-3 win.

The Indians were 0-for-12 with men in scoring position.

The Astros climbed to ten games over .500 at 74-64, meaning a 14-10 finish would give them 88 wins.

September 7---Houston oil exploration company Apache announced one of the biggest oil and gas discoveries in years in the West Texas Permian Basin. The equivalent of more than 15 billion barrels of oil were discovered in a relatively unknown quadrant of the basin, Apache said.

Another injury blow, this time involving Carlos Correa, added to the September dilemma of the Astros. Correa was sent back to Houston to see doctors after making diving plays two nights in a row to his right. His left shoulder was inflamed. Alex Bregman started at shortstop in his place.

Doug Fister's September slump continued, with the Indians collecting nine hits and six earned runs off him in 4 1/3 innings. It was the seventh straight start of five innings or less for Houston. Carlos Carrasco gave up a long Colby Rasmus two-run homer, but the Tribe scored four in the fifth and won 6-5. Kevin Chapman gave up a pinch two-run double to Brandon Guyer in that inning. The Orioles and Tigers also lost, leaving the Astros two games behind Baltimore and one behind Detroit.

Midges, tiny bugs that attacked Joba Chamberlain in the 2007 playoffs in Cleveland, swarmed all over the players for the second straight night. Carrasco had to get some medical attention after a midge got in his left eye. He gave up a Gurriel single and a Rasmus homer shortly after play resumed.

September 8---David Paulino made his major league debut at age 22, becoming the last pitcher on the Houston 40-man roster to appear in a 2016 major league game. "I didn't know that this was going to happen,"Paulino said the day before the game. "This is a surprise, and I'm very happy to be here." He had not even pitched 200 innings in his career as a professional, starting three games at AAA Fresno. Earlier, he was suspended for breaking team rules and had more down time with a shoulder problem.

Trevor Bauer gave up a first inning run on Alex Bregman's double. Paulino threw two scoreless innings to start his big league career. With Cleveland ahead 2-1 in the third and the bases loaded, Paulino's pitch to Lonnie Chisenhall was fouled after it bounced. But home plate umpire Jim Joyce did not make the foul ball call. Instead, he made no call. Two runs scored on the play and the other runner kept running while catcher Jason Castro argued with Joyce that the pitch had been fouled. Joyce erroneously called time out during the argument after the second runner, Mike Napoli, scored. The umpires conferred but did not change the call. This type of replay was not reviewable. They put on headsets and conferred about placement of the other runners, since time should not have been called while a play was in progress. Napoli's run was allowed and the Indians led 4-1. A.J. Hinch was ejected and Joyce had a full blown mess on his hands again.

"It's a tough scenario for us, obviously, because I think everybody in the ballpark saw the play as it was, except for the four guys that make the call," said Hinch. "The hitter reaction, the catcher reaction, the bench's reaction, the baserunners' reaction, all sort of proved it was a foul ball.

"It just wasn't the call on the field. Once they couldn't definitively say it was different, they weren't going to overturn it. It's not a call I challenge, not a call I can review. There's nothing you can really do about it but wear it, and it cost us two runs. That type of game, this type of situation, common sense loses again, because it's really a situation we can't do anything about."

"If any of (the other umpires) had it hitting the bat, I would have turned around and called a foul ball," said Joyce. "My partners couldn't help me on it. Since I called time out, I score two runs and put the other guy on third." (Video review later placed the runner at second.) "I've got Jason (Castro), he jumped in front of me. I don't even see the bat, I don't hear the ball hit the bat. I have not seen the play yet. I will be looking at it tonight, you can bank on that."

Joyce blew an easy call at first base June 2, 2010. It cost Detroit pitcher Armando Galarraga a perfect game against Cleveland. Joyce called Jason Donald safe at first on a ground ball to the first baseman. Galarraga took the throw and stepped on first clearly ahead of Donald, but Joyce called Donald safe. When Joyce saw the replay after the game, he was tearful and apologetic to Galarraga, who forgave him. Galarraga finished his career in 2012 with a 26-34 record and a 4.78 ERA. The perfect game would have been his biggest claim to fame by far, but the behavior of the umpire and pitcher in the aftermath of the blown call is remembered as an example of great sportsmanship.

There was a rain delay in the sixth inning. The Indians finished off a 10-7 win to split the four-game series. The Astros headed home from a 3-4 road trip, falling 2 ½ games behind in the wild card race.

September 9---Houston Rockets great Yao Ming was inducted into the Naismith Memorial Basketball Hall of Fame, one of ten new members.

A full house at Minute Maid Park included thousands of Chicago Cubs fans. Jon Lester continued his excellent run in September by winning his 16th, 2-0. Lester stopped the Astros for seven innings. Joe Musgrove proved a worthy opponent, allowing a two-run homer by Kris Bryant for the game's only runs. Bryant was the second player drafted in 2013, after the Astros chose Mark Appel. "You can play that game until you drive yourself crazy in this line of work," said Astros GM Jeff Luhnow about the Appel pick.

"Kris Bryant's a great player. We certainly knew he was going to be selected high in the draft, either 1 or 2, and I think he's had a very good career and the Cubs have benefitted a lot from having him. So, I'm not going to really reflect on it more than that." Bryant was considered the frontrunner for the National League MVP award, and he was the winner in November. Appel had not reached the majors. He was traded to the Phillies in the Ken Giles deal and underwent surgery in 2016.

Musgrove became the first Houston starter to go six innings since August 30.

The Cubs' bullpen closed out the game, with Aroldis Chapman throwing all six of his pitches at 100 mph or faster to get the final three outs. Carlos Correa sat out another game with left shoulder inflammation. Dallas Keuchel remained inactive but said nothing was wrong structurally with his shoulder. Lance McCullers graduated to playing catch from 120 feet with increased velocity but was not throwing from a mound yet. There were 21 games remaining.

The loss kept the Astros 2 ½ games out in the wild card race, but the Yankees now had moved ahead of them. Detroit and Baltimore were now tied for the second wild card spot after the Tigers beat the Orioles.

September 10---On George Springer bobblehead day, the fans packed into Minute Maid Park. Many of them wore Cubs' gear. Collin McHugh started the game well. His opponent, John Lackey, gave up a home run to Alex Bregman in the third inning. Then the Astros turned to small ball. Jose Altuve bunted for a hit, went to third on a single by Yuliesky Gurriel and scored on a squeeze bunt by Marwin Gonzalez. Those were the only runs the Astros scored.

The Cubs got a run in the fourth. McHugh exited after five with a 2-1 lead and four relievers pitched hitless baseball to nail down a 2-1 win with a combined two-hitter. The Astros remained 2 ½ games behind in the race for the second wild card position.

September 11---The nation paid its respects to first responders on the 15ᵗʰ anniversary of the September 11, 2001 attacks on the United States that cost the nation almost 3,000 lives. There were ceremonies in every stadium.

The first NFL Sunday found the Chicago Bears playing the Houston Texans at NRG Stadium, with the Texans winning 23-14 in the afternoon. At night, the Chicago-Houston sports twinbill matched the Cubs and Astros on ESPN Sunday Night Baseball.

Mike Fiers fell behind early and the Cubs built a 7-0 lead after three for Jake Arrieta, who won his 17ᵗʰ. The 9-5 loss dropped the Astros 3 ½ games back in the wild card race with a 75-68 record.

The 2016 Chicago Cubs

The Chicago Cubs captivated many baseball fans with their 24-6 start in 2016. The Cubs and Astros took a parallel path in the previous three years, regrouping with young talent. The Cubs swept the Pirates and the Nationals in back to back series in early May. Their start was the best in the majors in 32 years. They hadn't had a start that good since 1907, when they won the World Series. They won the Series again in 1908, but had not won it since. Seven of the 13 teams with starts as good as 24-6 or better won the World Series since it started in 1903.

When they were 25-8, the Cubs had outscored their opponents by 99 runs. That was an average winning margin of three runs per game!

The highest ERA in their starting rotation after seven starts was John Lackey at 3.54. Jake Arrieta, the 2015 Cy Young Award winner, set the pace with an ERA of 1.13. Jason Hammel checked in at 1.85. Jon Lester was at 1.96 despite problems throwing to first base. Kyle Hendricks had a 3.03 ERA beside his name.

Theo Epstein's Cubs were clearly the class of baseball. They were headed for their first World Series since 1945. Epstein got all due credit for his roster construction.

In 1945, the Cubs lost to the Detroit Tigers in the World Series in seven games. What was called a curse was put on the Cubs by tavern owner Billy Sianis. Sianis owned the Billy Goat Tavern across the street from Wrigley Field. Sianis decided to bring his goat to Game 4 of the World Series at Wrigley, but he was asked to remove his pet goat from the stadium because of the goat's foul odor. Sianis said he was placing a hex on the team, and no Cubs team had been able to break the hex.

In 1984, The Cubs led the San Diego Padres in the NLCS two games to none in the best of five series. A ground ball went through first baseman Leon Durham's legs and the Cubs lost in five games.

In 2003, the Florida Marlins trailed the Cubs three games to two in the NLCS, only to win the next two. Chicago was five outs from the World Series with Mark Pryor on the mound. Cubs fan Steve Bartman tried to catch a foul ball in the stands near the left field line. Cubs left fielder Moises Alou was furious when Bartman touched the foul ball, with Alou's glove just below Bartman's hands. The Cubs lost the game and many blamed the loss on Bartman, who moved to another state and stayed far from Wrigley Field. A curse? A hex? "We've heard the history, but at the same time we're trying to make history," said Cubs center fielder Dexter Fowler.

"We're not going to run away from anything," said Cubs manager Joe Maddon. With their 103 wins, they won more games than any Cubs team since 1910.

The Cubs entered the playoffs as the strongest favorite since the powerful 1998 New York Yankees, who won 114 games during the regular season. Chicago won 57 of its 81 games at home. Since the wild card was introduced into the playoffs in 1995, only four of the teams with the best regular season records had won the World Series. But the Cubs were only the eighth team in the previous 40 years to win eight games more than the next best club.

Fast forward to November 2. The Chicago Cubs were World Champions! Television ratings soared as the Cubs and Cleveland Indians battled through a tense seven-game Series, only to extend the drama into the tenth inning in Game 7. Former Astro farmhand Ben Zobrist, traded to Tampa Bay in 2006 for Aubrey Huff, was holding the trophy as World Series MVP. Zobrist was on the list for his second straight World Series ring. His hit in the tenth inning gave the Cubs the lead. They won 8-7.

The Cubs led the majors in regular season wins with 103. But they did anything but cruise to their first title since 1908. They trailed 3-1 in games after losing the first two at Wrigley Field before finishing with three straight wins.

The comeback began with a 3-2 Cubs' win in their home World Series finale. Aroldis Chapman extended his outing to 2 2/3 innings to protect the lead and earn a "throwback" save with 42 pitches. Rollie Fingers, Goose Gossage and other top closers must have enjoyed that show!

Addison Russell belted a grand slam and drove in six runs in Game 6 in Cleveland, leading the Cubs to a 9-3 thrashing of Cleveland.

With Chicago celebrating in big numbers, baseball observers were wondering if the Cubs were entering an era of dominance. Could a team run off a string of World Series titles the way the Yankees did in the late '90s? The Cubs were in an excellent position. Recent years had brought baseball an unpredictable era of rotating champions. Since 2000, the winners were memorable. Boston three times. San Francisco three times. St. Louis twice. But in 22 seasons in the Wild Card Era since 1995, 12 different teams won the World Series and 20 different teams of the 30 had reached the Fall Classic.

Many things had to work out for a team to become a World Series winner. Staying away from major injuries. Having the right mix of players who worked well together. Getting production from the key players at the right times during the postseason. Staying focused.

The Cubs did all of these things in 2016. Their free agent signings were an important factor in their success. Jason Heyward had a terrible season, but the respect of his teammates showed after his weight room speech in the Game 7 rain delay. Jon Lester and John Lackey contributed in a major way. And it's doubtful that the Cubs could have brought home the trophy without the earlier pressure performances by trade acquisition Aroldis Chapman, regardless of his struggles in Game 7. There will be new challenges in 2017.

September 12---The Astros signed Cuban 20-year-old lefty pitcher Cionel Perez for a $5.15 million bonus. Because the Astros had exceeded their allotted bonus pool of $2.197 million on the first day of the international signing period July 2, they would pay a 100% tax on this signing, which brought the cost to $10.3 million. They would not be allowed to spend more than $300,000 on any international free agents between the ages of 16 and 22 through 2019. Their strategy was to inject three years' worth of international talent into their farm system before the restrictions would begin June 15, 2017. Several organizations were following the same plan, with the assumption that these rules would change before 2017 anyway under the new collective bargaining agreement that was being negotiated at this time. Cionel Perez defected from Cuba in 2015. In late October, the Perez signing was voided by the Astros.

The Texas Rangers opened a critical three-game series at Minute Maid Park. They were 13-3 against the Astros and led them by 9 ½ games. Their head-to-head dominance of Houston accounted for their lead over the second place team, and it was one of the five most dominant performances since 1969 when the division era began for a first place team over a second place team. Seattle was tied for second with Houston.

Doug Fister started for the Astros and allowed two runs in the first.

Martin Perez, his mound opponent, was removed in the seventh with a 3-1 lead. The Astros got a pinch RBI double from Tony Kemp in the seventh. The Rangers called on closer Sam Dyson with a 3-2 lead in the ninth. Evan Gattis ripped a one-out fastball onto the train tracks above the left field wall for a home run to tie the game 3-3.

Rougned Odor smacked a 12th inning 2-0 fastball from James Hoyt over the right field wall for his third hit and third RBI of the game. That sent Texas to a 4-3 win in 12. It was Odor's sixth home run of the season against the Astros and he had driven in 19 runs against them. The Rangers were the kings of one-run games with a 32-10 record. The loss dropped the Astros into third place and kept them 3 ½ games out in the wild card race with four teams in front of them for the second wild card spot. They seemed to have run out of losses for a while if they were to maintain a pulse.

The Rangers stopped Alex Bregman's on base streak at 25 games. It was the third longest in club history for a rookie.

September 13---As Brad Peacock took the mound against the Rangers, he faced a well-oiled offensive machine. He faced only three batters in the first, getting a double play to end the inning. His mound opponent, A.J. Griffin, took the 1-0 lead to the fourth but surrendered it on a home run by Jose Altuve. Jason Castro sent his go-ahead homer well into the right field seats in the sixth for a 2-1 Houston lead. Then, with two outs in the ninth, reliever Ken Giles threw a slider in the dirt. If Castro had been able to block it, Rougned Odor would not have been able to reach first on a strikeout and wild pitch with one out in the ninth. Given the extra out, the Rangers turned it into a 3-2 win. Elvis Andrus tripled with two outs and Jurickson Profar made it 3-2 with his RBI single. Tanner Scheppers closed out the game and Houston fell to 3-15 against Texas. Of the 15 losses, eight were by one run.

"Every loss is tough, especially right now," said Altuve. "Every loss right now is going to cost you a lot."

The Astros dropped 4 ½ games out in the wild card race with 17 to play. Their 4-8 September had cost them dearly.

September 14---Cuban free agent Lourdes Gurriel, Jr. worked out for major league teams in Panama. Ten years younger than his brother Yuliesky, Lourdes was a shortstop/outfielder. "Of course I would love for him to sign here," said Yuliesky. "But there's a lot of variables that go into it, and a lot of things can change." The signing was not expected until October or later, when Lourdes would be 23 and able to negotiate with all teams without penalty. He signed in November with Toronto.

The term "pyrrhic victory" comes from battles in ancient times. It describes an army winning one battle but sustaining so many casualties that it cost that army the war. This game might fit that description for the Astros.

With the Rangers 15-3 against the Astros, this final meeting between the two started with the Rangers taking a 1-0 first inning lead against Joe Musgrove on a Carlos Beltran double. Jeff Banister had changed his starting pitcher from Yu Darvish to Derek Holland, having won the first two games of the series. It appeared he was getting his rotation lined up for the playoffs. Darvish would be pitching over the weekend after Cole Hamels and before Colby Lewis.

George Springer tied the club record with his eighth leadoff homer of the season. Teoscar Hernandez clubbed a two-run shot in the second. The 3-1 lead grew to 5-1 after six. But Jose Altuve was out of the game by then with discomfort in his right oblique after his second at bat. Alex Bregman joined him in the training room with a right hamstring injury after running the bases in the sixth. A.J. Hinch decided to get his best defensive team on the field, and that involved losing the DH when he moved Yuli Gurriel from DH to third base. When a manager moves the DH to a position on the field, the pitcher must be listed as a hitter.

But by the eighth Will Harris was pitching and Hinch put him in the second spot in the lineup, which was due up ninth in the inning. Marwin Gonzalez drove in two in the three-run rally, giving the Astros breathing room at 8-4 instead of taking a one-run lead to the ninth as they did 24 hours earlier when they lost. Gonzalez played three positions in the infield. "I'm prepared to do that," he said. "That's my role on the team. I have to cover it like any spot."

Chris Devenski secured the final three outs and the Astros finished 4-15 against their rivals and went to 76-70 with the 8-4 win. They moved to 3 ½ games out in the wild card race but were in sixth place as they left on the long flight to Seattle. Altuve and Bregman were questionable for Friday's game. Hinch used three second baseman and three third basemen in this game. "It's not great," said Hinch. "I don't like walking our players off the field and have them come out of games, specifically the guys in the middle of the order. That is a punch in the gut."

The experts gave the Astros a 5-8% chance of making the playoffs. If the target was 88 wins for a wild card playoff spot, here's how the contending teams could get there:

Baltimore 8-9 Toronto 9-8 Detroit 10-7 Seattle 10-6 New York 11-6 Houston 12-4

The Astros would need a furious finish and they would need help against the top contenders. They needed to start by winning the series at Seattle. Two wins would put them at 78-71 and would leave Seattle at 79-70.

September 15---Major League Baseball suspended San Diego Padres executive vice president and general manager A.J. Preller for 30 days without pay for withholding medical information on Drew Pomeranz before trading him to Boston.

With the Astros resting in Seattle, they picked up a half game on three contenders. Detroit, Baltimore and New York all lost.

The Yankees suffered a damaging loss to Boston when the Red Sox rallied with five in the ninth at Fenway to win on a three-run Hanley Ramirez walk off home run.

September 16---Vice President Joe Biden spoke at Rice University, where President John Kennedy gave his "Moon Speech " 54 years ago. That was the reason for the selection of Rice. This speech dealt with new government measures to make clinical trials more accessible to patients. Biden touted a new user-friendly government website, Trials.Cancer.gov, which identifies where trials are being conducted for a patient's specific cancer. The goal was to increase participation in trials so more cancer therapies could be discovered. Biden's son Beau died of brain cancer after being diagnosed and treated at M.D. Anderson Cancer Center, which pioneered cutting edge development of cancer treatment.

The torrid Seattle Mariners, riding an eight-game winning streak, sent King Felix Hernandez to the mound at Safeco Field. They were two games ahead of the Astros.

Alex Bregman was not with the team. He stayed in Houston because of his hamstring injury. His absence was reported a few hours before game time. Colin Moran was called up to help in Bregman's absence. Moran had gone home to Florida after the end of the Fresno season.

"It's a loss for us on a lot of fronts," A.J. Hinch said of Bregman. "He's a really good player and he was hitting in the two hole. He was in the middle of a lot of things that were going right for us. So, it's definitely a blow for us." Bregman was expected to miss at least 15 days, which covered the rest of the regular season. "It just needs to heal and it needs to heal over time and with some of the therapies that we do," said Hinch. "But time is not on our side right now." Yuli Gurriel was in Bregman's spot in the lineup, batting second and playing third base.

Jake Marisnick lined a two-run double to the left field corner in the second to grab the lead against King Felix.

Gurriel drilled a single to left in the fourth and the lead grew to 4-0. Collin McHugh beat the Mariners for the fourth time in four starts in 2016, collaborating on a 6-0 win with two relievers.

Like Bregman, Jose Altuve did not travel with the team. Both saw doctors Thursday. Altuve caught a late Thursday flight to Seattle and went 2-for-5, scoring his 100th run. He also collected his 40th double and reached twice on errors. The errors were questioned on the Root Sports TV broadcast by Alan Ashby and Geoff Blum. The current process of appealing official scoring decisions involved the player's agent or his team filing an appeal with major league baseball and a committee reviewing the calls on video and sometimes questioning the official scorer about the decision. With Altuve shooting for his second batting title, those two calls could impact the race. The Astros planned to ask for a review of at least one of the two plays.

Altuve put on a furious round of batting practice before the game in order to be cleared to play. His right oblique discomfort was a red flag. But he displayed his readiness. "That wasn't my swing," Altuve said of the Wednesday swing. "I wanted to strike the ball on that exact pitch, and that's why maybe I felt something. But if I go back to my normal swing I don't think we're going to have any problem." Reporters wanted to know if Altuve would be limited in any way. "I just can't swing and miss," he joked. Blum pointed out on the telecast that not hitting the ball on a swing was more painful with that injury.

The Astros were still four games behind the co-leaders in the wild card race in fifth place, with Seattle one game ahead of them.

September 17---Mariners lefty James Paxton brought a blazing 97 mph fastball into the game, starting with five perfect innings against the Astros. Mike Fiers matched him. The Astros broke through in the sixth on a two-out Yuli Gurriel two-run double. Seattle didn't score until the eighth and lost 2-1.

The win gave the Astros a 78-70 record, tied with Seattle. The Mariners were one of five wild card contenders who lost. The Astros gained a game on all of them, pulling to within three games of co-leaders Toronto and Baltimore. The Houston win meant a three-way tie with both Seattle and Detroit. Now there were no teams between the Astros and the co-leaders.

September 18---The Houston Texans won their second straight, beating Kansas City at NRG Stadium.

Cuban lefty Ariel Miranda stopped the Astros on three hits through seven innings in a 7-3 Mariners win. Seth Smith ripped two home runs off loser Doug Fister, who allowed seven earned runs in 3 2/3 innings. "I just didn't execute today," said Fister. "That's what it comes down to. The ball's down, the ball's up, all over the place. I let my team down." Fister was 0-4 in his last five starts with a 10.71 ERA with a .404 batting average by his opponents.

Carlos Correa blasted a 450-foot home run – his 20th. Correa joined Alex Rodriguez as the only two shortstops with two 20-home run seasons by the end of their age 21 campaigns. He also became the Astros fourth 20-home run hitter in 2016. The Astros set a club record with 1,284 strikeouts by their pitching staff.

The Astros stayed three games behind Toronto for the second wild card spot. But Detroit and Seattle were now ahead of Houston by one game. Toronto would be at Seattle for the next series while Houston was headed for Oakland.

September 19---Young Jharel Cotton, the centerpiece in Oakland's trade with the Dodgers, took the mound at Oakland Coliseum for a hot Athletics club that had won six of its last seven games. He had allowed just two earned runs in his first two major league starts. Former Oakland pitcher Brad Peacock opposed him. Evan Gattis clubbed a home run off Cotton in the second. But Oakland took the lead with two solo homers in the last of the second.

Trailing 2-1 in the eighth, pinch hitter Tyler White pulled a line drive into the left field corner, scoring Teoscar Hernandez from first base. In the ninth the Astros loaded the bases against Oakland closer Ryan Madson with nobody out. Marwin Gonzalez broke the 2-2 tie with a two-run single through the middle of a drawn-in infield.

The Houston relief quintet of Kevin Chapman, Pat Neshek, Will Harris, Luke Gregerson and Ken Giles pitched no-hit ball in the final 3 2/3 innings to nail down the 4-2 win, which kept the Astros three games behind in the wild card race.

"For the team, it's great," said Gonzalez. "Everybody is doing their part. We're fighting until the end. Nobody's quitting. The pitchers are making good pitches, and the defense is there too. We have to fight until the end."

Jose Altuve, with a September slash line of .222/.279/.365, broke an 0-for-11 slump with a ninth inning single to start the winning rally. He began the night with a ten-point lead over Dustin Pedroia in the batting race, .337-.327. Mike Trout was third at .318. Altuve was hitting only .192 on fastballs in September.

September 20---It was Ken Giles' 26th birthday. The Astros had 12 games remaining and they needed to make up three games on either Baltimore or Toronto and ½ game on Detroit to force a tie for the second wild card spot. There was little margin for error. They might have to win nine of 12, which would give them 88 wins.

In 1964, the St. Louis Cardinals pulled off one of the wildest finishes in baseball history. They had 12 games to go and they trailed Philadelphia by 6 ½ games. The Cardinals went 10-3 while the Phillies cratered. Philadelphia manager Gene Mauch relied on Jim Bunning and Chris Short to start eight of the 12 games, and it was too much to ask of starting pitchers with two days rest between starts. Mauch was hounded by that decision for the rest of his career.

The Cardinals overtook the Phillies and went on to win the World Series, beating the Yankees in seven games.

The Sean Manaea-Joe Musgrove matchup moved swiftly through five scoreless innings. Musgrove had a no-hitter for 5 1/3 innings but left with the bases loaded and one out, tied 0-0. Chris Devenski allowed a runner to score on a groundout, but he retired all 11 men he faced in a brilliant outing, lowering his ERA to 1.98. The Astros tied the game 1-1 on a seventh inning pinch double by Tony Kemp. The game went to the tenth. Kemp doubled again and moved to third on a sacrifice bunt. Oakland manager Bob Melvin brought in his infield. George Springer grounded a single up the middle for a 2-1 lead. "I understood I just had to hit it through the infield somehow," Springer said. "Just like I was taught before, you find a way and help the team."

Birthday boy Ken Giles took the mound and got a strikeout to start the bottom of the tenth. Then two walks and a single loaded the bases with one out. A.J. Hinch brought in his infield. Giles got a popup and a strikeout to escape the threat and give the Astros their 80th win. Baltimore lost to Boston, moving Houston to within two games of the Orioles for the second wild card position.

Jose Altuve singled in the eighth inning for his 200th hit. He became only the third second baseman to collect at least 200 hits in three consecutive years, joining Charlie Gehringer and Rogers Hornsby. His batting average dropped to .336 with a 1-for-5 game, but he lined out twice. "It took a long time," said Altuve. "I tried to get hits in Seattle, I couldn't. I tried to get hits here, I couldn't. But finally. I think now I'm going to get more hits." He was correct. He got his next hit without swinging the bat! The official scorer in Seattle changed his ruling from the September 16 play in the fourth inning. Altuve was credited with a hit on the play originally ruled an error by third baseman Kyle Seager.

September 21---The race got tighter. In a day game at Oakland in the road trip finale, Evan Gattis blasted two home runs to give him 30 in 418 at bats. Both were vital in a 6-5 Houston win.

"This is the first time I've ever (hit 30), so I'm very excited," said Gattis. "I'm really proud of him," said Hinch. "Thirty home runs is a big deal. It means he's stuck it out the entire year and been productive." Gattis now had 100 career home runs. He hit eight in September, joining Chris Carter as the only Astros in the last nine seasons to reach 30.

Another big play was George Springer's base running, scoring on a seventh inning groundout by Yuli Gurriel. Springer was at third with one out in the seventh with Houston up 4-2. Springer waited for shortstop Marcus Semien to throw Gurriel's grounder to first before taking off for home. His headfirst slide got him to home plate a hair before Bruce Maxwell's tag. The call survived a replay review. "I understand they could throw the ball around a little bit and I had some success with that earlier, and I just figured now is the time to take a risk and it worked out," said Springer.

Collin McHugh won his fifth straight decision with support from five relievers. "We know the road we have in front of us," said McHugh. "I think our challenge is going to be staying focused on that, staying focused on the team that we have to beat, and not trying to let our vision get diverted a little bit to what other teams are doing. It's going to be tempting to do that, but we know the job we have, and we know the teams we've got to beat."

Luke Gregerson pitched around a Jose Altuve error to earn his 15th save.

Baltimore lost to Boston and Detroit was rained out. That left Baltimore in the second wild card spot, one game ahead of both Houston and Detroit. If those three teams tied, Houston would get its choice of playing the winner of the game between the other two on the road or staying at home to play one team, then the other if it won the first game. Hinch had already decided he would choose to play the winner of the first game on the road. He wanted to rest his starting pitching.

September 22---Lance McCullers threw a bullpen session from the mound for the first time. The plan, if he continued to show progress, was for him to be available for the postseason in limited use. Alex Bregman rejoined the club and continued to rehab his hamstring injury, with no plan to return to the lineup for the regular season because he needed more time for the injury to heal.

The Los Angeles Angels sent Ricky Nolasco to the mound and he became the story of the night. Nolasco, with a 6-14 record and a 4.78 ERA, held the Astros scoreless for seven innings and won 2-0. The runs were provided in the first inning by an Albert Pujols home run off Mike Fiers, who retired 13 in a row later. Nolasco was facing the Astros for the first time since 2012. He captured more success against them, running his record to 6-1 lifetime against the Astros and 4-0 at Minute Maid Park.

The loss slipped the Astros 1 ½ games behind the new leaders for the second wild card spot, Detroit. The Tigers swept a doubleheader in Minnesota to move into that spot, ½ game ahead of Baltimore. "We're not perfect," said A.J. Hinch. "I don't know if anybody's going to run the table."

September 23---The Astros suffered a devastating loss, 10-6. They overcame a 3-1 deficit with a five-run sixth to grab a 6-3 advantage. Marwin Gonzalez tied the game with a dramatic two-run single involving a long at bat.

But when Ken Giles took the mound for the ninth with a 6-4 lead, the Angels put together a six-run barrage against him, with a two-run homer from Yunel Escobar to tie the game and a three-run double by pinch hitter Rafael Ortega off Michael Feliz. Ortega sent a pop fly into shallow center field. Carlos Correa's legs were churning and he launched his body for it, gloving the ball but losing control of it when his body slammed to the ground. Correa reinjured his left shoulder on the play and came out of the game.

The raucous crowd of 29,000 plus fell quiet during the Angels' ninth. "Toughest inning of the year, for a lot of reasons," said A.J. Hinch. "Just a tough loss for this time of year, that fashion. We have six outs and our two primary relievers left. We felt really good about the position we were in, but it will teach you it's never over...That was a gut wrencher."

"Plain and simple: Just didn't do my job," said Giles. "That's all I can say. Didn't do my job. I put us in a hard position. Right now I'm going to make up for it. I'm going to do my best to carry this team and pick up my slack, even from just one bad outing. I can't let this happen at this time."

Detroit, Baltimore and Seattle all won. The Astros were 2 ½ games out with eight to play. Many thought they had just received their death knell.

September 24---Another chance to restart the Astros' fading wild card chances was going well through seven innings. They led the Angels 4-1 going to the eighth. Brad Peacock left with a 2-1 lead after five. Chris Devenski took over and stayed in for 2 1/3 innings before allowing three straight hits. Luke Gregerson could not stop the Angels' momentum. They got two more hits and a sacrifice fly off him, grabbing a 5-4 lead. Then the Angels blew the game open in the ninth for a 10-4 win. Giles was not available after being hit on the right wrist by a line drive during batting practice. The loss dropped the Astros three games behind Baltimore with seven to play. It appeared the Astros would need to win all seven remaining games just to keep their faint hopes alive. Detroit and Seattle also remained ahead of them.

September 25---On a warm but rainy Sunday morning, news came that tragedy had struck in South Florida. The Miami Marlins' star right-handed pitcher Jose Fernandez was dead at age 24 of a boating accident. The Marlins canceled their game and the mourning extended through the baseball community to all the friends and fans Fernandez had touched during his brief life. Cuban born Yunel Escobar of the Angels was scratched from their lineup.

Rumor had it that he was grief-stricken by the loss of his friend. All teams observed a moment of silence before their games. "It's awful that he's gone, but he lived every day," said Lance McCullers. McCullers and Fernandez worked out together in Tampa during the offseason and were good friends. "The thing that everyone will remember about him the most is just his joy he had about him and how much fun he had playing the game," said former teammate Jake Marisnick.

By the evening hours, golf legend Arnold Palmer was dead at age 87. One of the most revered figures in sports was a worldwide treasure. Fernandez had been robbed of his chance to fulfill his sports dreams the way Palmer had done.

Joe Musgrove took the mound at the same age as Fernandez, keeping the Angels at bay with one single between Mike Trout and Albert Pujols in eight at bats. His mound opponent, Daniel Wright, pitched much better than his 7.36 ERA. Evan Gattis and Tony Kemp ripped home runs off Wright and the Astros led 3-1 after six. Tyler White added a home run later and Houston won 4-1 with a save from Ken Giles, nursing a bruised right wrist. Yuliesky Gurriel hit into four double plays to tie a major league record. Baltimore won, staying three games ahead of Houston. Detroit suffered a damaging loss to give Baltimore a 1 ½ game lead for the second wild card spot.

The Los Angeles Dodgers played their last regular season home game, and it was Vin Scully's last game of his career at Dodger Stadium. The script was written in Hollywood. The Dodgers' magic number was one to eliminate the San Francisco Giants, who were playing in San Diego. The Giants were trailing by one in the ninth and the Dodgers went to extra innings against Colorado. The Dodgers won in the tenth to clinch the National League West, touching off a celebration. With the players on the field and their champagne bottles in hand, Scully addressed the crowd from his TV booth following his 67th season. His farewell to a tearful crowd included a recording of Scully singing "Wind Beneath My Wings."

Scully, regarded by most as baseball's best broadcaster of all time, was a nationally known figure who was a network broadcaster for football and golf as well. He spent many years broadcasting some of golf's famous tournaments. As Palmer's death was announced, Scully headed for San Francisco at age 89 to work his final games.

September 26---In Miami, the Marlins returned to the field with all players wearing the number 16 on their uniforms to honor Jose Fernandez. The grief-stricken players gathered around the pitching mound at the beginning of the evening in a tribute to Fernandez. They beat the Mets on an emotional night. Their leadoff hitter, Dee Gordon, wore Fernandez' batting helmet for the first pitch to him. Gordon, a left-handed batter, batted righthanded for one pitch. Then he took off Fernandez' helmet and put on his own. He homered on the 2-0 pitch from Bartolo Colon of the New York Mets, sending the Marlins on to victory. After the game, the Marlins players all circled the mound again and removed their caps, leaving them on the mound.

In Houston, Alex Bregman ran sprints before the game and declared himself ready to play, but the Astros did not activate him from the disabled list. Colby Rasmus was not listed among the bench players on the lineup card and was not in the clubhouse. A.J. Hinch was asked about Rasmus' absence. He told the media that Rasmus would not be back for the remaining games because he was going to Philadelphia for a second opinion on a hip and groin injury.

In pregame ceremonies, Bregman was honored as player of the year and Brady Rodgers as pitcher of the year in the Astros' minor league organization.

Mark Berman of KRIV-TV was inducted into the Media Wall of Honor at Minute Maid Park.

Collin McHugh, who was undefeated in 13 September starts as an Astro starting in 2014, gave up runs to Seattle in the first and third innings in the matchup of second and third place teams in the AL West and fourth and fifth place teams in the wild card race. Whoever won this game faced long odds of making the playoffs, but whoever lost had virtually no chance. Hisashi Iwakuma kept the Astros scoreless until the sixth.

Seattle led 3-1 when Houston put together a tying two-run rally in the ninth, with Jose Altuve and Carlos Correa each driving in his 95th run.

Robinson Cano's second home run of the game in the 11th off Luke Gregerson gave Seattle a 4-3 win. Cano now had eight homers and 22 RBI against Houston. The Astros' "tragic number" was reduced to three. Any combination of Baltimore wins and Houston losses adding up to three would eliminate the Astros from playoff contention. They trailed the Orioles by 3 ½ games with five to play.

Jose Altuve had two hits, stole a base and drove in a run. He injured his right wrist in the sixth inning diving for a hit but stayed in the game. "Like I've said before, and I've said this a hundred times, this is the team we are," said Altuve. "If we're going to win a game or lose a game it's going to be this way – the way we did it today." Altuve slammed his glove to the ground and his right hand went numb. "No chance," said Altuve when asked about leaving the game. "Not at this point."

September 27---The Harris County Commissioners voted to spend $105 million on the first phase of a plan to raise the floor of the Astrodome and use the lower area for parking. The area above ground could be used for convention and retail space for events such as the Houston Livestock Show and Rodeo. The Texas Historical Commission must approve the plan in order for it to be implemented.

The Houston Texans suffered a tremendous loss when J.J. Watt reinjured his back. The injury led to more back surgery later in the week, ending his season.

The Seattle Mariners had Mike Fiers in trouble from the outset. They built a 4-2 lead after three innings. But the Astros responded against Felix Hernandez with two runs in the first and trailed 4-2 going to the sixth.

They erupted for six runs in the sixth with five hits and two Seattle errors. George Springer and Marwin Gonzalez each drove in two runs. The 8-4 Houston win moved them to within 2 ½ games of Baltimore.

September 28---In the Astros' final home game of the season, Seattle jumped on Doug Fister with a three-run home run from Robinson Cano after three Mariners batted. Cano had nine home runs and 25 RBI against the Astros in 2016. The Mariners built a 7-0 lead in the third and finished with a 12-4 thumping to send the Astros to the brink of elimination for a wild card spot. The team headed for Anaheim after the game for a day off.

September 29---The Baltimore Orioles beat Toronto 4-0 to eliminate the Astros from playoff contention. Their off day in Anaheim closed the door on their aspirations. There were still four American league teams in the running for two wild card spots.

September 30---The Los Angeles Angels beat the Astros 8-1.

October 1---Collin McHugh pitched shutout baseball for 7 2/3 innings in a 4-0 win.

October 2---The season ended with Brady Rodgers making his first major league start. The Angels beat the Astros 8-1. Jose Altuve collected two hits to finish with a major league high 216. He also secured the batting title with a .338 average. George Springer played in all 162 games. The Astros finished the season with an 84-78 record. Their 41-40 road record was their best since 2004.

Baltimore and Toronto finished with the two wild card playoff spots.

October 3---General manager Jeff Luhnow and manager A.J. Hinch discussed the season for the media at a news conference the day after the season ended. "I'm not handling it very well at all, to be honest," said Hinch. "I hate losing. I don't like being here and having this meeting when I know there's a game being played tomorrow, but I'm proud of the fact that 84 wins isn't good enough. I'm proud of the fact where the standards have been raised in two years that I've been here to have those emotions."

"We are as motivated as we've ever been," said Luhnow. "We're sort of open for business across all areas, with the exception of our middle infield, which is in pretty good shape at this point." Luhnow said that he would have done more to improve the club in trades before the August 1 deadline if he had known that injuries were about to strike Dallas Keuchel and Lance McCullers in August. "Absolutely," said Luhnow. "But I didn't have that perspective at that point."

The team had struck out 60 times more than in 2015 and hit 32 fewer home runs. They scored 724 runs, just five fewer than the year before. But their ranking in the American League dropped from fourth to eighth in runs. They finished fifth in ERA at 4.06, a dropoff from the league-leading 3.57 a year earlier.

The Astros ranked in the middle of the pack in the majors in 2016 in runs and OPS. They ranked 11th in ERA and WHIP. By statistical measures they were an average to slightly above average major league team.

Potential free agents Jason Castro, Colby Rasmus, Luis Valbuena and Doug Fister would force Luhnow to think about replacements soon.

The Houston chapter of the Baseball Writers Association of America voted Jose Altuve the team MVP. Chris Devenski received pitcher of the year and rookie of the year honors for the team. Collin McHugh won the Darryl Kile Good Guy Award.

September statistics

The Astros were 13-16 in September and October. They scored 114 runs while allowing 138. Their ERA was 4.85. Their top hitters were Alex Bregman (.323-3-14 with .973 OPS) and Evan Gattis (.256-10-14). Their top pitchers were Collin McHugh (3-0, 3.10 ERA) and Will Harris (0-0, 1.46 ERA in 13 games)

Final Standings in AL West

Texas   95-67 -

Seattle   86-76 - 9

Houston 84-78 - 11

LAA   74-88 -15

Oakland 69-93 -20

Chapter 11

Altuve's Ascendancy

As 2016 approached, most observers thought Jose Altuve would have a hard time improving his performance. After all, his career batting average was now .305. He had won a batting title, Silver Sluggers and a Gold Glove. He had back to back 200-hit seasons. His 15 home runs in 2015 was a new career high, as well as his 66 RBI. Altuve wasn't thinking like that. He decided to improve by being more selective.

"I think everything is about the program that I have in the offseason. I feel like the offseason is the time you have to prepare yourself for all season long and then during the season you just have to maintain," he said of his winter work.

Altuve's work ethic and quest for excellence carried him to the highest level of achievement in 2016. Michael Baumann of The Ringer wrote an analytical article about Altuve's improvement in late August.

"The pitches I'm swinging at now are strikes," Altuve told Baumann. "If you try to swing at a ball outside the zone, sometimes you're going to hit it hard, but most of the time you're not." It took a while to change his thinking. Before that time, he knew he could top a pitch outside the strike zone and roll it slowly up the third base line, beating it out for an infield hit. When he revised his thinking, he realized he could let those marginal pitches go and wait for a pitch in his power zone which he could hit harder. "I go to home plate with a purpose, with a plan, and not get out of it," he told Richard Justice of MLB.com. "I'm putting myself in good hitting counts and getting good pitches to hit."

What caused the different approach? "Watching these guys play last year like Carlos (Correa) and other players from the other teams, I realized when you swing at better pitches you're going to have the ability to hit the ball harder.

"I was thinking about taking those borderline pitches. That way you can take your game to another level," said Altuve.

Among the 335 players who had 1,000 plate appearances from 2011-15, he ranked 30th in walk rate at 5%. He swung at 35.4% of pitches outside the strike zone. But he was the 17th toughest in baseball to strike out and his hand-eye coordination took him places other players can't reach. It was tough to argue with success. Not many batting champs decide they need to improve their approach at the plate!

"Coming off last year and the year before, when he won the batting title, he came in this year and he wanted to work harder, " said outfielder Jake Marisnick. "He said, 'I've got things I want to fix in my swing,' and we all looked at him like 'You're crazy.' Then he comes in and he's doing what he's doing this year."

Dave Hudgens introduced a helpful drill for Altuve and some other hitters in spring training 2016. Some of the pitchers were recruited to throw at a distance shorter than the 60 feet six inches they normally faced. They threw at less than full speed so as not to tax their arms in practice. But they threw all the same pitches they normally throw in games. The hitters had little reaction time due to the short distance. Their assignment was to recognize whether the pitch was going to be a strike or a ball, then call out what they saw. This helped Altuve and the other hitters with their strike zone judgement.

In late August, Altuve had the highest wRC+ in baseball, 162 (weighted runs created with league and ballpark effects factored in). His walk rate climbed from 4.8% to 9.3%. After a downturn in September, he finished with a walk rate of 8.4%.

"The game is evolving, and I wanted to go with the game," said Altuve. "Right now, people look at OPS, OBP, that kind of stuff. Mostly I used to hit for average, not too many home runs, not too many doubles, so I felt like I could get better."

It's exceptionally rare that a young player on a Hall of Fame pace improves as much as Altuve did from 2015 to 2016. "I think my adjustments were more mental than anything else," said Altuve. "When I showed up to spring training, I tried really hard to swing at good pitches, and that's been the key for my season, just trying to lay off borderline pitches, put the ball in play. I'm trying to do damage at the plate. Before, if I hit a weak ground ball, I knew I could be safe.

"Then I understood that if you hit a double or drive in a run, it's better than hitting a single. I'm not trying to hit a home run every time. I'm trying to look for my pitch and put a good swing on the ball."

By the third week in August in 2016, Altuve was hitting .363 and he had a 42-point lead over David Ortiz in the batting race. He had enough plate appearances to qualify for the batting title, meaning he did not have to play another game to be the batting champion with his huge lead. His line drive percentage increase from 2015 to 2016 was the second largest in the majors.

The last MVP with a height of 5-6 was Phil Rizzuto of the New York Yankees in 1950. With Altuve at 5-5 and Betts 5-9, the little guys were in position to do big things.

September brought the biggest test of the season for Altuve. Through September 18 he was hitting .222 with a .279 on base average and a .365 slugging percentage in the month. His lead in the batting race was down to ten points, .337 to .327 over Boston's Dustin Pedroia. But that night his ninth inning single triggered a winning rally against Oakland. "We've seen it this season out of him and been around it every day," said A.J. Hinch. "It's as impactful in all facets as anyone can be – his power, the speed, the hits."

Entering the final week of the season, Altuve recalled the last days of 2014 when he won his first batting title.

"I remember that year I had Victor Martinez about two or three points behind me going into the final game," said Altuve. "That was kind of close. I don't know where the guys are behind me right now but it's more than one guy. You have to go out there and do your job. Maybe because of the situation we have I'm just trying to go out there and win the game. In 2014 we were 20 games behind and I really wanted to win the batting title and I know the guys around me were expecting me to win the batting title. I know right now everybody's paying attention to winning.

"The last day of the season the whole focus was on the batting title – the manager, the fans, everybody. Now they don't pay much attention to the batting title and neither do I."

As September came to a close and the Astros were eliminated from the playoffs, Altuve led the AL in hitting over Boston's Dustin Pedroia .338-.318. In his last at bat of 2016, he flared a broken bat single to right field. When he arrived at first base, he banged his hands together and the visiting dugout reacted with cheering. Altuve pointed toward his team's bench and nodded toward them. There was no special ceremony after the game. He had such a commanding lead that A.J. Hinch honored him after the previous days' game with a champagne toast in the locker room. "I wanted to make sure that he got recognized in front of our team," said Hinch. "Very rarely do you get a batting champion in front of you."

Originally the plan was for Altuve to rest on the final day, but he chose to play. He deflected the credit to his teammates, as is his custom. "They really made my job easier this year – Georgie (Springer), Carlos (Correa), Marwin (Gonzalez). Every single guy that was in the lineup helped me win the batting title," he said. "The way that these guys played this year, they went outside to the field, played hard, and that kind of encouraged me and pushed me to keep playing hard every day."

"He's done a great job of being a complete hitter this year wherever I've put him," said Hinch. "He's taken it personally to improve his plate discipline."

A Venezuelan has claimed the AL batting title for the last six years. Miguel Cabrera won from 2011 to 2013 and again in 2015. Altuve won in 2014 and 2016. He is the first second baseman to win multiple batting titles since Rod Carew won five 1969-75. It's only fitting that starting with Altuve in 2016 the AL batting champ will receive the award now named for Carew.

Altuve became the fifth second baseman in history with three 200-hit seasons. He joined Charlie Gehringer, Rogers Hornsby, Napoleon Lajoie and Billy Herman. All are Hall of Famers.

The last to accomplish the feat was Gehringer in 1937.

No second baseman had ever put together this combination of statistics until 2016: 100 runs, 200 hits, 40 doubles, 20 home runs, 95 RBI and 30 stolen bases. Of the six 20-20 Club members in 2016, Altuve was the rare superstar who walked 60 times while striking out only 70 times in 717 plate appearances.

Here's how Altuve compares to major league baseball's all time hit king, Pete Rose, through their first 829 games:

	Altuve	Rose
Slash line	.311/.354/.437	.299/.356/.419

(batting average, on base average, slugging pct.)

Hits	1,046	999

Note: Altuve was 287 days younger than Rose at the end of the 2016 season

The only second basemen with more hits through their age 26 seasons were Hall of Famers Roberto Alomar, Bobby Doerr and Bill Mazeroski.

Those who were promoting Altuve's candidacy for MVP honors pointed to his slash line (.338/.396/.531) compared to the rest of the team (.247/.319/.417). No other Houston hitter had a batting average as high as .275. Altuve ranked third in major league baseball in batting average with men in scoring position at .372. His slugging percentage of .531 represented a major improvement in his career. His previous high was .459 in 2015.

Altuve Month By Month in 2016

April: .305-6-13 20 runs .400 oba .611 slugging % Hit 5 home runs in first 62 plate appearances

May :   .345-3-18 12-game hitting streak set club record with 23 extra base hits in first 29 games

June :   .420-4-15 reached base in 32 straight games 1.004 OPS

July :   .354-5-16 10-game hitting streak .341-14-51 at All-Star Break with 119 hits

August: .333-4-27 back to back 4-hit games. Ended streak at 202 consecutive games played

September: .269-2-7   the only slowdown of the season came when facing the top pitchers and best teams

October 27---*Sporting News* announced that Jose Altuve was its 2016 Major League Player of the Year, determined by a vote of players from both leagues for the player who had the most outstanding season.

"It is great, especially when you get voted by the players," Altuve said. "I really appreciate that from my teammates and players on other teams. These are the kind of things that make you keep getting better.

"You wake up every morning and realize you won this award by the players, and you want to keep getting better. Not only for the team, but for the fans and for everybody that's been (helping) you."

"I think it's one of the greatest signs of respect is when the players around the league bestow this kind of award around him," said A.J. Hinch. "He's earned it. He's certainly had one of the best seasons imaginable, but still left room to get better. And so, I think the fact his peers recognize that should make him feel good, and rightfully so."

"He's achieved a level that not many have achieved in their career and he's already thinking about this offseason and how he's going to improve for next year," said General Manager Jeff Luhnow.

Altuve became the second player in Houston history to win this award. Jeff Bagwell was the first in his National League MVP season of 1994. "When you see Jeff Bagwell's numbers for his career and you just mention my name next to Jeff's that means I'm doing something kinda good for my team," said Altuve. "It's an honor for me being next to Jeff. Everything I can do to keep getting better and helping my team I'm going to do."

Altuve answered questions from the Houston media at Minute Maid Park. He talked about his offseason, which would include his first child. "I have a baby," said Altuve. "I also have to work out and do the same routine that I've been doing my last three years. It would be stupid if I changed it. I'm gonna go there (Venezuela) for at least a month and do what I do every year and talk to the guys that I talk to every year." Baby Melanie was born a few days later to Jose and his wife Nina.

Altuve and Detroit slugger Miguel Cabrera, good friends, both were born in Maracay, Venezuela. They occasionally got together in their country during the offseason. They also collected the last six batting titles in the American League. "We talk a lot," said Altuve. "Sometimes he calls me, sometimes I call him. Great guy. We talk hitting more in the offseason than during the season." Did the older Cabrera praise Altuve?

"He told me that I'm a better hitter than him," said Altuve. "But no. No chance. He has a Triple Crown and two MVPs."

Altuve said there was no celebration in Maracay of batting titles by its natives. He also pointed out that Carlos Gonzalez of Colorado added a seventh title by a Venezuelan in recent years. Maracaibo native Gonzalez won the National League batting title in 2010.

Altuve was asked about winning the American League MVP award, which would be announced in three more weeks.

"If I win it's going to be great, if not I'm going to feel proud because I feel like I did what I had to do to help my team and I don't want to stop here," said Altuve. He admitted he wanted to join the 30-30 Club for home runs and stolen bases. "You guys know that I don't like to talk about numbers. That's like a dream, something that you want to do," he said. "When I was signed by the Astros when I was 16, if you told me I was going to be 20-20 everybody would be like, 'Nope." I still doubt about myself I could be 30-30, but you never know. It could happen."

Of all of his statistics, Altuve said he was proudest of his 161 games played. His determination to be available every day may have cost him in September of 2016, with the team struggling and Jose playing through some minor injuries. There were signs that he was pressing to provide meaningful hits as the team dropped back in the wild card race.

Many MVP voters value the Wins Above Replacement (WAR) statistic, because it is designed to measure all of the player's assets with one number. The defensive aspect of WAR has been debated heavily and is not readily accepted by some. Altuve finished 2016 with a 7.6 WAR, trailing Mike Trout at 10.6 and Mookie Betts at 9.6 in the American League. Those three players were announced as finalists for the AL MVP about ten days before the final voting was announced.

November 9---The MLB Network introduced the Players Choice Award winners for 2016 in an evening telecast. The Players Choice Awards, introduced in 1992 by the Major League Baseball Players Association, were dominated by Jose Altuve.

Altuve became the first Astro to win the MLBPA Player of the Year Award, beating Mookie Betts and David Ortiz of Boston in the voting. Altuve also won the American League Most Outstanding Player Award, beating Betts and Mike Trout in the voting by fellow players. The third award for Altuve was the Majestic "Always Game" Award. It was the second straight year Altuve captured that honor.

The Majestic award goes to the player who constantly exhibits grit, tenacity, perseverance and hustle.

"It's an honor that they think I was the best player this year," said Altuve. "These are things that make you want to get up in the morning and keep getting better."

In a TV interview Altuve was asked what he did differently in 2016. "Last year I realized if I put a good swing on the ball I can drive it," he said.

November 10---The Silver Slugger Awards were announced by Louisville Slugger. Jose Altuve became the first Houston Astro to win three straight Silver Sluggers. Craig Biggio won a total of five silver bats, but never three in a row. Jeff Bagwell won a total of three. Managers and coaches vote for Silver Slugger awards.

November 17---The long-awaited announcement by the Baseball Writers Association of America of the two league most valuable players came early in the evening on the MLB Network.

This award has been exclusively the domain of the baseball writers since it started. The BBWAA has always been a very powerful organization due in no small part to its selection of the most important awards in the sport. A strong case can be made to include voters other than writers.

Astros Diary

In college football, Heisman Trophy winners from the past vote each year on that award. Hall of Famers in baseball do not vote on the major awards. Broadcasters, executives and others are not a part of the voting process. The Hall of Fame voters also are members of the BBWAA exclusively. It is a closely held honor.

The writers who vote do not take it lightly. In modern times most of them reveal their votes publicly. That leaves them open to criticism. Typically the voters spend many hours researching the candidates. When they dive deeply into the statistical mountain, they can choose whichever favorite stats they choose. They vote for up to ten players for the MVP awards.

As the announcement approached, many speculated that Boston's Mookie Betts appeared to be the favorite. Not only did he rank high in most of the important categories, of the three finalists Betts was the only member of a playoff team. On the other side of the ledger, Betts was part of a Red Sox team that scored a major league high 878 runs. The high-powered Sox surrounded Betts with several talented hitters, which gave him an advantage. Boston finished with five of the top 30 American League players in wins above replacement (WAR).

By contrast, Mike Trout played for the fourth place Los Angeles Angels with 717 runs. He ripped 29 home runs and drove in 100 runs, compared to Betts' 31 and 113 and Altuve's 24 and 96. Altuve's Astros scored 724 runs, and his club was in the wild card race until the final days. Brian McTaggart of MLB.com pointed out that Altuve hit .388 in the Astros' wins, .281 in their losses. Was Altuve more valuable to his team? That's what the voters had to decide. It would have been easier for the voters if the term "most valuable" had been replaced by "player of the year" or some such designation allowing the voters to consider their personal statistics in a different light than what they meant to their team. But, the voters were faced with determining how valuable each player was.

The results were announced and the winner in the American League was Mike Trout. Betts finished second and Altuve wound up in third place. Regardless of the disappointment felt by many Altuve fans, his achievement was noteworthy. And the previous awards voted by the players were more meaningful to some than the writers' vote.

Trout won his second MVP and also had three second place finishes in a five-year period. He became the first MVP from a losing team since Alex Rodriguez in 2003. It seemed that his stature in the game at age 25 was just too powerful for the voters to ignore.

On the same day as the MVP announcements, the Astros traded two pitching prospects, Albert Abreu and Jorge Guzman, to the New York Yankees for catcher Brian McCann. McCann, a 33-year-old lefthanded hitter with 245 career major league home runs, fills the vacancy left by Jason Castro's exit via free agency. That same day, word leaked out that the Astros had signed free agent outfielder Josh Reddick, another lefthanded hitter, to a four-year contract. The day before, they signed free agent pitcher Charlie Morton to a two-year agreement. Earlier in November, they claimed another lefthanded hitter, Nori Aoki, on waivers from Seattle.

Now the lineup took on a different look. The presence of McCann, Reddick, and others like perhaps Aoki would give the Astros' lineup better balance on paper. Now the hitters surrounding Altuve were changing, and it seemed that the Astros were better positioned to maximize Altuve's value to the club.

Altuve's career batting average of .311 through 2016 is the best in Houston club history for a minimum of 1,000 plate appearances. Jeff Bagwell and Bob Watson are tied for second at .297.

Here are numbers from Jose Altuve's 2016 season with American League rankings in parentheses:

.338 batting average (1) by 20 points over Betts

216 hits (1)   340 total bases (4) 42 doubles (tied 3)

.396 on base average (4) .928 OPS (5)

.372 with runners in scoring position (2)

.376 road batting average (2)

30 stolen bases – (tied 2)

Here is where the three AL MVP finalists finished in several categories:

Batting average: Altuve .338 (1) Betts .318 (2) Trout .315 (tied for 5th)

On base percentage: Trout .441 (1) Altuve .396 (4)

Slugging percentage: Trout .550 (4) Betts .534 (8)

Total bases: Betts 359 (1) Altuve 340 (4)

Runs scored: Trout 123 (1) Betts 122 (tied for 2nd) Altuve 108 (7)

RBI: Betts 113 (4)

Where does Altuve's career go from here? It won't be on cruise control. "I have seen a lot of players that have four really good seasons, but that's it. Maybe five, six," he said. "I don't want to stop. I want to keep going. I feel I haven't reached my goal, which is the World Series."

John Mallee, Altuve's hitting coach in 2013-14, recalled the goals he and Altuve set during those years. "Number one, make adjustments in his swing," said Mallee. "Number two, be an All-Star. Number three, win a batting title. He got that far because of who he is."

His first major league manager, Brad Mills points to "Such tenacity. Such work ethic. Such drive. The way this guy's developed. Look at the stolen bases. It's so impressive the way he uses all the intangibles he has to get better."

Here's how Altuve improved in his walk rate: 2.1% in 2011, 6.3% in 2012, 4.8% in '13, 5.1% in '14, 4.8% in '15 and 8.4% in '16. In 2016 his walk rate of 8.4% almost matched his strikeout rate of 9.8%. In his first season, his walk rate was 2.1% and his strikeout rate 12.4%.

In the MVP voting, he progressed from 13th in 2014 to 10th in 2015 to third in 2016.

Gigante has giant dreams and a heart to match them. He's breathing orange fire.

EPILOGUE

by Greg Lucas

I'm going to let you onto a secret. When Bill first thought of writing this book it was going to be a day to day account of the Astros winning a pennant or maybe even the World Series. After their success in 2015, which took them to a few outs of the American League Championship series and the corps of solid young talent with more on the way, that was a definite possibility.

As things turned out the club didn't have that kind of season. There is still great hope that maybe 2017 will be the year. After all didn't Sports Illustrated plaster the cover of an edition on June 20, 2014 with a photo of George Springer taking a big swing with the inside featuring a story by Ben Reiter declaring the Astros "Your 2017 World Series Champs"? So, maybe the team was a year ahead of schedule?

It didn't turn out that way, but Bill was able to focus on what WAS right about the Astros and why fans should continue to be very encouraged the second golden age of Astros baseball is very close. It centered on Jose Altuve. The man who won his second American League batting championship and was named AL Player of the Year.

I really enjoyed Bill's look at what fans hope will be the next golden era of Houston Astros baseball and particularly the man who will be heavily responsible for it happening, Altuve.

Already at such a young age Jose has had achievements no other players in the 55 year history of the franchise have reached. And he is not finished yet.

Coupled with other young players scouted, drafted and signed then developed in the Houston farm system owner Jim Crane and his baseball leadership has the team on the right track.

Sometimes teams in all sports seem to be headed into the right station but the team jumps the track. By building the system with talent in volume the Astros have no plans in letting that happen.

Learning of the dedication players like Altuve and Carlos Correa put in starting in their youth with strong familial leadership should not only be encouraging but instructive as well. Many have wondered had Altuve come around a few years later would the modern computer driven models called him a potential player or not? At only 5'5" tall and perhaps 145 pounds at the time the answer probably would have been , "No." But Jose and his father would likely have not taken that as a good enough answer. They didn't at the tryout camp in which he wasn't invited back the next day. They both showed up anyway. Altuve was made to play baseball and play it well. He would have been a major leaguer and beaten those statistical print outs. The Astros are all the better for the determination of their scouts—particularly Al Pedrique who signed him—and Altuve himself who made himself one of the best players in all of major league baseball.

The 2016 season may have turned out to be a struggle, but the club was still over .500 and only a few games off their record of 2015 despite having to battle several injuries to key players like Luis Valbuena, Colby Rasmus and pitchers, defending Cy Young Award winner Dallas Keuchel and Lance McCullers.

In his last season calling Astros games on television after 30 years at the post Brownie retired but still had this story to tell. He'll be following the Astros as a fan like the rest of us and hoping next year's story will prove Sports Illustrated writer Ben Reiter to have been a prophet.

(Greg Lucas worked 17 of Bill Browns 30 seasons as a field level commentator, pre-game host with occasional analysis and play by play on Astros television from 1995 through 2012. His new book, *The Hearts of the Houston Baseball- Craig Biggio and Jeff Bagwell* is being released in 2017)

Made in the USA
Lexington, KY
25 June 2018